THE SIBLING CONSTELLATION

Brian Clark is a counselling astrolo… …ron Centre in Melbourne… …the four-year programme i… …on Centre, and a tutor in th… …d extensively overseas to … …d has received awards fro… Canada and Australia, as w… Regulus Award.

Brian is Canadian by birth and Australian by adoption. He is married, has three step-children and one granddaughter.

CONTEMPORARY ASTROLOGY

Series Editor: Erin Sullivan

THE SIBLING CONSTELLATION

BRIAN CLARK

ARKANA

PENGUIN BOOKS

ARKANA

Published by the Penguin Group
Penguin Books Ltd, 27 Wrights Lane, London W8 5TZ, England
Penguin Putnam Inc., 375 Hudson Street, New York, New York 10014, USA
Penguin Books Australia Ltd, Ringwood, Victoria, Australia
Penguin Books Canada Ltd, 10 Alcorn Avenue, Toronto, Ontario, Canada M4V 3B2
Penguin Books (NZ) Ltd, Private Bag 102902, NSMC, Auckland, New Zealand

Penguin Books Ltd, Registered Offices: Harmondsworth, Middlesex, England

Published by Penguin Books 1999
1 3 5 7 9 10 8 6 4 2

Set in 9.5/12 pt PostScript Monotype Garamond
Typeset by Rowland Phototypesetting Ltd, Bury St Edmunds, Suffolk
Made and printed in Great Britain by Clays Ltd, St Ives plc

Contents

List of Figures

For Suzanne, Cameron and Melissa,
three bright stars in their sibling constellation

Acknowledgements

Without Erin Sullivan's active encouragement and direction this book would never have been conceived, and certainly not delivered – brotherly thanks. Grateful thanks go to Christine Bright and Frith Luton who assisted me with presentation and layout. Mary Symes generously gave her time to read some original drafts and offer encouraging feedback. As a writer, Peter O'Connor heartened my own struggle to write, with his friendship, support and wisdom. For fine tuning, copy editing and her professional input I thank Monica Schmoller; I am thankful destiny saw fit to assign a double Gemini to the task. My own journey back to university to study classics also gave me the courage to return to writing.

I would like to thank the many students I have had the privilege of teaching; their openness and sharing always added to my own understanding. Their own experiences, coupled with their astrological insights, continue to reveal the subtle nature of astrological patterns. My thanks also go to the students and clients who shared their familial and sibling stories with me, and a special *merci beaucoup* to those who allowed me to present their case material.

Throughout the period of compiling the book, my friends and colleagues were a great help and I would like to acknowledge my appreciation. My associates at the Chiron Centre were especially supportive; thank you for listening to my monologues on the subject. Members of my family saw less of me while I was writing and I am grateful for their patience and continuous support.

And finally I wish to thank Glennys for her constant team effort in all that we share together, be it familial, personal or professional.

Introduction
Sister–Brother–Other

And the Lord said unto Cain, Where is Abel thy brother? And he said, I know not: Am I my brother's keeper? Genesis 4:9

In every photograph taken when I was young, my brother is at my side. On a wintry Canadian afternoon, the first picture was taken of me when I was three months old. My brother stands at our mother's side as she holds me. Not until the age of five do I appear solo in photographs. My brother is my constant photographic companion; wherever I am, he is there too. These images serve as a visual record, as I have few memories before the age of five. In many of the photographs my brother has his arms around me or he is holding me. Yet my earliest memories conflict with this visual evidence. My first memory with my brother is of embarrassing him. I remember feeling inferior to him, feeling rejected by him, trying to emulate him, but not being close to him. Therefore I could never understand the discrepancy between what the photos reveal and my memories of feeling left behind by him.

My experiences and observations of my step-children's sibling relationships are quite different. No matter how intense their anger or how palpable their indifference with one another, their loyalty to and love for each other was never compromised. From childhood through to adulthood, they have maintained their individuality and have forged their own unique personalities, while sustaining the sibling relationship. All three have vivid memories of their childhood experiences together, and have constantly managed to nurture their sibling relationship. They seem to have negotiated that first partnership much better than I; their close relationship is a striking contrast to my estrangement from my brother.

Of course, my own confusion and grief with the sibling relationship has been mirrored by clients in my practice. I am not alone in struggling to reconcile and heal the sibling relationship. It is a theme that is perennially part of my astrological counselling practice, and many of my colleagues, be they astrologers, therapists or other professional helpers, have also struggled with this theme, in both their private lives and practices.

The sibling relationship is a powerful bond that influences our adult relationships and our sense of well-being. It is a bond that has not been adequately delineated or honoured, yet it is the *one* relationship that has the most chance of spanning a complete lifetime. While it is a relationship that has been ignored by psychology in the past, things are beginning to change. With much of the fabric of the traditional family in tatters through divorce and separation, the sibling is often the link to continuity and security. As the global family becomes more of a reality and the quest for equality continues, it is natural that the image of the sibling, as the carrier of peer relationship, will be constellated in the collective.

What often prompts an individual to make an astrological appointment is the complexity of a relationship. The human labour of forging a fulfilling relationship is the task that most often brings us face to face with our own selves. Abundant literature on human relationship exists, yet seldom includes an exploration of one of our most fundamental relationships, that with the sibling. In examining the influential relationships from the family of origin and our childhood, the sibling relationship is of primary significance. Siblings mature within the same system and generation, and sisters and brothers belong to the same hierarchical level of the family. It is a peer relationship. Siblings are witness to our lives, the custodians of our earliest memories and the touchstones of our childhood experiences. Brothers and sisters are powerful figures in our lives, whose influences contribute to the emotional foundation upon which intimate relationships are built. In adulthood another task emerges: how to recreate the sibling relationship as adults.

Each sibling system is its own unique constellation, whether there are many siblings or none at all, whether the siblings are blood related or not. This unique constellation of individuals belonging to the same system was an important image in antiquity. The ancients told many mythic stories of sisters and brothers which range from devotion to fratricide. One Greek myth tells of the twins, Castor and Polydeuces.[1] Their story was projected on to the constellation of Gemini, inspiring the zodiacal sign that today represents the powerful image of the sibling bond. When I began to write this book, Gemini became my point of departure and Castor and Pollux were my fixed stars in examining and researching 'siblinghood'.

My first port of call was to research what psychoanalysis had documented about the influence of the sibling. Aware of Alfred Adler's interest in both the family constellation and birth position, as well as Sigmund Freud's depiction of sibling rivalry, I was curious to find what theories and cases these early psychoanalysts articulated. I also researched Carl Jung, as he was the third member of the psychoanalytic triumvirate that influenced the course of psychoanalytic theory. Not aware of any sibling theories ascribed to Jung, I was astounded at how the sibling theme had permeated his own life as well as his theory of archetypes.[2] While my intent was to examine Freudian, Adlerian and Jungian theory, their own sibling constellations appeared as a dominant influence, with the result that I drew on both their personal sibling constellations and horoscopes to better appreciate their sibling stories and theories. All three had such powerful sibling issues and experiences, to varying degrees, that the influence reverberated throughout their psychology. The first part of the book explores this territory.

Many references to the potent impact of the sibling were made by the psychoanalytic founders, including case studies where both Freud and Jung traced the presenting neurosis back to a sibling relationship. Yet, ultimately, the psychoanalytic patriarch and followers seem to have overlooked the sibling, caught up in the parent–child model and its transference. The psychology of the sibling seemed to be lost until sociology and family therapy started referring to the individual in the context of a system, not solely orientated to the parents. Only when the hierarchical focus began to wane during the course of the twentieth century, could the image of the sibling begin to emerge.

Myth was the second resource that was immensely valuable in informing me of sibling relationships. All comparative mythologies contain moving and gripping stories of the sibling bond. These deserve their own tome. Myth also informs our astrological understanding, and sibling myths underlie some of the prevalent astrological archetypes. Astrology was the constant resource that enabled me to appreciate the powerful influence of the sibling. Each horoscope contains a treasury of information about both the literal and archetypal sibling. The second part of this book explores the astrological landscape of the sibling.

Sibling relationships are the first experience of equal relationship which in turn affects the world of friends, peers, colleagues, partners and companions. Equality, including gender equality, is part of the sibling archetype which then informs all our other equal relationships in life. In the horoscope, the sibling archetype is located in the third house. This acts as a template for the other two houses of equal relationship – the seventh house of partnership and the eleventh house of friendship. The astrological horoscope inherently contains the image of the sibling/s since it contains all archetypes within its system. Reflecting on the natural wisdom of the astrological model can also expand our understanding of the sibling.

With such a focus on the sibling as the first partner, companion and other, only children may feel left out. But this is part of the fate of being an only child. The sibling is an *a priori* image in the psyche whether there is a literal sibling or not, and the psyche will attempt to embody this image through others in the life of an 'only'. An only child may even be closer to the very nature of the sibling archetype, since that concerns the sense of separateness and the eternal search for the lost other. In birth order theory, the only child is just one of the many arrangements of the sibling constellation.

Synchronicity is ever present in astrological work. In fact, it is at the heart of the work. Therefore it may be of interest to point out the following astrological recurrences: my current year's Solar return ascendant is in the same degree as my progressed ascendant. Both are the same degree as my natal third house Placidian cusp – the gateway to the sibling. Transiting Saturn opposed my natal Mercury, the ruler of Gemini and the sibling, three times during the period of writing this book. Each time was concurrent with an actual phase of writing. And today, as the book draws near to completion, the progressed Moon rests on the cusp of the third house! It is this synchronicity that defies interpretation.

I hope that *The Sibling Constellation* serves both as a way to help you understand and heal your own sibling relationships, as well as creating awareness of the sibling archetype in each horoscope that you examine.

Note on the Text

Sibling is a genderless word and I have relied on this word to convey the symmetry and equality inherent in this archetype.[3] Where necessary and for grammatical purposes I have used the masculine he/his and the feminine she/her interchangeably when referring to a sibling. This is most evident in Chapter 8, which explores the astrological archetype of Gemini. On reflection, this is appropriate as the experience of Gemini is where we also locate the conscious ability to differentiate, be separate and articulate individuality. Exceptions are found in Chapters 3 and 4 when discussing Freud and Adler's theories, as their sibling theories, while applicable to both sexes, for the most part dealt with males in identification with their own personal experiences as brothers. When gender specific, I have used sister or brother. For the most part I have tried to vary the gender of the pronoun or possessive adjective accompanying the noun *sibling*. Gemini, and the third house, is the territory of the sibling; however, it also symbolizes language and the consciousness of duality.

Melbourne, April 1998

Notes

1. Known in Latin as Pollux.
2. To be true to Jungian theory, the sibling would have to be included as an archetype.
3. For amplification on this point, see Chapter 7, 'Gender, archetype and the sib'.

1

The Sibling Bond

Lifelong Companions

Such a Sister, such a friend, as never can have been surpassed – She was the sun of my life, the gilder of every pleasure, the soother of every sorrow, I had not a thought concealed from her, & it is as if I had lost a part of myself. Cassandra Austen[1]

Darius, the Persian king, had imprisoned Intaphernes, along with his children and all his kin, except his wife. All had been arrested, put in chains and condemned to death for their suspected treachery. Each day Intaphernes' wife would stand outside the gates of the palace, weeping and wailing. Darius was so moved by the vigilance of the lamenting woman that he sent a messenger to tell her he would grant her a boon. The king would pardon one of her kinsmen but she must choose which one. After some deliberation, Intaphernes' wife told the messenger: 'If the king grants me the life of one alone, I make choice of my brother.' The king was astonished and sent the messenger to ask the woman why she had chosen her brother and not her husband or one of her children; after all, her children were closest to her and her husband was dearest. She sent a reply back with the messenger: 'O king, if the gods will, I may have another husband and other children when these are gone. But as my father and my mother are no more, it is impossible that I should have another brother. This was my thought when I asked to have my brother spared.' The king was so moved by her sentiment that he pardoned another family member – her eldest son.[2]

Loyalty between siblings was one of the ways myth portrayed the fate of this lifelong bond. Sophocles' plays often centred on the sibling relationship and in *Antigone* he expresses a similar sentiment through his eponymous heroine. Her twin brothers, Etocles and Polynices, have just killed each other. Etocles has received a state funeral being a defender of the city, Thebes, while Polynices is condemned to remain unburied for betraying the city. Antigone defies the law of the city, risking her own life in order to bury her brother. Burial was to honour the laws of the gods and ensure his safe passage into the Underworld. Her only remaining sibling, a sister Ismene, chooses not to help. Antigone is arrested and entombed for her crime against the city. She tells us she would never have risked her life in the same way for her husband or children; however, for a brother she could never replace, Antigone is willing to risk her life:

> 'Never, I tell you,
> if I had been the mother of children
> or if my husband died, exposed and rotting –
> I'd never have taken this ordeal upon myself,
> never defied our people's will. What law,
> you ask, do I satisfy with what I say?
> A husband dead, there might have been another.
> A child by another too, if I had lost the first.
> But mother and father both lost in the halls of Death,
> no brother could ever spring to light again.'[3]

Myth consistently recognizes siblings and their influence throughout the life span. The stories honour the sibling bond through a complexity of relationships, both mortal and divine – the sibling marriage of Zeus and Hera, the solidarity of brothers Agamemnon and Menelaus or the fraternal rivalry of Romulus and Remus, the devoted companionship of Apollo and Artemis, the fate of sisters Iphegenia and Electra or the envy of Psyche's sisters.

Myth speaks of the taboos of this relationship and the complex emotions that are all part of the sibling story. Love, jealousy, power, envy, trust, betrayal, faith, suspicion, deceit, cheating, lying, pride, support, competition, grief, all constellated in the exchange between siblings. The lost sibling, the wounded sibling, the rejected sibling, the father-identified and mother-identified siblings all enter the mythic tales. Myth tells us that the sibling relationship is a cornerstone of our relational life and always a part of who we are and who we will be.

Folk tales, fairy tales and fables also tell us of the sibling constellation. Who could forget feeling empathy for Cinderella at the hands of her brutal step-sisters, or trepidation for Hansel and Gretel as they found themselves outcast in the woods. These folk tales of siblings also appear in numerous cultures, once again echoing the universality of this relationship. The sibling bond is a relationship an only child longs for, but, none the less, is still part of the child's soul and fate. Sibling relationships, whether realized or not, are fed by the same archetypal spring, filled with similar complex emotions and eagerly sought in the external world. Without an incarnate sib we find a replacement, real or imagined, to cast the archetype over.

The ancients also immortalized the sibling relationship in the sky. Seven sisters, the Hyades, were in such grief over the loss of their brother that they were placed in the sky by Zeus. Another sisterly constellation, the Pleiades, is an eternal reminder of sisterhood.[4] It is the two bright stars, Castor and Pollux, in the constellation of Gemini, that became not only a symbol of fraternal solidarity and love, but also an emblem for the archetype of sibship.

Astrology honours the innate bond between siblings through the *third* zodiacal sign, Gemini. The importance of the sibling relationship is implied in the myth and through the experience of Gemini. Its inclusion in the zodiac, the wheel of life, suggests that the image of the 'twin' other, as symbolized by a sister or brother, is inherent at birth, an *a priori* aspect of the psyche. Gemini is an earlier sign of the zodiac, and this image is a primal part of an individual which helps shape relational patterns throughout life. Gemini's initial experience of otherness also gives form to an eternal quest to reconnect with the twin other. The sibling, whether we are the eldest or youngest, a step-sibling or a surviving sibling, is inherently part of our fate and the sibling bond is an aspect of each individual that is a template for future relationships. Psychoanalysis seemed to forget this truth in early theoretical development, perpetuating the psychological disenfranchisement of the sibling bond.

The word 'sibling', from the Old English *sibb* or *sib*, was used by anthropologists from 1903.[5] Synchronous to Pluto transiting Gemini, the sign of the sibling, anthropology revived this word to describe one of two or more children in a family. Originally the word sib referred to any relative or kin and by medieval times was used for acquaintances who were not blood related. A god-sib referred to a godparent or baptismal sponsor. The word *gossip* is derived from god-sib and originally was a form of addressing a familiar acquaintance. Getting acquainted, becoming familiar and feeling akin all begin in the primal relationship to our siblings. Astrologically this process also begins with Gemini and the third house.

The sibling bond becomes an important and powerful relationship to honour in our exploration of human nature through our own, our families' and our clients' horoscopes. Brothers and sisters are potentially our only lifelong companions. They may share both our entry into and our exit from the world; they are witnesses to our childhood and share in the familial history. Siblings are the companions and 'others' that populate our earliest environs and impress upon us some of our earliest attitudes, values and beliefs. Like the sign Gemini, the sibling constellation is full of paradoxes. Siblings may be both ally and enemy or both confidante and betrayer. We want to be identical to them, we want to be completely different. With the sibling we initially experience the polarity of feeling.

Such powerful figures as our brothers and sisters and their influence upon our psychological development are represented in the horoscope in numerous ways. In the internal world, the sibling is a Hermetic companion–guide who we continually seek in our external world. Astrology can help us define and imagine both the internal and archetypal sibling images as well as their external representatives.

To begin our exploration into the sibling, I would like to turn first to what psychoanalysis had to say about the sibling bond. Theory is, in part, biographical and often speaks from the theorist's own unconscious. Therefore the psychoanalytic fathers' own sibling constellations and their horoscopes will provide a reference point for their articulation of the sibling bond.

Notes

1. *Jane Austen's Letters*, R. W. Chapman (ed.) (Oxford University Press, London: 1952), 513–14. This letter is from Cassandra Austen to her niece after the death of her sister, Jane.

2. Herodotus, *Histories*, trans. George Rawlinson (Wordsworth Editions, Ware: 1996), Book 3.119.

3. Sophocles, *Antigone*, in *The Three Theban Plays*, trans. Robert Fagles (Penguin, Harmondsworth: 1984), 105.

4. Maia, Hermes' mother, is one of the Pleiades. Owing to precession, the brightest of the sister stars, Alcyone, will be on the cusp of Gemini in the new millennium.

5. *The Barnhart Dictionary of Etymology*, Robert K. Barnhart (ed.) (H. W. Wilson, New York: 1988), 1003.

PART ONE
Psychology and the Missing Siblings

Ultimately sibling rivalry is about surviving childhood.
Frank J. Sulloway, *Born to Rebel*

2

Psychoanalytic Siblings

Images of Siblings in Psychology

None of the classical theories of personality or of psychological development portrayed siblings as important agents of socialisation. Traditionally psychological theories have emphasised parental influences on child development. Michael Lamb[1]

Theories of personality developed early in the twentieth century by the founders of psychoanalysis, like Sigmund Freud and Carl Jung, stressed the powerful imprint the parental relationship etches upon the psyche. At the turn of the twentieth century, the political and cultural atmosphere contributed to this focus on authoritarian and hierarchical structures. Familial relationships were viewed in this light, stressing the relationship to the authoritative parent while virtually ignoring the association to the sibling. The sibling system, where the patterning for equality in relationship begins, was overshadowed by the psychoanalytic focus on the parental pair.

Classical psychoanalytic literature which explores the impact of the sibling is rare. If mentioned, the sibling influence is static, fixed in childhood and not explored as a continuous influence across the life span. Left in childhood or interred under the familial rubble, psychoanalysis abandoned the sibling even though early psychoanalytic cases were pointing to the importance of the sibling relationship. For example, both Freud and Jung referred to analytic cases where the sibling had been the catalyst for the patient's disorder. D. W. Winnicott documented the study of a young girl, 'The Piggle', where the marked changes in her behaviour began with the birth of her sister.[2] Not recognizing the powerful influence of the sibling on development over the life span ignores valuable material that could amplify psychic complexes.

The fathers of psychoanalysis, Sigmund Freud, Alfred Adler and Carl Jung, were also colleagues. Their fraternal relationship was fractured by rivalries as each one brought his personal sibling experiences to his collegial relationships. Experiences within their own sibling systems influenced some of their psychoanalytic theories. Their lack of focus on the sphere of siblings may have been an unconscious defence to maintain the seat of authority. The analyst–patient relationship, exclusively modelled on the parent–child dyad, is power based, a system which maintains a sense of hierarchy.

The psychoanalytic triumvirate

Sigmund Freud was the first-born son in his family of origin, entering a complex family situation. His father had two grown sons from a previous marriage and was already a grandfather when Sigmund was born. Freud had five sisters and one surviving brother that followed him over the next ten years, as well as a younger brother who died shortly after birth. Feelings of rivalry unleashed at the birth of a sibling formed the cornerstone for his theory on siblings. As the eldest son displaced by seven successive siblings, jealousy is evoked as the eldest confronts the loss of his primary love, fated to share his mother with the succeeding siblings.

Alfred Adler was the second surviving son. His sibling constellation included an older brother, two other surviving brothers and two sisters, as well as two brothers who died. From his view, in second place, he developed the theory of 'organ inferiority and the inferiority complex'. Adler, as he noted himself, was the second son trying to catch up. Freud, from the vantage point of the first son, alluded to the omnipotent feelings of the child, whereas Adler's perspective in second place contributed to his theoretical development on the feelings of inferiority. As a later arrival, feelings of envy and inferiority may be more readily constellated.

Carl Jung was the first surviving son who had one sister born nine years later. His sibling constellation also included a brother born before him, who survived for a few days, as well as two stillborn sisters. He was the only surviving son, and for nine years an only child. As elder sons, Freud and Jung eclipsed the second-positioned Adler.

What all three had in common was a brother who died. Freud's brother Julius was born seventeen months after him but survived only seven months. Adler's younger brother, Rudolf, died of diphtheria in the cot next to him, just before Adler's fourth birthday.[3] His family tradition suggested another brother was stillborn. Jung had a brother, Paul, born two years before him who survived only five days. While sibling loss was a more common experience in the late nineteenth century, it is uncanny that all three had lost a brother. How this loss may have affected their psychological theories is conjecture; however, Freud and Adler do speculate that the loss deeply affected them. Until recently, sibling loss and its impact on the surviving siblings was not explored to any extent. It was a grief not spoken of, abandoned to the unconscious annals of ancestral history. Jung also had two stillborn sisters precede him. While Freud and Adler's theories sought the lost brother, it was Jung who found himself deep in the territory of the lost feminine, the unknown woman.

As these psychological technicians were formulating their maps of the unconscious, Pluto was in Gemini (1882–1914), the sign connected to the myth of the lost brother.[4] The planet Pluto had not yet been discovered, therefore its archetypal pattern was still collectively unknown, expressed through only a few individuals of the time. Pluto's domain is the underworld; Gemini's is consciousness. At the turn of the century, the underworld broke into consciousness through the ideas, theories, maps and thinking of Freud, Adler and Jung. Gemini is also the constellation of the sibling, its myth recounting the story of Pollux's quest to rejoin his dead brother, Castor. For both psychoanalysis and its founders, the psychic impact of the loss of the sibling was left relatively uncharted. The psychoanalytic founders' lost sibling became a part of psychoanalysis itself, as manifested in the exclusive focus on parental figures and the accompanying hierarchical structures.

While Freud referred to the sibling's urge to rid himself of the competitive rival, Jung wrote about the theme of the hostile brothers who killed their sibling in order to individuate. Within the trinity of the psychoanalytic fathers, each had survived a potential rival. However, the lost sibling rival arrived in the midst of their psychoanalytic circle as the colleague. Freud, the elder, and Adler, the second son, belonged to the Viennese psychoanalytic 'family' that grew up around Freud in the early 1900s. Freud and Adler's views collided and Adler left the circle. Curiously, Adler's eldest brother was named Sigmund, a chilling constant reminder of the elder sibling with whom Adler could never catch up. Jung and Freud moved from a close bond to their eventual estrangement, eventually 'killing' each other off. Irreconcilable differences, perhaps unresolvable rivalries, drove them apart. Freudians, Adlerians and Jungians who built on their original theories, continued to echo the sibling conflict. The unresolved sibling conflicts were now part of the community of psychoanalysis. Three variations on the theory of psyche were caught in the web of incomplete sibling issues at the heart of the psychoanalytic family.

Early in his career, Jung wrote a paper on the 'Family Constellation' and was attuned to the impact of the family atmosphere. Freud also wrote of familial complexes, commenting on the sibling mainly in terms of rivalry and the child's awakening ego consciousness at the birth of a sibling. It was Adler who provided a more definitive delineation of the family constellation by formulating a theory of birth order, describing the destiny of siblings from their ordinal position. Adler aligned himself with the horizontal view of family life that includes the sibling system. His belief in the unconscious, therefore, was fundamentally different from that of Freud and Jung. His theory of 'Individual Psychology' strove for the equality of the individual. Adler's theories are more aligned with the trinity of relationship houses (three, seven and eleven), which are houses that describe the quest for equality in relationship. This trinity of houses begins with the sibling's influence represented by the third house. Theorists like Jung and Freud, who espoused the latent and hidden powers of the unconscious, are more likely to be found excavating the terrain of the houses of endings (fourth, eighth and twelfth), unearthing the more archaic patterns beneath the surface of family life.

Psychoanalysis matured in a Eurocentric and patriarchal culture dominated by males. Christine Downing suggests this masculine-dominated perspective stresses the bond between the spouses and the nuclear family where the eldest son takes precedence. This minimizes the importance of the sibling experience. In contrast, a matrilineage honours the familial bond over the marital bond, where blood kin, parents and siblings come before partners.[5]

Neither Freud nor Jung wrote about the sister bond, yet each struggled with these bonds in their own personal lives. Sisterhood remained a mystery to the psychoanalytic fathers and their followers. The three psychoanalytic founders were elder brothers of sisters, and in an uncanny way it was their 'younger sisters' who became their patients, arriving in their consulting rooms as the 'hysterics' who ultimately inspired psychoanalysis.

The female players in the psychoanalytic world were also caught up in their own sibling issues. Two prominent female psychoanalysts, Melanie Klein and Anna Freud, also succumbed to sibling politics. One of these, Melanie Klein, became a prominent analyst and member of the British Psycho-Analytical Society. She was the youngest child in her sibling constellation, which included an older sister she envied, a brother she adored and a sister she lost. In describing Klein's envy of her older sister, her biographer suggests this sibling envy became incarnated in her work:

she still retained the envy of a powerless baby sister. Melanie Klein was an embodiment of her own latter theories: the world is not an objective reality, but a phantasmagoria peopled with our own fears and desires.[6]

Anna Freud was the youngest daughter of the great father, Sigmund Freud. Anna had two older sisters and three older brothers. In both Anna and Melanie's sibling constellations, the first born was a sister. As Anna became recognized in the areas of child development it was inevitable that sisterly envy would be constellated, causing splits in the psychoanalytic family. Female analysts, psychoanalysis's younger sisters, struggled for visibility in the complex psychoanalytic family atmosphere.

Adler's delineation of sibling positions led to a series of research studies into sibling rivalry which increased its universal awareness, if nothing else. The other main area of research into sibling influence is the significance of birth order. Much of this research is criticized because many other familial factors have not been taken into account. Birth order research holds a perennial fascination with clinicians since there are obvious characteristics forged from our placement in the family. The order of birth confers a sense of place upon the individual. There is a fate that accompanies the place we take in the sibling order, a place that we unwittingly try to recreate in our social lives.

A new horizon

At the end of the twentieth century, the focus on authority and hierarchical structures has shifted. The political and cultural atmosphere is ambivalent about authority; on one hand, there is a grief at the loss of strong authoritarian figures, on the other hand there is a strong urge for equalitarianism on all levels of society. With this shift in focus from hierarchy to equality, the issue of the sibling, as the first equal relationship, will emerge.[7] The sibling influence on personality development and socialization has been addressed more by researchers from the fields of sociology and social work. Sociology and family therapy have stressed the importance of the family system and the interactive dynamics between all family members. Identifying the family as a holistic organism, comprised of the central parental pair, their families of origin, as well as the other immediate family members, extends the socializing agents for an individual beyond the parents to all familial relationships. In this system, siblings are seen as important contributors to our patterns of relating.

The family structure, as it was in the early days of psychoanalysis, no longer exists. In the rapid rearrangement of family structures, values, morals and goals, the role of the sibling is becoming more important. Siblings act as 'safety valves' in a separation or divorce, providing continuity when the family structure alters or splits apart. More than ever, this system holds much of our familial coherence. In some ways the link between sisters and brothers is one of the most unusual familial bonds, as it often survives throughout our lifetime, becoming a link that encompasses the longest period of time in comparison with other relationships. Sibs share similar genes, similar parental beliefs, and a similar early lifestyle; this shared history imprints them with a common destiny, a shared foundation in life. This influence is a cornerstone to later relationships. The sibling influence is of utmost importance, for within the sibling system we learn to share, strive for equality and have our first experiences of equal and peer relationships.

From an astrological point of view, this exploration of siblings is also timely. Uranus' passage through the sign of Aquarius will last until the year 2003, while Neptune's transit in the same sign will last until 2011. Both planets stress the collective's need for equality and equal relationship. The quest for equality begins in the sibling system and our own personal sibling constellation. Our place within the groups we join, the community we belong to, and many other group constellations will be examined, drawing into consciousness early imprints from our experiences within the sibling unit.

The planet Pluto transits the sign of Sagittarius until 2008, in opposition to the sign Gemini, symbolizing the need to delve into earlier peer relationships, especially those with siblings, more intently. As Pluto begins to aspect our personal planets in Gemini, unresolved material, including unexpressed grief or loss, from earlier relationships with our siblings will be drawn to the surface for healing. This transit will resurrect the Geminian images of the lost twin or the missing half that has been carried by 'significant others' in our lives. Honouring the other half of self that has been constellated by partners and peers throughout our lives is a significant part of the process. It suggests a need to understand the spectrum of feelings transferred into contemporary relationships from our primary relationship with siblings. Pluto in Sagittarius also offers an opportunity to reflect on the ideas and theories seeded when Pluto was in Gemini, the period when psychoanalysis was born.

Notes

1. Michael Lamb, 'An Overview and Introduction', in *Sibling Relationships: their Nature and Significance across the Lifespan*, 4.
2. See D. W. Winnicott, *The Piggle: an Account of the Psychoanalytic Treatment of a Little Girl*, 6. In presenting the case to Dr Winnicott, the mother said in her letter: 'She had a little sister when she was twenty-one months old, which I considered far too early for her.' Interestingly, at a later time, Winnicott found out the mother had a sibling born after an identical gap. Family timing repeats itself, as do the feelings that the mother experienced when she had a sibling at the same time.
3. Alfred Adler, *What Life Could Mean to You*: foreword by Rita Udall, 9.
4. Neptune was in the sign of Gemini from 1888 to 1902, and in 1891–2 conjoined Pluto three times in the eighth and ninth degree of Gemini. This further emphasizes the theme of the missing or estranged sibling.
5. Christine Downing, *Psyche's Sisters: Reimagining the Meaning of Sisterhood*, 62.
6. Phyllis Grosskurth, *Melanie Klein: her World and her Work*, 62.
7. See Robert Bly, *The Sibling Society* (Addison-Wesley, New York: 1996). Bly does not talk about siblings, but uses this as a metaphor for a society that has become horizontal and lacks authority figures.

3

Freudian Beginnings

Mars, Rivalry, Aggression and Leadership

Transference is not necessarily bound to mother or father images, but may also proceed from the 'brother imago'. Sigmund Freud[1]

Sibling rivalry

Hostile feelings towards brothers and sisters must be far more frequent in childhood than the unseeing eye of the adult observer can perceive. Sigmund Freud[2]

When the American Psychoanalytic Association's Committee on Indexing produced a cross-referenced index on Freud's work there was no category for sibling, brother or sister included.[3] While Freud's references to siblings were not at the forefront of his psychological theories, none the less, his case studies and theories often presented sibling issues. For instance, his famous cases of 'Little Hans' and the 'Wolf Man' demonstrated the important psychological impact of the sibling upon the individual's well-being and psycho-sexual development. In retrospect, perhaps it was Freud's disciples who did not pick up the trail of the sibling influence that Freud's work hints at.

Freud's comments generally concerned the phenomenon of sibling rivalry and hostility 'when the next child appears in the nursery'.[4] He stressed that the eldest child has strong jealous and competitive feelings when the next child is born into the family. The eldest child, formerly the centre-piece of the family, is usurped by the entrance of the younger sib. Freud suggested the rage constellated by being displaced and feeling the parental focus shift to the younger child is expressed by the older sibling through jealousy and competitiveness. Competitive feelings are described as hurtful, resulting in a sense of loss of parental love and resource, rather than a spur to achievement. Unlike mythic sibling stories that speak of love, loyalty and sacrifice, Freud leaves us with an impression of the wound that is inflicted in the primary sibling relationship, a wound which resonates with his own experience.

These aggressive and hostile feelings provoke curiosity, leading the elder child away from mother. Hostile feelings experienced towards the sibling form part of our earliest memories and promote the beginning of ego awareness. This could parallel the elder child's beginning to approach father, the sibling's birth motivating the older child to relate more fully to father. The intrusion of a younger sibling encourages a movement away from mother, stimulating the consciousness of self and the Sun. This shift in parental focus is a primal initiation of separation and individuation. The urge to recognize our own individuality begins the process of differentiation from the sibling as well as other family members. Feelings of rivalry, awakened by the intrusion of an equal into the family, constellate the archetype of Mars. The aggressive, competitive and hostile feelings that accompany rivalry provide the stimulus to experience Mars. As Mars is activated a more conscious experience of separateness instigates a movement away from the symbiotic relationship with mother. Mars' traits of courage, adventure and, eventually, leadership are also experienced.

What is initially apparent in Freud's horoscope (see figure 1) is Mars, the focal planet, being most elevated and a singleton planet by hemisphere.[5] It is the only planet retrograde at birth, opposing the other planets grouped together in a bundle. Nearing the end of its retrogradation cycle, Mars has gathered the powerful charge associated with a stationary planet. Freud's observations are from his position as the eldest child. Other children in the sibling system may not feel the impact of the next sibling's entrance as severely as the eldest since they have learned to coexist with another sib since their birth. The eldest is in a unique position as he holds the position of an only child, then has it taken away by the birth of a younger sibling. Feelings of rage and jealousy are therefore stronger for the eldest child.

Freud's professional references to sibling rivalry and the feelings of jealousy, aggression and competitiveness that the dethronement of the oldest child constellates, are illustrated in some of his lectures on psychoanalysis. His own references to sibling jealousies are in his letters, implied in family anecdotes or alluded to in his essays and lectures. Some of these memories surfaced during his own self-analysis.

In his 'New Psychoanalytic Lectures' of 1923, when speaking of why a girl may turn from her mother to her father, Freud states:

The next accusation against the child's mother flares up when the next baby appears in the nursery. If possible the connection with oral frustration is preserved: the

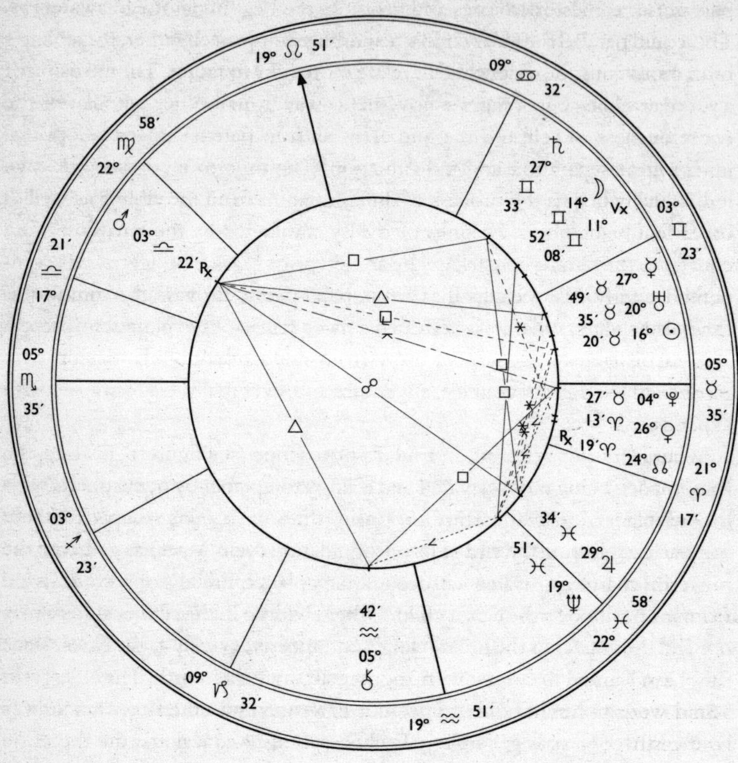

Figure 1: Sigmund Freud's horoscope, 6 May 1856, 6.30 p.m., Freiberg, Moravia.

mother could not or would not give the child any more milk because she needed the nourishment for the new arrival. In cases in which the two children are so close in age that lactation is prejudiced by the second pregnancy, this reproach acquires a real basis, and it is a remarkable fact that a child, even with an age difference of only 11 months, is not too young to take notice of what is happening. But what the child begrudges the unwanted intruder and rival is not only the suckling but all other signs of maternal care. It feels that it has been dethroned, despoiled, prejudiced in its rights; it casts a jealous hatred upon the new baby and develops a grievance against the faithless mother which often finds expression in a disagreeable change in its behaviour.[6]

Freud clearly draws a picture of this primal jealousy towards the new sib and also suggests that it may influence later stages of development. He may be unconsciously alluding to his own shock as his siblings continued to arrive almost annually.

In 1910, during Freud's lecture series on psychoanalysis, he remarked that the curiosity drive is often stimulated by the jealous feelings aroused with the impact of a new sibling. These feelings of hostility and jealousy are also associated with the archetype of Mars. When talking of the awakening of sexual curiosity in a child, Freud suggests that the important event that arouses this curiosity and its accompanying questions is 'the actual birth of a little brother or sister'.[7] He makes the point that this nascent curiosity may be directed into a new understanding for the older child. The curiosity is also a means to becoming informed and therefore empowered 'as if the child were looking for ways and means to avert so undesired an event [as the birth of a sibling]'.[8] The birth of a sibling can spark the conscious questioning of human origins, calling our own existence into question. The sib's arrival prompts an inquiry that may correlate with the beginning of differentiation, hence consciousness. This budding curiosity, conscious inquiry and intellectual exercise are also part of the territory of the astrological third house. Upon the terrain of the third house we not only meet the sibling but experience curiosity that leads us out into a wider context of neighbourhood, to examine, explore and question who we are and the world we live in.

Freud articulated the complex feelings that are catalysed when a new child arrives in the family. While the family celebrates this new addition, the displaced sibling may literally see this new 'arrival' as 'a rival'. There may be a defined shift in the relationship with mother as conflicting feelings now exist towards her being the care giver to both the elder and younger siblings. This experience of 'other' can now be defined in reference to the sibling. Awareness of the ego as separate from the sibling does not feel as dangerous as being separate from mother. This awareness of being separate from the sibling can facilitate the psychological task of being separate from mother/Moon. This new feeling of separateness in relationship to the sibling promotes more individuality and begins the journey of knowing who we are as distinct from others in the family unit.

Julius, his younger brother, was born seventeen months after Freud and died at seven months.[9] Freud greeted the baby 'with rage and wicked death wishes'.[10] In 1897, when Freud was in the process of his own self-analysis, he wrote to his colleague Fleiss mentioning his feelings of rivalry towards his younger brother and the guilt associated with his death. In a stream-of-consciousness writing style he explains

> that I greeted my one-year younger brother (who died after a few months) with adverse wishes and genuine childhood jealousy; and that his death left the germ of (self-) reproaches in me . . . This nephew and this younger brother have determined, then, what is neurotic, but also what is intense, in all my friendships.[11]

Freud's comments on sibling rivalry seem to stem from his relationship with his nephew, John, and his younger brother Julius. Fifty years after his birth he wrote: 'the unwelcome arrival of a baby brother or sister is the oldest and most burning question that assails immature humanity'.[12] Freud also recognized the impact of his younger brother and elder nephew on his adult friendships. His struggle with close friends and colleagues could partially be linked to these earlier feelings of jealousy and rivalry. His nephew, John, was a surrogate older brother. Freud commented how this relationship 'determined all my later feelings in intercourse with persons my own age'.[13] Mars retrograde in the eleventh house symbolizes the themes of intensity, rivalry and jealousy that plagued many of Freud's friendships and colleagueships. It also symbolizes his research on sexuality and his theory of libido, the theory that created the most dissension and conflict amongst his psychoanalytic colleagues.

Fraternal rivalry

Friendships and collegiate support were intensely important to Freud; however, they often eluded him. In a letter to his colleague, Karl Abraham, Freud expressed the sentiment: 'All my life I have been looking for friends who would not exploit and then betray me.'[14]

In many friendships this hope never eventuated. During his early years as a psychoanalyst, his intimate friendship and close colleagueship with both Wilhelm Fleiss and Josef Breuer were destroyed by jealousy and rivalry. When Freud was a more mature and prominent figure in the psychoanalytic movement, Alfred Adler became an important colleague; however, this relationship ended in an unpleasant split. Freud's 'crown prince', Carl Jung, once the treasured colleague and anointed successor, soon became a bitter rival after their estrangement. As Freud himself said:

> All of my friends have in a certain sense been reincarnations of this first figure [a composite of his nephew, John, and younger brother, Julius]. My emotional life has always insisted that I should have an intimate friend and a hated enemy. I have always been able to provide myself afresh with both, and it has not infrequently happened that the ideal situation of childhood has been so completely reproduced that friend and enemy have come together in a single individual.[15]

The earlier and incomplete ambivalent feelings around his siblings surfaced in the arena of the astrological eleventh house of friends and colleagues. Younger colleagues became his surrogate siblings who constellated the archetype of Mars, stirring feelings of rivalry and his need for control and domination.

Freud also commented how the 'herd instinct' may be a derivative of this initial jealous impulse towards the sib. Continuing to keep aggressive feelings alive evokes the fear of becoming alienated from the family which encourages the movement towards allying with a common group goal. Social feeling may be partially the result of sublimating our sibling conflicts and transforming sibling rivalry.[16]

This developing spirit of community is extended into the world of peers, first with other children in the school yard and then eventually into our friendships and with colleagues in the workplace. Social bonds are born out of the renunciation of sibling jealousies and rivalries. Each sibling's love and need for the parents puts the sibs on an equal footing within the family.

This spirit of equality is a basis for group participation. Freud depicts how this instinct allows a group of individuals and potential rivals to rally around a common focus: 'Originally rivals, they have succeeded in identifying themselves with one another by means of a similar love for the same object.'[17]

Sibling rivalry and the way we manage the associated feelings affect our ability to be within a group, to promote equality and mutual concerns. Festering sibling hostilities are met in the group, the rival–other appearing as a member or members of the group. Astrologically, this is the link between the third and the eleventh houses. The eleventh house experience is no longer based around the parent or blood ties but around a mutual goal, a common objective, a shared spirit. The eleventh house is the setting for adult relationship that has developed out of the sibling world. Left-over sibling hostilities are often dragged into this arena. The reactivated feelings towards the sibling find their way into conscious expression, through the stimulus of the group that has re-enacted the family atmosphere. In group dynamics, and certainly in group psychoanalysis, this places sibling transference at the heart of the work.

Freud and his family

Freud's position on the collective phenomenon of sibling rivalry was influenced by his personal experience. He was the eldest child in his family of origin, the first-born son of his mother but the third son of his father, Jacob, who had previously been married twice with two sons from his first marriage. Freud had two adult half-brothers when he was born: Emanuel was two years older than Sigmund's mother, while Philip was one year younger. Emanuel had one child at the time of Freud's birth and therefore Freud became an uncle at birth to John, aged one. A niece, Pauline, was born six months after Sigmund. This confusing family picture placed Amalie, Sigmund's mother, in the same generation as his half-brothers. The family atmosphere that contained his parents' trans-generational marriage, spawned fantasies for Freud of his mother having a relationship with his half-brother, Emanuel. The situation also fed fanciful fantasies of his half-brother as father, confusing the parental and sibling roles, a theme that would recur in many ways in Freud's life. In Freud's publication, *Psychopathology of Everyday Life*, the book that inspired the popular phrase 'Freudian slip', he illustrates how forgetting and making unconscious errors reveal deep complexes. Freud describes two errors that he found after his book *The Interpretation of Dreams*

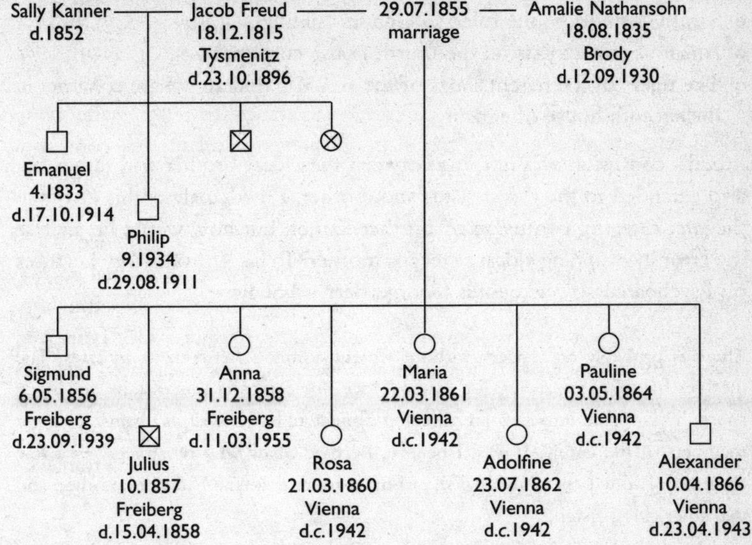

Figure 2: Freud's sibling constellation.

was published. One of the errors was to name Hannibal's father incorrectly as *Hasdrubal*, who was in fact Hannibal's brother. Hence the brother was substituted for the father, fuelling a fantasy; as Freud says: 'how much pleasanter it would have been had I been the son of my brother instead of the son of my father!'[18]

The other error was to name Zeus as the one who castrates Ouranus, virtually missing out one generation. How could this have happened when Freud consciously knew it was Chronus, Zeus' father, who castrated Ouranus. Freud explains that his half-brother had once admonished him in a way he never forgot. His brother had clearly pointed out that Freud belonged 'not to the second but really the third generation of [his] father'.[19]

The confusion between the role of the father (authority) and the sibling (equality) is apparent in Freud's role as a surrogate authority figure to his sisters and brother. Later, he continued to remain the authoritarian father towards his peers and colleagues. The blurred boundaries between his role of sibling and parent are suggested by the following statements in his horoscope:

- o Capricorn (authority) on the cusp of the third (sibling) with
- o Saturn (authority), the ruler, in Gemini (sibling).
- o Aquarius (equality) is on the fourth house cusp (parent).
- o The rulers of the parental axis of the IC–MC (hierarchy) are conjunct in the seventh house of equality.

Freud's confusion was not just between the eldest brother and father but also extended to the eldest sister and mother. Freud analysed his errors in the first category confusion of brother/father, but how would he analyse the error in swapping eldest sister for mother? In his 'Introductory Lectures on Psychoanalysis', he quotes George Bernard Shaw:

> There is probably no nursery without violent conflicts between its inmates. The motives for these are rivalry for parental love, for common possessions, for living space. The hostile impulses are directed against older as well as against younger members of the family. It was, I believe, Bernard Shaw who remarked: 'As a rule there is only one person an English girl hates more than she hates her mother; and that's her eldest sister'.[20]

Shaw did use this line in *Man and Superman*. But Freud transposed the elder sister and mother, echoing the confusion in roles between the sibling and the parent. In Shaw's play his character Tanner says: 'as a rule there is only one person an English girl hates more than she hates her elder sister; and that's her mother!'[21]

Freud's 'eldest sister' Anna may have been a more convenient hook for some of the hostility that Freud could not divert towards his mother. On 31 December 1858, shortly after Julius Freud's death, Anna was born.[22] Four more sisters followed, one nearly every year after that, and finally the youngest child, a brother, was born ten years after Freud. It has been postulated that Freud's idealization of his mother concealed his rage towards her, feelings he was unable to come to terms with.[23] These feelings may have stemmed from losing her to his sibling rivals.

Many losses in the family coincided with the death of Freud's brother Julius on 15 April 1858. Freud's mother also lost her own brother, Julius, for whom the new baby had been named. Sigmund lost a brother and an uncle, both named Julius, at the same time. These losses were compounded by the failure of Freud's father's business during the same period. With the loss of a child, a black hole appears in the constellation of the family; the missing sibling holds a void of unlived potential. Without adequate mourning, the grief over the dead child and its lost potential creates a vacuum in the family system. The mother often feels unavailable, lost in her own depression. Her anxiety, provoked by the loss, is also experienced by the surviving children, often quite intensely. The mother's ability to bond with the surviving children is threatened as she may now fear their loss. Possibly at the time of Julius's death, Freud felt the loss of his mother and, rather than direct his anger at her, redirected the hostility towards the next arrival, Anna. His sister Anna also arrived synchronous to Freud's nanny mysteriously disappearing; this nanny had been a surrogate mother to Freud. Thus the family atmosphere around Anna's birth was charged with grief and bewilderment.

Freud's sister Anna arrived on New Year's Eve, the day the Sun was transiting Sigmund's third house cusp. This birth was significant for Freud for many reasons: she was the first of five sisters and the first surviving sibling to follow him. As the oldest male sibling to five sisters, he gradually displaced his weakened father, becoming their protector and adviser. Sigmund's position as the favoured and talented sibling was secured at the expense of his sisters.

Aggression and Eros

Freud directed most of his hostility towards his sister, Anna. She was his least favourite sibling. Whether this was because of her challenge for the mother or because of his guilt reaction to an erotic bond is not certain. However, the covert hostility between the two siblings remained throughout their adult years.

Anna is described in Freud's interpretations of one of his own earliest memories.[24] His father had allowed Sigmund, aged five at the time, and Anna, almost three, to rip up an illustrated book. He described tearing the book, leaf by leaf, like an artichoke. Paralleling this memory were fantasies of masturbation. Freud was to postulate later that these erotic fantasies felt guilt laden and therefore were converted into hostility. Freud's Oedipal complex centred on the young boy's desire for the mother; yet sexual desire for the sister could be even more overwhelming owing to their closer proximity, equality and symmetry.

In one of Freud's most famous cases, the 'Russian Wolf Man', he comments on the damaging Eros of a brother–sister relationship. After being rejected by an intelligent and seductive older sister, Freud suggests the Wolf Man was then compelled to choose relationships that were inferior substitutes for the sister.[25] Freud's adherence to the Oedipal complex did not allow him to see the erotic impulses between brother and sister in their own right. Ernest Jones states:

> The characteristics of the father–daughter complex are also found in a similar one, the brother–sister complex. As analytic work shows every day, this also, like the former one, is a derivative of the fundamental Oedipus complex. When the incest barrier develops early in the life of the young boy it begins first in regard to his relationship with the mother, and only later sets in with the sister as well; indeed, erotic experiences between brother and sister in early childhood are exceedingly common.[26]

Freud's adherence to the Oedipal tale limited his vision into the abundant myths that told of the brother–sister marriage as well as the love and Eros between opposite-sex siblings.

An interesting enmeshment between the siblings continued into their adult lives. Anna and Sigmund married a sibling pair. Eli Bernays, the older brother of Martha Bernays, married Anna three years before Freud married Martha, even though Sigmund and Martha were the first couple to be engaged. Eli and Martha, unlike Sigmund and Anna, had a close sibling bond. This intimacy was threatening to Freud, especially when his fiancée would seek her brother Eli's advice. For reasons never mentioned, Freud did not attend his sister's wedding! He transferred much of his hostility and rivalry to Eli, twice a brother-in-law. It is common that a sibling's marriage ignites the taboo feelings too dangerous to express to the sibling. Certainly, in opposite-sex sibling pairs, the sib's marriage partner is a prime target for unexpressed sibling hostilities or feelings. Anna, writing about her brother in later years, criticized his dominance and favouritism in the family, resenting what she had to sacrifice for him and his education.

Another sibling triangle formed part of Freud's marriage. In November 1895, nine years after Sigmund and Martha married, Minna Bernays, his wife's sister, came 'for a stay of several months'.[27] In reality, she lived with her sister and brother-in-law for the rest of her life. This arrival occurred a few weeks before the sixth and last child, Anna, was born. The sisters shared the management of the household. Martha knew little of her husband's vocation or seemed little interested, while Minna was actively involved and supportive of his work. Minna was intellectually aligned with Sigmund while Martha was more pragmatic, attending to the care of their children. Freud has referred to Minna as 'my closest confidante'.[28] Her presence was part of his daily life – he discussed his analytic practice with her, they spent evenings playing cards together and she accompanied him on his daily walk. In essence, Freud had two wives; his wife's sister became his spiritual wife. As we would imagine, this situation gave rise to rumours and speculation of an affair between Sigmund and Minna by biographers. The enmeshment of the sisters' relationship with Freud may have been partially fuelled by his earlier incestuous wishes towards his sister as well as his triangular relationship with his siblings and his mother. It may have been easier for Freud to speak about the hostile feelings between siblings rather than the erotic ones.

Opposite-gender siblings contain a potent heterosexual erotic component. Aggressive feelings may be directed more easily than erotic impulses. Guilt over these erotic feelings may unconsciously result in cruel or distant behaviour. This defensive behaviour helps protect the acting out of the taboo erotic feelings. Opposite-gender sibs close in age may act out their erotic impulses with their sib's friends as surrogates. This begins the channelling of the Eros away from the sib on to other potential partners. A triangle is still part of this scenario with the sibs now having a friend/lover in common. Freud's relationship with his sister reminds us of the potent astrological link between the sibling patterns of the third house and the formation of adult relationship patterns in the seventh house.

Freud also commented on homo-erotic experience in relationship to older same-sex siblings. In his essay on 'Homosexuality' he cites his observations where hostile and jealous feelings directed at brothers 'sometimes reach the pitch of actual death wishes'. It is too dangerous for the boy's development to maintain these death wishes and therefore 'these impulses yielded to repression and underwent a transformation so that the rival of the earlier period became the first homosexual love-object'.[29] Rivalry, thus, is not only avoided but transmuted into homo-erotic feelings. The rival is eliminated by choosing brother as a love object rather than identifying him as a competitor. Aggressive and potentially murderous feelings are sublimated into sexual feelings. The erotic impulses towards the sib are later safely displaced into another relationship that may take the form of the earlier relationship with the brother. Some recent research has collaborated Freud's observations, confirming a higher percentage of male homosexuals were second-born sons with an older brother.

The great leader, the compliant follower

We know little of Freud's other sisters besides descriptions of family life given by Freud in his letters. Rosa was the second sister, born 21 March 1860, and his favourite, followed by Marie, Adolfine (Dolfi) and Pauline. Freud was also fond of Dolfi, who never married and who lived with their mother and whom Freud helped support. Freud was automatically the authority figure to whom his sisters and the extended family would turn for advice and resources. It was these four sisters Freud left behind when he emigrated to London in 1938. All four died later at the hands of the Nazis, after his death.

It was Freud's younger brother Alexander who became his closest sibling. Alexander was born ten years after Freud on 19 April 1866. At a family council, ten-year-old Sigmund suggested the name Alexander for his baby brother, after the military leader Alexander the Great whose power and leadership had made an impression upon him. Unconsciously he also chose a conquering hero who surpassed the glory of his father. Later, Freud was to name all his children after significant men or women connected to him. Anna, his youngest daughter who followed in his professional footsteps, bore the same name as her father's sister, but was named for the daughter of one of his intimate friends.

As a younger brother, Alexander became Sigmund's supportive follower, travel companion and suppliant ally and helper. Sigmund's fatherly role to this brother is reminiscent of the confusion between the father–brother roles he experienced with his half-brother, Emanuel. This relationship may have been the pattern that Freud hoped to find with his younger colleagues, with them as compliant followers. Perhaps it was this model of a colleague that he referred to when writing to his younger colleague and heir apparent, Carl Jung:

> Just rest easy, dear son Alexander. I will leave you more to conquer than I myself have managed, all psychiatry and the approval of the civilised world, which regards me as a savage.[30]

Now it is Jung whom Freud names Alexander, the son who is to surpass the father. Referring to Jung as Alexander blurred the boundaries between his role as an older sibling and a father-figure. Alexander, Freud's youngest sibling, was the prototype of how Sigmund would deal with his younger male friends and colleagues. Freud's role as a surrogate father to his sibs also created a distortion with his younger colleagues – he often placed himself in the role of leader/father rather than equal/colleague. In a letter to Sabrina Speilring, Jung lamented: 'I want to be a friend on an equal footing while he [Sigmund Freud] wants to have me as a son.'[31]

Ambivalent feelings

Sibling research has suggested some elder children's behavioural problems stem from sibling rivalry. Overt hostility, increased acting up, demanding behaviour, regression to baby talk and regressive steps in eating and toilet training were all reported as reactions by an older child to a younger sibling's birth.[32] Murderous feelings towards the sibling, however, may be replaced later with strong positive feelings. Darker feelings of envy, hatred, rage and jealousy cluster around the negative pole while brighter feelings of love, admiration, tenderness and warmth constellate around the positive pole. The feelings towards the sibling swing back and forth between the poles. Children experience the tension of paradoxical feelings in relationship to the sibling.

Negative feelings towards the parents are more difficult to sustain as they endanger the sense of safety. However, in the sibling system we have more latitude in experiencing both extremes of feeling. Both poles of the feeling life can be felt and experienced consciously without the negative pole destroying the relationship. Within the sibling system we can realize that both negative and positive feeling can coexist, and that negative feelings towards siblings do not destroy our relationships with them.

The range of ambivalent feelings towards siblings is often denied. However, the denial is quite contrary to children's actual aggressive behaviour to their younger siblings. Aggression to the younger sibling is behaviour we often label as 'just part of growing up'. The bullying and triumphing over the younger sibs is often taken into the school yard, and later into work situations and organizations, or is repressed and replaced consciously by more acceptable feelings. It is through dreams and other unconscious imagery that the murderous feelings towards the sibling may surface. Freud comments:

> Many people, therefore, who love their brothers and sisters and would feel bereaved if they were to die, harbour evil wishes against them in their unconscious, dating from earlier times; and these are capable of being realised in dreams.'[33]

Repressed feelings towards a sibling are often transferred on to a new rival, presenting as a partner, friend or colleague.

The range of emotion for our siblings may be our first experience of the duality of feeling, for passionate and often murderous feelings live alongside joyous and loving ones. D. W. Winnicott points out that only children, not having the experience of being dethroned, may lack the early childhood experience of what conflicted feelings feel like. They may not be as prepared for rivalries later in life, not having experienced them in relationship to a sibling.

The archetype of Mars

The rivalry and competitive feelings, the beginning of turning away from the total sense of immersion in the mother-matrix and out into what lies beyond the mother, are characteristic of the archetype of Mars. Mars, the first planet outside the orbit of the Earth, is our first experience of individuality as it lies beyond the container of the Earth's orbit. The cycles of the other personal planets of Venus and Mercury, while contributing to the sense of personal identity, do not symbolize the development of hostile and competitive urges that actually help cut the ties that bind. The Mercurial and Venusian developmental cycles are still held within the orbit of the Earth and therefore develop within the parameters of this system. Mars is outside this system and represents the initial experience of independence from the familial system.

This is why the birth of a sibling, especially for the eldest, is often synchronous with a transit or progression to natal Mars. The urge to risk exploring beyond the familiar arises. A transit to Mars, at the time of a sibling's birth, suggests that rivalry and competition will be a natural part of the relationship; this transit being the younger sib's horoscope and forever in aspect with the older sib's Mars. When Julius was born (October 1857), Sigmund's progressed Moon was square his natal Mars while the progressed Sun was sesqui-square natal Mars. Both luminaries were aspecting Mars, stressing both the conscious and unconscious layers of his rivalry. A common progression I have seen in many elder children's horoscopes is the progressed Sun aspecting natal Mars at the time of a younger sibling's birth. This confirms Freud's premise that there is a conscious awakening and ego identification (progressed Sun) at the birth of a younger sib. His theories on rivalry, jealousy, competitive feelings, hetero- and homo-erotic urges all resonate with Mars.

If a sibling is born before the older sib's Mars return,[34] the elder could experience difficulty in forging ahead and taking the first initial steps towards separation. Without a full cycle of Mars, the elder child may not be ready to break the symbiosis or exclusive relationship with mother. It may be more difficult to separate, fuelling the already present aggressive feeling towards the usurper. Hostile feelings that are ignited by the sibling's birth may be turned upon the self and the child regresses to a state of helplessness in order to engage in a more covert competition for the mother. Alternatively, this could result in the two siblings becoming bonded to such an extent that a twinning relationship occurs, finding it difficult to separate from each other, since the primal separation has not taken place. Separation may feel threatening. The need to identify with the younger arrival, to experience commonality, or perhaps idealize the new sibling, may be a safer defence than the actual wish to get rid of the competitor. These hostile feelings experienced before the age of twenty-two months may not yet feel part of who we are, but something that is larger than us and, if expressed, may be destructive. Complicating this may be a sibling born in the pre-Mars return phase who arrives on the first Solar return (one year old), the Mercury return (anywhere between eleven and thirteen months) or the Venus return (ten to fourteen months), impinging upon the sense of individuality. Aspects to the natal Mars will help identify to what degree the stimulus to separate was complicated by the sibling's birth. These aspects may describe how we experienced our first aggressive feelings, or, if we are younger, how aggression was acted upon us. The aspect may also suggest how these aggressive and hostile feelings could be channelled.

Freud commented that hostile attitudes towards new sibs were more apparent in children aged between two and a half and four or five years.[35] Here the child is able to express hostility, to voice disapproval and act out angry feelings. These ages are post Mars return. Before the Mars return, the ability to act upon these feelings is diminished and aggressive feelings may be introjected rather than expressed, compounding the complex around the expression of Mars.

Freud was over two and a half years old when Anna was born and he was more vocal in his hostility towards her as his theory suggests. However, the feelings towards the missing brother Julius, born before his Mars return, were more complicated.

The horoscope of Sigmund Freud

Sigmund Freud was born on 6 May 1856 at 6.30 p.m. in Freiberg, Moravia. His father, Jacob, recorded the event and his son's birth time in the family Bible along with the details of his circumcision.[36] Freud was named after his father's father who died only two and a half months before Sigmund was born. The name inscribed in the Bible was Shlomo Sigismund, Schlomo his grandfather's name. His father's first wife had died three years earlier, while mystery and secrecy surrounded the second wife. An unconfirmed story to do with his birth tells of a shopkeeper's prophecy: upon hearing of the child born in a caul, he announced to Amalie, Sigmund's mother, that a great man had been brought into the world. (For Freud's horoscope, see figure 1.)

With Scorpio rising and the ruler Pluto on the horizon of the horoscope, the imagery of death, mystery and prophecy surrounding the birth is not surprising. Pluto, regent of the Underworld, is on the western horizon, the astrological threshold where setting planets descend into the unseen world. This symbol is consistent with Freud's descent into the underworld of others' psyches to excavate what was not yet consciously visible to them. Pluto had not yet been discovered at his time of birth, but was known by his death. Freud's excavations of the underworld and psyche in the early decades of the twentieth century paralleled the ongoing research into Pluto. When he died on 23 September 1939, Pluto had been known of for nine years. The planet was then in the third degree of Leo, having entered Leo for the last time and beginning the waxing square to the natal Pluto.[37] Both Jupiter and Uranus were retrograde and were returning to their natal positions within the month. This would mark the close of Jupiter's seventh cycle around his horoscope and the completion of the Uranus cycle of eighty-four years.

When Freud died, transiting Pluto was within one degree of Carl Jung's Sun. Transiting Pluto was just below the descendant, in the *exact position* as it was in Freud's natal horoscope (see figure 6). Partially, Jung's Pluto transit to the Sun/descendant was losing his erstwhile friend, colleague and mentor. Now Jung could continue where Freud left off, fulfilling Freud's earlier promise to Jung (see quote, page 26).

To explore the sibling system it is interesting to look first at the third house of the horoscope. Capricorn is on the cusp, a fitting reminder of Freud's authoritarian role in his sibling constellation later taken into other groups of friends and colleagues. When Freud refused to share any more personal information with Jung to assist in amplifying a dream, Jung reported that Freud's response was 'But I cannot risk my authority', preferring, as Jung said, to place personal authority before truth.[38] Capricorn on the third house cusp is an immediate image of this authority, as well as duty and responsibility in reference to his siblings. The archetype of Capricorn or Saturn connected to the third often correlates with an elder or only sibling. Freud was a father-figure to his sibs, providing both resources and advice for them, just as earlier, his half-brother had become a father-figure to him.

Capricorn on the third house cusp could signify feelings of aloneness, alienation or even exclusivity in his sibling interactions. Saturn, ruling the third house, is in Freud's eighth house in Gemini, compounding these feelings with guilt over the loss of his brother. The sign Gemini is on the cusp of the eighth house, connecting the experience of loss and death to a sibling. In Freud's case, the death of the sibling was literal. With such a significant primary loss, the eighth house area of intimacy could be well defended. With Saturn in the eighth, the fitting defence mechanism may be authority and control. Two other astrological statements in Freud's horoscope are synonymous with the loss or alienation of a sibling – the Moon in Gemini, also in the eighth, and Chiron in the third house.

Chiron in the third house in Aquarius is a statement of a wound unintentionally opened through the sibling experience. Chiron also squares Pluto. Like Pluto, Chiron was not discovered at the time of Freud's birth and remained undiscovered throughout his lifetime. Pluto, squaring the third house Chiron, reiterates the theme of sibling loss. Chiron's placement in Aquarius in the third is evident in Freud's life: his mental health vocation promoted healing through the mind and its associations. Freud listened to the language of his patients to find a link to a possible cure. Bertha Pappenheim labelled this method the 'talking cure', which, in part, was a confession. The third house Chiron describes not just the healing power of the word but also the wounding evident in his caustic remarks to both his siblings and colleagues, no longer in favour. His writing and lecturing on the wounding and healing properties of the unconscious inspired a new field of psychoanalysis. Freud, like Chiron, was mentor and foster father to numerous Solar heroes of the psychoanalytic movement. Like the mythic Chiron, he was fatally wounded.

Freud developed cancer of the jaw and mouth and, after numerous operations, talking became difficult and painful. The cancerous wound was in the same area where his healing abilities were also located. His youngest daughter, Anna, became his mouth, speaking for him at meetings and lectures. He described her as his Antigone, still in identification with the Oedipus myth. Antigone was her father's guide after he blinded himself, becoming his companion and his sight while he was exiled. Antigone was Oedipus' daughter, but they shared the same mother, therefore she was also his sister. Anna had the Moon in Gemini which was exactly conjunct her father's Saturn.[39] Again the theme of the confusion between the parent and the sibling is evident.

Chiron in the third also refers to his sibling legacy. The wound inflicted through his experience of siblings was evident, resulting in feelings of alienation, separation and guilt. Chiron in Aquarius suggests these feelings may have surfaced in his associations with adult peers who may have unwittingly reopened the wound. Freud's fascination with death wishes was apparent in his relationship with Jung. On two occasions he fainted after accusing Jung of harbouring death wishes against him. Freud's Chiron was conjunct Jung's ascendant, igniting his earlier sibling wound and the conflicted feelings with his dead brother.

This may also be an image of what prompted Freud to write his essay 'Family Romances'.[40] The family romance emerges when the child feels slighted having to share his parents with his siblings. To liberate himself from identifying with his siblings and/or the parents, the child romanticizes his origins. Generally he is adopted and his 'real' parents are far grander than his current ones, also the parents of his siblings. Or he is the only legitimate child and his brothers and sisters are bastards, born of mother's love affairs. He also mentions how this romance can rid the boy, sexually attracted to his sister, of the incest taboo, for now they have different origins. Chiron in the third feels adopted, alien and outcast in its sibling system. Individuals with Chiron in the third house may feel marginalized. Freud commented that the civilized world regarded him as 'a savage', and felt on the fringe of humanity. His earlier wounding in the sibling system was taken into the wider arenas of life as well as visibly contributing to his psychoanalytic theories.

The sibling story is also spun around Gemini. Freud has both Saturn and the Moon in Gemini. With the Moon in Gemini, an enmeshment between mother and siblings may occur, or the roles of siblings and mother are not well defined. Mother preferring the role of a sister, or the sister becoming a mother to her siblings, is a common scenario with the Moon in Gemini.

In Freud's case he became a parental figure to his siblings. By secondary progression the Moon had progressed to natal Saturn when Freud was eleven months old, exactly the age referred to by Freud in his lecture on 'Femininity', when a child can feel mother's withdrawal due to the presence of another sibling. Certainly this is biographical, for Freud's mother would have been three months pregnant at this time. This progression signals a deep sense of isolation and separation from mother, and may be an emotional watermark for his confusing respect and authority with love and acceptance. The Moon in Gemini conjures up the mythic search for the lost twin. In the eighth we also see the intimate relationship entangled with the sibling relationship, and in Freud's case this manifested in his 'marriage' to the two sisters. These confusions of roles between mother–wife, sister–daughter were part of Oedipus' story and also part of the legacy of his Moon in Gemini.

The Vertex is also in Gemini in the eighth house. While psychological astrology does not often refer to the Vertex, this angle frequently carries strong images of compulsive relating. It symbolizes where there may be a compulsive or blind aspect in our relationships. The Vertex symbolizes the hidden agenda in relationships that is not visible until the relationship has excavated deeper emotional territory. An image I often equate with the Vertex is the alchemical 'left-handed handshake' – the king and queen are bound together by a similar complex and unconsciously agree to collude on a particular agenda. However, the agenda they are agreeing on is not yet visible or known to them and is quite contrary to the conscious contract in their relationship. The astrological imagery of the Vertex helps to articulate the hidden agenda. The Vertex is an image of what we struggle to complete in a relationship, as well as what keeps us bound to the relationship, or a form of it, until it erupts through the ego defences to be confronted. Often it is described by individuals as the relationship they 'cannot let go of'.[41] The Vertex gathers images of what is unconscious within relationship. Gemini symbolizes the sibling, therefore the Vertex in Gemini reiterates the theme of incompleteness and compulsion around the area of sibling relationships.

The Moon is conjunct the angle of the Vertex, which amplifies the theme of confusion between the sister, wife and daughter already apparent in the horoscope. When his sister Anna was born and he 'lost' his mother, Jupiter in Gemini was conjunct the Vertex. When his daughter Anna was born (at the same time that his sister-in-law Minna moved in), Pluto in Gemini was conjunct the Moon/Vertex conjunction. His Moon conjunct the Vertex would be an image of the powerful transference with women that he encountered throughout his life, first with mother, then sisters, analysands, colleagues, wife, sister-in-law and daughters. In Gemini it points to the duplicity inherent in his relationships and first encountered with his sisters. It is interesting that his beloved daughter would carry the name that would remind him of his difficult relationship with his own sister. The amalgam of sister/daughter was also consistent with the Oedipus myth: Antigone being both Oedipus' daughter and half-sister.

Sigmund Freud, while not specifically devoting his writings to siblings, left a mark to start from – a mark, or perhaps a scar, from his own sibling experience. Few psychoanalysts were to follow his leads. While Freud contributed interesting material on siblings, his followers continued to concentrate on the parental axis. Melanie Klein, influenced by her own sisterly envy, continued to emphasize the jealousy, hostility and sadistic aggressiveness that children feel towards their siblings and how the intensity of hatred is inevitably repressed in order to remove these feelings from consciousness. She also portrayed siblings as objects that interfere with mother, but also are able to free each other from narcissistic enmeshment with mother. Siblings can be transitional figures who help to draw the monumental feelings of security and dependency away from the mother, redirecting these intense feelings on to the world of siblings and, eventually, extra-familial peers.

It was Alfred Adler in his pursuit of 'Individual Psychology' who first helped define the nature and role of the sibling within the family system, and it is to Adler that we turn in Chapter 4.

Notes

References to *The Standard Edition of the Complete Psychological Works of Sigmund Freud* will be abbreviated as *SE*, followed by the volume and page number.

1. Freud, 'The Dynamics of Transference', *SE* 12.100.
2. Freud, 'The Interpretation of Dreams', *SE* 4.252.
3. Stephen Bank and Michael Kahn, 'Freudian Siblings', *Psychoanalytic Review* 67, no. 4 (winter 1980–81).
4. One of Freud's expressions from his lectures on 'Psychoanalysis'.
5. Chiron is not referred to here as a planet.
6. Freud, 'Femininity', *SE* 22.123. From this quote it is often deduced that Freud may have been alluding to his brother's birth when he was eleven months old. Astrologically, eleven months is exactly half the Mars cycle.

7. Freud, 'Leonardo da Vinci and a Memory of his Childhood', *SE* 11.78–9.
8. Ibid.
9. Two differing times are given for when Julius may have been born. The other suggestion mentioned is that Julius was born eleven months after Freud (see note 6). Ernest Jones, Freud's colleague and biographer, mentions this in *Sigmund Freud: Life and Work*, vol. 1. This information is based on Freud's own recollections from his self-analysis and then is mythologized in his biographies as it 'fits' well with his quote of 'eleven months'. Peter Gay in *Freud: a Life for Our Time*, 8, confirms the October 1857 date. Marianne Krull in *Freud and his Father*, 214, confirms this from records.
10. Peter Gay, *Freud: a Life for Our Time*, 507.
11. Freud, *The Origins of Psychoanalysis: Letters, Drafts and Notes to Wilhelm Fleiss* (Basic Books, New York: 1950), 219.
12. Giovanni Costigan, *Sigmund Freud: a Short Biography*, 4.
13. Ibid.
14. Duane Schultz, *Intimate Friends, Dangerous Rivals: the Turbulent Relationship between Freud and Jung*, 216. This was referring to the 'brutal, sanctimonious Jung and his disciples'. The letter was written on 26 July 1914, which happened to be Jung's thirty-ninth birthday. Jung shared the birthday with Freud's wife, Martha, who was born on 26 July 1861.
15. Ibid., 29.
16. Freud, *Group Psychology and the Analysis of the Ego*, trans. James Strachey (W. W. Norton, New York: 1989), 66.
17. Ibid., 67.
18. Freud, *The Psychopathology of Everyday Life*, trans. A. A. Brill (T. Fisher Unwin, London: 1928), 253.
19. Ibid.
20. Freud, 'Archaic Features and Infantilism of Dreams', *SE* 15.205.
21. George Bernard Shaw, *Man and Superman*, in the Complete Plays of Bernard Shaw (Hamlyn, London: 1965), 355.
22. Differing December dates have been suggested. The 31 December date is confirmed by both Gay and Krull. Anna's Sun is conjunct Freud's third house cusp, a constant reminder of the conscious intrusion by his sister.
23. This is suggested by Lucy Freeman and Herbert Stream in *Freud and Women*. Samuel Slipp in *The Freudian Mystique*, 108, states: 'instead of individuating from his mother and establishing a separate identity, Freud seems to have remained fused and identified with her. He continued to use the internal defence mechanism of splitting, repressing his hostility and consciously idealizing his mother.'
24. Freeman and Stream, *Freud and Women*, 26.
25. Freud, 'From the History of Infantile Neurosis (1918)', *SE* 17.22–3.
26. Ernest Jones, *Hamlet and Oedipus: the Oedipus Complex as an Exploration of Hamlet's Mystery* (Doubleday, New York: 1949), 157–8.

27. *Complete Letters of Sigmund Freud to Wilhelm Fleiss*, Jeffrey M. Masson (trans. and ed.), 152.
28. Ibid., 73.
29. Freud, *SE* 18.231.
30. *The Freud/Jung Letters: the Correspondence between Sigmund Freud and C. G. Jung*, William McGuire (ed.), 300.
31. Aldo Carotenuto, *A Secret Symmetry*, 184.
32. Judy Dunn and Carol Kendrick, *Siblings: Love, Envy and Understanding*, 24–7.
33. Freud, 'Interpretation of Dreams', *SE* 4.251.
34. Traditionally, astrologers state the Mars return to occur at twenty-two months. In actuality, the period of the Mars return can vary considerably, ranging from seventeen to twenty-three and a half months, dependent on orbits that are used.
35. Freud, 'Interpretation of Dreams', *SE* 4.251.
36. Ronald Clark, *Freud: the Man and his Cause*, 8–9.
37. This aspect occurs for individuals with Pluto in Virgo and Libra as early as the age of thirty-five.
38. Jung, *Memories, Dreams, Reflections*, 158.
39. Anna Freud was born on 3 December 1895 at 3.15 p.m. in Vienna. Freud noted the time of birth in a letter to Wilhelm Fleiss that day.
40. As included in *SE* 9.236–41.
41. Because the Vertex has this 'fated' quality, it is useful in synastry and chart comparisons, especially among bonded relationships that 'last a lifetime': parent–child, siblings, soul mates, etc.

4

Adler, the Second Son

Birth Order and the Family Atmosphere

The position in the family leaves an indelible stamp upon the individual's life style.

Alfred Adler[1]

Individual psychology

Alfred Adler's contribution to psychology is often lost between the giants of Freud and Jung. Adler saw a more visible horizon to the psyche than his contemporaries. His psychology was an 'Individual Psychology' that placed the individual at the centre of his own life, responsible for his own choices. True to his Aquarian nature, Adler forged a fulfilling life out of social interest, feeling for humanity and contributing to society. Society's foundation rests on the structures forged out of our first experiences within the microcosm of a social system – the family.

The divergent orientation to the psyche's horizon that Freud, Jung and Adler saw can be accounted for, in Adlerian theory, by their different birth order positions. Each position in the family has its own environment that influences one's attitudes and goals in life. Both Freud and Jung were the eldest. As an eldest child, the parental relationship dominates the horizon. It is the child's only primary familial relationship at birth. Adler, as the second child, entered the family where another sibling was already part of the family constellation. The sibling relationship is already innate to the experience of the later-born child who has to share his parents from birth. Adler implies that Freud's view of the domination of the parental imprint on the psyche is an eldest child's view. This superior and only position of the eldest child could contribute to the regressive urge to return to that once favoured position before the advent of the sibling intruder. One of Adlerian psychology's main tenets is the striving from a position of inferiority to superiority, a view from his position in second place. Later-borns learn to interrelate and share with a peer from the beginning. Whereas first-positioned

Freud's Oedipal complex put the eldest son in the shadow of father, Adler as the second son was in the shadow of brother.

> A typical second child is very easy to recognise: he behaves as if he were in a race, as if someone were a step or two in front and he had to hurry to get ahead of him. He is going full steam ahead all the time. He trains continually to surpass his older brother and conquer him.[2]

An eldest child may be engaged in trying to regress to an exclusive relationship with the primary parent by removing the obstacle of the rival, the other parent. However the second born is engaged more in acts of striving forward to surpass the older sibling. From this different perspective, rival psychologies were forged. Freud, as the eldest, developed the Oedipal complex suggesting the child's inherent urge to kill off the father to marry the mother, as the mythical Oedipus had unwittingly done. Adler, from the experience as the second son, developed the 'inferiority complex'.

Alfred Adler was born in the Vienna suburb, Rudolfsheim, on 7 February 1870. Unlike Freud or Jung, there is no record of his birth time although various astrological books and periodicals have presented differing times.[3] The lack of recorded birth time is also consistent with the dearth of biographical details on Adler. There are no volumes of his letters, unlike Freud or Jung, no archives dedicated to his research and few photographs, voice or film recordings. Adler's work has been disseminated most effectively through education rather than writing. In order to refer to Adler's horoscope I shall use the local midday on the day of his birth to present the chart. With the grace of serendipity, Gemini is appropriately ascending in the horoscope.

Ironically, the psychological pioneer who talked mostly of the sibling influence is also the one who is ignored in mainstream psychology, like the theme of siblings itself. Adler's overshadowing may be due, in part, to the focus on the parental pair by psychoanalysis, where the engagement with parental transference is at the heart of the work. With the first born's concentration so focused on the hierarchy of parental authority, the horizon of the sibling is overlooked. As we move beyond this focus on the parents as the key to psychological health, a wider vista of familial interrelationships opens up, including those with our siblings.

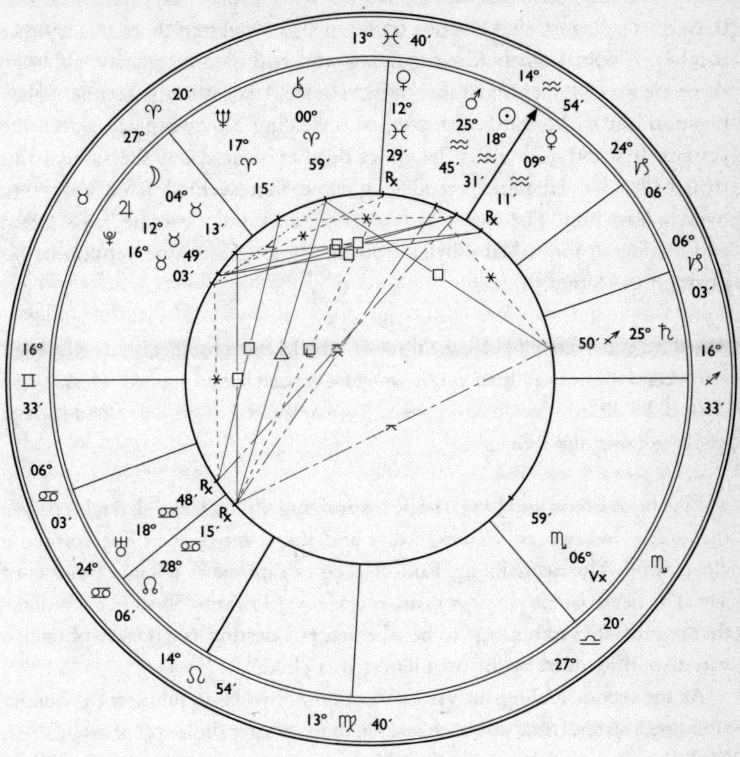

Figure 3: Alfred Adler's horoscope, 7 February 1870, midday used, Vienna, Austria.

Adler and his siblings

Adler's sibling constellation included his older brother Sigmund who was born on 11 August 1868. Family tradition also suggested there was another brother, Albert, born before Sigmund, who had died in infancy, although there are no civil records of this birth.[4] Hence Adler is in the second sibling position but is the third-born son, complicating his own place within the system. It is interesting that his older brother's name was the same as his rival colleague, Sigmund Freud – a name that seemed fated always to overshadow him. The eldest brother, Sigmund, was described as a gifted and intelligent individual. Phyllis Bottome notes Adler's perception of his position in second place:

> Alfred Adler felt himself put in the shade of a model eldest brother, a true 'first born' who always seemed to Alfred to be soaring far beyond him in a sphere which Alfred – for all his efforts – could never attain. Even at the end of his life, Alfred had not wholly got over this feeling.[5]

Like both Freud and Jung, the next surviving sibling was a sister, Hermine; but unlike his two colleagues, Adler and the sister next in line formed a close bond. The next sibling, Rudolf, died of diphtheria at eight months of age. The death of his younger brother was one of the childhood benchmarks that contributed to his urge to be a healer. His destiny as a healer/physician was also influenced by his own illness as a child.

As the second sibling, he was also a middle child contending with younger siblings. A sister, Irma, was born just ten months after the death of his brother, Rudolf, and then another brother, Max, was born on 17 March 1877. While Adler was fond of Max, this feeling was not always reciprocated. Bottome reports that Max was 'highly envious and jealous of the popular Alfred'.[6] Richard was born fourteen years after Alfred and the role in the family of 'mother's favourite' was transferred from Sigmund, the eldest, to Richard, the youngest. Alfred felt rejected by his mother, yet formed a powerful relationship to his father whom he saw as protective, becoming his father's favourite. Parental favouritism fuels rivalry. The supportive Solar quality of Alfred's father found its way into the Solar-orientated Adlerian psychology.

One of Alfred's earliest memories was when he was four years old. His father would take him for a daily walk to encourage a sense of recovery from the rickets that had kept him immobile for a long time. During these

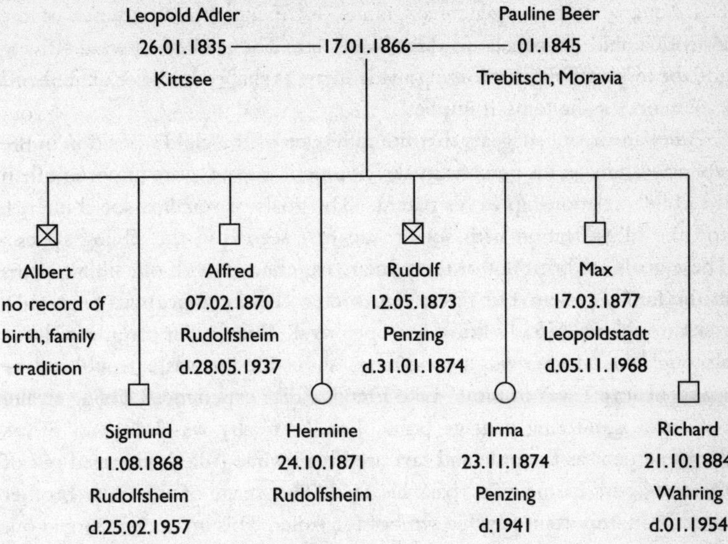

Figure 4: Adler's sibling constellation.

walks his father would repeat an invocation that came to be important to Adler: 'Alfred – never believe anything anyone tells you!'[7] This axiom would become important to Individual Psychology as conduct and actions, the striving towards a goal, are more authentic than words. Action and motivation resonates with Adler's Sun–Mars conjunction and as a four year old, who had just lost a brother, action may have been an effective replacement for mourning.

In his book, *The Practice and Theory of Individual Psychology*, Adler reiterates the imprint that childhood marks upon the individual:

> Every marked attitude of a man can be traced back to an origin in childhood. In the nursery are formed and prepared all of man's future attitudes. Fundamental changes are produced only by means of an exceedingly high degree of introspection or among neurotics by means of the physician's individual psychological analysis.[8]

Adler's psychology grew from the premise that the individual was responsible for his own transformation and motivation. While we are influenced by the society about us, none the less we are the chief protagonist in our own story. His Aquarian Sun is quincunx Uranus, fortifying the importance of the individual and his conscious direction in life. The goal of forward striving and the responsibility for forging an identity was shaped by Adler's childhood experiences as he himself implies.

Adlerian theory suggests that the influence of the child's position in the sibling system on his personality development is even more important than the child's relationship to his parents. The goals of equality, social interest and the identification with society are first seeded in the sibling system. These goals are born out of the primary experiences with our sibling-peers in the family system, our first micro society. Bottome portrays Sigmund's role throughout Alfred's life as his 'open rival'. Even Adler commented that although this brother was a good man, 'all his life [he was] a trouble to me – as I believe I was to him'.[9] Like Freud, Adler experienced sibling rivalry but from a differing vantage point. Freud's rivalry was born out of his dethronement as the only and favoured one, while Adler's emerged out of the competitive urge to surpass his rival. The image of the older brother became an important psychic symbol for Adler. This image was forged out of his experience of weakness and immobility due to his early illness while his older brother was healthy and active.

Alfred and Sigmund: sibling synastry

The personal masculine planets, the Sun and Mars, may be constellated by both the elder brother and father. Father is the most likely candidate for the transference of the Solar energy, but if the father is weakened, unavailable, or unable to carry the Solar projection, the elder brother becomes the next choice. When father is available, then the individual's Sun–Mars aspects could symbolize the relationship between father and brother, and how the dynamic flow of masculine energy between the two is experienced. Mars could easily be captured by an older brother, especially if he was vibrant, energetic or a passionate warrior. From the younger brother's view, the older brother seems paces ahead, more physically capable and a formidable rival, all magnets that attract the projection of Mars. Alfred, as the younger brother and sickly child, may easily have shaped his Mars through the experience of his elder brother.

Sigmund Adler had the Sun in Leo at the exact opposite degree to Alfred's Sun in Aquarius. Since Alfred also had the Sun–Mars conjunction, Sigmund's

Sun was also opposite Alfred's Mars. This Solar opposition helped stimulate a sense of mirroring and an identification of opposites. Alfred's Mars was also conjunct Sigmund's South Node; Alfred may have displaced his Mars on to his brother, recognizing Sigmund as 'soaring far beyond him'. What he saw as innate in his elder brother had to be consciously developed in himself through effort and striving.

Adler was plagued by rickets which left him immobile in the early years of his life. It was during this illness that he locates his first memory:

> One of my earliest recollections is of sitting on a bench, bandaged up on account of rickets, with my healthy elder brother sitting opposite me. He could run, jump, and move about quite effortlessly, while for me movement of any sort was a strain and an effort. Everyone went to great pains to help me, and my mother and father did all that was in their power to do. At the time of this recollection I must have been about two years old.[10]

This memory around the age of two, the Mars return, confirms the imprint of the image of the healthy brother, a polarity to Alfred's illness. The first Mars return near the age of twenty-two months synchronizes with the child's accelerating consciousness of mobility and the urge to move farther afield. The image at the heart of Adler's psychology, that of the individual's striving for mobility and power, was first experienced with his brother, who was a catalyst for his future ideas. Brother, mother and father are all part of this first memory, but the main focus is on brother.

The urge for separateness and movement away from early attachments is part of the first Mars return, a time when the aggressive, competitive and individualistic feelings begin to emerge. These feelings are often reflected in the relationships to our siblings at this time. Through this period, Adler's experience was one of being bound. Mars, as reflected in the healthy brother, stimulated the impetus to harness the frustration, to create goals of forward striving and the movement towards perfection. The elder brother served as the shadow image, carrying health and movement. Sigmund had Mars in Gemini which opposed Alfred's Saturn. While Alfred experienced a sense of restriction and being bound by the limitations of his illness (Saturn), his brother's vibrancy was even more evident. The reality of Sigmund's vitality was in stark contrast to Alfred's reality of being immobilized. This may have helped evoke authentic urges for health and movement that lay in himself. It would have also highlighted his sense of inferiority to brother, urging

Alfred to strive for a sense of authority over this feeling. Later, Adler developed his theories of organ inferiority and the inferiority complex inspired by his own experience of illness.

There came to light a remarkable relationship between somatic inferiority and psychic overcompensation, so that I gained a fundamental viewpoint, namely that the realisation of somatic inferiority by the individual becomes for him a permanent impelling force for the development of his psyche.[11]

During his first memory, Jupiter and Uranus were transiting his North Node – an image of striving towards freedom, away from the restrictive image of his Capricorn South Node. The North Node was transiting Gemini and had previously transited the synastry aspect between the brothers – the North Node conjoining Sigmund's Mars in Gemini (freedom and movement) while the South Node transited Alfred's Saturn (binding and restriction). Brother was a facilitating shadow figure, and therefore became a vital contributor to the dynamics that helped forge Adler's psychology.

In 1908 Adler formulated and presented his ideas on the aggressive instinct as an autonomous drive. Similar to his own experience, he postulated that a greater aggressive drive accompanies organ inferiority. But this aggressive drive may align with a higher principle-motivation. During this year Pluto in Gemini turned stationary retrograde at the exact degree and minute opposite Alfred's Saturn, and conjunct his brother's Mars in Gemini. Adler's authority over his own experience of the aggressive instinct (Mars), confronted earlier in his relationship to his brother, was ready to surface. Adler continued to develop his concepts regarding aggression, later aligning the aggressive drive with motivation and striving to succeed. When social interest was not developed in the individual, aggression became a destructive force. Freud, who originally did not accept the theory of the aggressive instinct when Adler first presented it, later called it the 'destructive' or 'death instinct'. Sigmund Freud had his Saturn at the same degree of Gemini as Sigmund Adler's Mars. Sigmund's Mars was a mirror for his brother. Alfred came to know the principle of striving forward out of a sense of deprivation, a highlight of Adler's philosophy.

The astrological web between the two brothers is a reminder of the powerful imprint the sibling makes on the formation of our world view. As Mercurial personifications, siblings help formulate, both consciously and unconsciously, our ideas, our attitudes and our modes of thinking and

Alfred Adler	*Sigmund Adler*	*Sigmund Freud*
Sun – 18° Aquarius	Sun – 18° Leo	MC – 19° Leo
Sun conjunct Mars		
Alfred's Sun–Mars conjunction opposite brother's Sun and conjunct Freud's IC		
Saturn – 25° Sagittarius	Mars – 28° Gemini	Saturn – 27° Gemini
Mars – 25° Aquarius	South Node – 26° Aquarius	

Figure 5: The synastry of Alfred Adler, Sigmund Adler and Sigmund Freud.

expression. Siblings are our first peers who encourage and criticize us. They are witnesses to our first attempts to walk, speak, draw, write and express. They inhabit the third house territory where we first become conscious of ideas, the process of thinking, learning and speaking. The sibling may be the mirror, the Mercurial trickster or change maker that facilitates consciousness.

Losing a brother

The major imprint from Adler's childhood experience was the death of his younger brother who died of diphtheria on 31 January 1874. This was the exact date of Adler's Mercury return. Adler, born with Mercury retrograde, had Mercury return to its natal position for the fifth time exactly on the day his brother died. Transiting Uranus was retrograde, opposing his natal retrograde Mercury, for the second time. During the Uranus opposition to Mercury a separation from a sibling or sibling pattern could occur. Transits to Mercury awaken sibling themes; Uranus transits to Mercury encourage a separation or reparation of our sibling patterns. Coupled with the return of Mercury it suggests that the consciousness of the event will leave a powerful imprint on Adler's ideas.

As the retrograde planet is closer to a person's internal core (as symbolized by the retrograde being closest to the Earth), Adler's natal Mercury retrograde intensifies the sibling images. Often my experience of Mercury retrograde does correlate with an estrangement or loss of a relationship to a sibling, or simply an intense and powerful identification with a sib. It is a clue that alerts me to investigating other sibling themes in a chart.

The sibling, as an embodiment of Hermes, may act as a *psychopomp* in many ways. Literally, he may be our guide through dangerous transitional terrain or bring complex and difficult issues to the liminal of consciousness.

He may become a 'transitional object' that carries us through one stage of childhood to the next, our guide into territory we have not yet experienced. A missing sibling may continue to become our guide to the other world. Adler experienced his younger brother die, lying in the cot next to him. A profound imprint is etched on his psyche, the sibling image could now be one of soul guide into the depth terrain of psyche. This was Alfred's first conscious experience of the profundity of death, loss and mortality.

The second profound experience of Adler's childhood occurred near the age of five when he came close to death himself with pneumonia. Throughout this year, Saturn was transiting his Sun–Mars conjunction while transiting Pluto was squaring his progressed Sun, as well as the midpoint of the Sun–Mars conjunction. The impact of the Pluto–Saturn transits upon the Sun–Mars helped consolidate the earlier images of the sense of striving (Mars) for individuality (Sun), born out of his illness of rickets. This sense of striving forward could also be compensatory for the feeling of being swallowed by death. His own brush with death came a year after his younger brother died.

Adler developed the theory of organ inferiority which suggested, in part, that the 'inferior organ' provides a symbolic clue to the psychic complex the ego/body is compensating for. I wonder what he thought pneumonia symbolized: could it be a somatic image of unexpressed grief over the loss of the brother? The second child is highly attuned to what is repressed in the family and unexpressed grief could find a way into consciousness through the body and illness. It is common for a child to express a familial loss or trauma through a physical or emotional illness, injury or intellectual setback. The child's unconscious is flooded by the buried feelings of the family and expresses itself visibly for the family to recognize. Like his two adult colleagues, Freud and Jung, Adler may have been more influenced by the unexpressed grief of the family than he realized.

The images of Alfred's two brothers make a striking contrast for Adler. Compared to the eldest he is bound, while his older brother is mobile; in contrast, his younger brother dies from an illness, while he survives. The progressed Moon was in Gemini at the time of Rudolf's death, confirming the emotional impact of the loss of his brother. A year later Adler was close to death with pneumonia. The Uranus transit at his brother's death suggests the detachment from his feelings of loss, facilitating his recovery by not identifying with his brother's death. Adler believed one's unconscious is formed out of the social experiences we encounter, and that it is largely determined by the meaning we ascribe to these experiences. The way we direct these experiences is our own choice. Adler's Sun–Mars in Aquarius aspecting Uranus suggests a clarity of thinking through its ability to distance and separate from overwhelming feelings. This supports his conviction that humans have the ability to choose their responses. For Adler, striving forward may also be a means to disconnect from the trauma of loss and grief.

> No experience is in itself a cause of success or failure. We do not suffer from the shock of our experiences – the so-called trauma – but instead make out of them whatever suits our purposes. We are not determined by our experiences but are *self-determined* by the meaning we give to them; and when we take particular experiences as the basis for our future life we are almost certain to be misguided to some degree. Meanings are not determined by situations. We determine ourselves by the meaning we ascribe to situations.[12]

A second child's strategy is to develop a rational perspective or orientation to distance the self from emotional pain. Seconds, often barometers for the unlived emotional life of the family, may need to create this mechanism to avoid drowning in the family grief.

These early childhood experiences in the sibling environment inspired many of Adler's theories: organ inferiority, the inferiority complex, the striving for superiority and the effect of the sibling and the family constellation. Like both Freud and Jung, his personal experiences played a central part in his theories. Having overcome his illness, he aligned himself and his psychology with the superiority of the ego. This same attitude permeated his ideas on neurosis. Adler states that neurosis is symptomatic of not being able to overcome the feelings of inferiority, not conceiving that effort will change the dynamic. The Sun–Mars conjunction in Aquarius had become a theology of effort, motivation and forward striving, harnessed by the ego of the individual. This ego ideal was reinforced in his sibling relationships to his healthy brother Sigmund and his dead brother Rudolf.

In second place

Adler's sibling constellation was the seeding ground for the ideas he later formulated on ordinal position in the family. As a second son he was rival to his eldest brother and caught in an unsought competition with his younger brother Max. This sibling theme was replayed through his later association with Freud and Jung in the psychoanalytic family. Not only was Freud his senior, but carried the same name as Adler's older brother; Jung was five years junior. Birth position is part of our fate that recreates itself in the adult world of peers:

And was not his position of a second boy between a brilliant older brother and a competitive younger one revived later when he found himself between Sigmund Freud and Carl Gustav Jung.[13]

Adler's first contact with Sigmund Freud may have come as early as 1899.[14] This was the year of Adler's Saturn return. Adler's Saturn was opposite Sigmund Freud's Saturn in Gemini; half a cycle of Saturn separated them, a ripe transferential image of an elder sibling. There was also fourteen years' difference between Adler and his younger brother. Adler's association with Freud and the Viennese psychoanalytic circle lasted from 1902 to 1911. During the final years, Pluto was conjunct Freud's Saturn, thus opposed Adler's. A power rift developed and Adler left with other members of the circle to found his own Society for Free Psychoanalysis. He was no longer 'bound' to the patronage of Freud. The precipitating conflict was centred on Adler's theories, especially the 'masculine protest', which had become his main dynamic focus. Uranus was transiting Adler's South Node; half a cycle before, when Uranus transited the North Node, he had his first recollection of being bound while his brother Sigmund was free. The masculine protest was the ego striving for freedom. The figure this time that Adler strives to move away from is not his brother Sigmund, but his colleague and one-time friend, Sigmund. Adler was now 'free' of his second position. He founded the Society for *Free* Psychoanalysts and *Individual* Psychology, symbols of Uranus' need to break free. Adler, a later-born, needed to fulfil his destiny described by both birth position and his Sun–Mars conjunction in Aquarius. Sigmund Freud had the Uranus–Sun conjunction in the seventh house exactly square to Alfred Adler's Sun in Aquarius.

Adler took the path of education rather than analysis to help individuals overcome their obstacles. This attitude often led both Jung and Freud to perceive Adler as 'non psychological'. Two years before Freud and Adler split, Freud wrote to Jung about Adler: 'He is a theorist, astute and original, but not attuned to psychology; he passes it by and concentrates on the biological aspect.'[15] In responding to Freud over political intrigues in the psychoanalytic circle, Jung stated: 'The most I can do is criticise – Stekel for his own sweet self and his theoretical superficiality, and Adler for the total absence of psychology.'[16]

The 'total absence of psychology' may have been the absence of 'eldest son' psychology to which both Jung and Freud ascribed. No doubt Adler was more of a social theorist. His description of the unconscious was not focused on the ancestral past but more on the conscious striving towards a social interest first experienced in the family.

Jung uses the metaphor of the eldest brother and the younger brother when contrasting the Freudian theory of the 'pleasure principle' and the Adlerian theory of the 'striving for power' in his paper 'Problems of Modern Psychotherapy'. The first-born brother sounds like Freud, who as an eldest is plagued by his desires that unconsciously become the doctrine of the 'pleasure principle'. Adler is the later-born son craving the power that his birth position has not given him. Jung contrasts the eldest and the younger son, an insight probably gleaned through his association with both colleagues:

> The elder brother who follows in his father's footsteps and wins to a commanding position in society may be tormented by his desires; while the younger brother who feels himself suppressed and overshadowed by the other two may be goaded by ambition and the need for self assertion.[17]

When reading this passage, I was struck by the phrase 'overshadowed by the other two'. While I assume the 'other two' refers to the elder and the father, I wondered if the pen had slipped and Jung had fallen into an identification with Freud as the elder brother, unconsciously suggesting he and Freud were the two who overshadowed Adler. We express our birth position instinctively, recreating our position in our organizations and associations.

Freud and Adler's different approaches to psychology are best seen by the metaphor of how they saw their patients. Freud's patients lay on a couch where he could see them but the patient could not see him. Adler insisted on a face to face interview with the chairs being equal. Freudians also have a more rigid adherence to boundaries, whereas the Adlerian school is not as rigid concerning their appointments. Again this reflects Freud's hierarchical view of the patient–doctor relationship based on parent–child, whereas Adler attempts to equalize the scenario which aligns more to the sibling relationship.

*

It was after the First World War, in which Adler served as a physician, that his 'theory of social interest' became important to him. It was also in 1918 that he presented his theories on birth order for the first time.[18] During this year Uranus conjoined his natal Mars while Saturn opposed it. From 1918 to 1928 he continued to formulate his theories on birth position within the family.

Birth order position became a cornerstone in his delineation of a personality. Adler would know immediately the individual's position of birth by the behaviour and manner shown. In defining the most important points to ask about when obtaining data from the client, birth position was a priority:

> the most trustworthy approaches to the exploration of the personality are to be found in a comprehensive study of the earliest childhood memories, of the place of the child in the family sequence . . .[19]

Adler was the first to categorize specifically the birth order positions within the family. Birth order implies its own sense of fate just as the time of birth does. This position cannot be changed; however, the understanding and acceptance of its influences can. Unaware of its influence, its fate continues to meet us in the recreation of similar scenarios in our experience within other group constellations.

Exploring Birth Order

Since Adler's delineation of ordinal positioning, birth order has been one of the most researched areas of the family. This research, however, has been perennially criticized and moves in and out of favour with researchers. Within the *Bibliography for Adlerian Psychology* I counted 140 categories for research on Birth Order.[20] These ranged from the birth order effect on academic achievement through to its effect on virginity, with homosexuality, illness, personality and psychopathology in between. Researchers have studied whether birth order affects our choice of marriage partners, our levels of stress or our involvement in group therapy. In some presentations, it seems that the understanding of birth order may be the answer to all our ills! Researchers following Adler's lead turned out volumes of material in the field of birth order, often widely contradictory.[21] Swiss researchers Cecile Ernst and Jules Angst published their extensive research into birth position in 1983 and were severely critical of other research that had erroneously excluded the appropriate variables that are inherent in sibling position. While they generally agreed that birth order, along with the size of our sibling constellation, had a considerable impact on personality, they highlighted most birth order research as ineffective and inconclusive in this regard.[22]

Birth order theory was part of antiquity and part of the stories we grew up with. Myths, fairy tales, fables and biblical stories tell us of birth ordinance. The first sibling constellation in the Bible, Cain and Abel, conflict over their ordinal position in the family. The struggle between the first born and the youngest or last born becomes a clear feature of the Old Testament. In Exodus, God unleashes ten plagues on the Egyptians as a result of the Pharoah denying the Hebrews release from slavery and Egypt. The last plague 'smote all the firstborn in the land of Egypt' (12:29). Birth order is part of our fate and a strong influence on the way we orientate ourselves to life, whether researchers are able to prove it or not.

In 1961, Walter Toman first published his theory and research on birth order in his book *Family Constellation.* Toman furthers Adler's theories by delineating the sibling constellation in terms not only of rank, but also of sex and size. He attempts to delineate the difference between an older brother of a brother as compared to an older brother of a sister, trying to include the variants of sex and sibship size as much as possible. He also suggests that when our position in the sibling system is recreated in adult relationships (partners and friends), there is potentially greater compatibility. The relationships that recreate our sibling position in rank and sex have the greatest chance for a successful outcome. He postulated that the 'worse case' scenario between adult partners was when they were both only children. Only children, according to Toman, are at the greatest risk in adult relationships, ranking low on compatibility with others. They have grown up without a partner, used to being the only focus, and now are called upon to be in relationship to an equal. Other worst-case scenarios were when there was both a rank conflict (two partners who were both eldest or both youngest etc.) and a sex conflict (both partners had same-sex siblings, or each partner only had sisters or brothers). Best scenarios were when partners recreated the rank and sex situation of their sibling constellation (the eldest daughter who has a younger brother marries a younger brother who has an older sister). He applied the same model to friendship. Toman's findings were criticized for having too much of a theoretical base and not enough research. However, his work picks up the ancient theme of the brother–sister marriage, and echoes the truth astrologers already know about the houses of relationship which link the sibling, the partner and the friend in a trinity. The third house of sibship, the seventh house of partnership and the eleventh house of friendship are linked together in a triangle of houses known as the houses of relationship. The truth of Toman's premise is also borne out in astrological chart comparison and synastry. Aspects of the sibling's horoscope are often chillingly duplicated in the partner's horoscope. Toman's model of sibship position and gender taken into the adult world of relationship is a potent tool to view the immediate link between our adult relationships with partners and friends and our sibling relationships.

While I was in the midst of writing this chapter, a book by Frank Sulloway was published called *Born to Rebel.* This book is Sulloway's creation after twenty-six years of research and involvement with birth order. Because of its long gestation it has much more of interest than most of the research done into birth order influences. It is an articulate and scholarly excursion through birth order from the Darwinian world on. However, the bottom line seems to repeat the constant theme that first borns carry the parental and traditional expectations of the prevailing authority and that later-borns are born to rebel and bring forth revolutionary thought. First borns find their niche by sabotaging change, while later-borns consistently challenge the established order.

Between Adler and Sulloway lie countless methods of approaching birth order and many more theories as to what our birth position may mean. Where then can we begin our examination? Adler points out that it is not only the birth order that dominates the formation of character but the atmosphere into which the child arrives and how this is interpreted. The family atmosphere, the attitudes of the parents, along with the dynamic of the inheritance of the ancestors, contribute to whether the task associated with the sibling position has a light or dark face. Louis Stewart makes this point extremely well in his book *Changemakers*:

> What makes the difference between a Hitler and a Ghandi, both of whom were younger sons engaged in revolution? Here we must look to the family atmosphere, that indescribable amalgam created by the behaviour, values, cultural development, and (perhaps most significantly) the unconscious parental complexes which carry the unanswered questions of the ancestors, and represent the unlived lives of the parent. It is to these influences of the family that we should look for the difference . . .[23]

One of the first variants in birth order research is how do we actually count the sequence of the sibling if the order has been interrupted by a termination, a miscarriage, neonatal or perinatal sibling death, an adopted sibling or a step-sibling? How old do children have to be before they are included in the sequence? I suggest the labelling of the position is more important for the researcher than the counsellor or therapist. The death of a sibling, whether *in utero*, at birth or shortly after, has an impact on all the siblings. The shade of the child finds its place in the sibling constellation. The family atmosphere is altered forever by the loss of the child, no matter at what age. When there has been a schism in the sibling order due to a sibling death, life arranges itself in position of those who have survived, but the unconscious life records the missing sibling. For therapists and counsellors, it is the sibling loss that is important to acknowledge and work with.

Generally, birth order is defined in terms of the first born, the middle child, the youngest and the only child. Other systems have delineated the first, second and third positions in the family with later birth positions being undifferentiated. Some systems have delineated a fourth position.[24] Karl Konig suggests that only three birth positions exist. He suggests that these three positions are repeated with subsequent siblings so that the fourth child is similar to the first; the fifth, the second; the sixth, the third and so on.[25]

Astrologically, we can also offer a theory of birth order applying the technique known as the 'derivative house system'. In this system we can locate anyone in the horoscope by deriving them from the house of the primary relationship which is counted as the first house. For example, children in general are the fifth house and therefore the eldest child is located in the fifth house. The second child is the sibling (third house) of the eldest, therefore is three houses from the fifth house – the seventh house. This house is derived from the fifth house, which is counted as the first. The third child is the next sibling and so we would count three more houses from the seventh. This aligns the first child with the fifth house, the second child with the seventh house, the third child with the ninth house, the fourth with the eleventh house and so on. While on the surface this may appear contrived, this model is worth exploring. It implies that the eldest child constellates the myth of the hero and is at risk of becoming the narcissistic mirror of the parent (the fifth house). The second child, aligned with the seventh house, is at risk of triangulation with the opposite-sex parent when there is a dysfunction in the parental marriage. Often it is the second child most at risk in parental conflict, separation and divorce, as this child manifests the undercurrents of the parental marriage. Second children are more prone to taking the role of mediator, negotiator, go-between, but also to becoming the surrogate partner. The third child, as the ninth house, is the explorer, the one who steps beyond the beliefs and mores of the family, in a cross-cultural exploration that exposes the family to wider horizons. Here the archetype of Sagittarius is called forth in the third child to be acted out. Astrological themes are often synchronous with birth order.

Birth order offers an added insight when looking at an individual's horoscope. A first born may be more prone to favouring Saturn while later-borns may favour their Jupiterian or Uranian constellations. Middle children may be at risk of over-identifying with their Libran planets in their sibling role of mediator and go-between. Familiarizing oneself with the roles assigned due to birth order will complement the understanding of astrological statements. To introduce birth order I have used four categories: the eldest, the middle, the youngest and the only child. There are a multitude of other factors that contribute to defining the birth position: gender, sibship size, age spacing, sibling loss, the family atmosphere, etc.; therefore this can only be a general introduction. The second of *two* siblings will experience being the youngest very differently from the youngest of seven siblings. From the second child's point of view, the gender of the older child exerts a great influence. If there is an age gap of more than seven years (a Saturn square), this second child may feel more like an only child. All these factors should be recognized. Sibship size is decreasing while the phenomenon of step-siblings is increasing, altering the destiny that birth order bestows upon us. None the less, reflecting upon our own birth position can be highly thought-provoking.

The oldest child

Parents' expectations of both themselves and their first-born child are high. By the birth of the second child, the expectations, idealism and fantasy have waned with the reality of actual child rearing. Many parental expectations of the first child are overt; however, the first born is also in a position to constellate the unlived lives of the parents, to be imprinted with their unrealized dreams. Upon the newborn's shoulders rests the parents' expectations to accomplish what they did not achieve and to possess what they could not have. Performance anxiety of the eldest child is due to the pressure to succeed, be productive and become a high achiever.

The eldest child is the first member of a new generation, and until the first sibling arrives, the only member of this generation. The eldest are the focus of parental attention and the centre of the family. The first child receives more of the parents' resources and energy but the price demanded is to follow their values, mores, customs and traditions. This is why the eldest is often described as father-identified, aligned with the figure of traditional authority (equally could align themselves in direct opposition to the authority's values). Certainly the eldest position comes with more obvious responsibility and traditional 'masculine' traits. As the second child, Adler's 'masculine protest' could have been a protestation of his lower rank. No wonder Freud, as eldest, categorically opposed his theory.

The pressure for the first child to identify with maintaining the status quo and continuing the familial traditions encourages the first born to be more family orientated. First borns tend to have more children than their other sibs.[26] Being first also encourages the Solar qualities, as the child is the centre and at risk of becoming the narcissistic child that is called upon to mirror the parents' attitudes. With the Sun and Saturn highlighted in this position, approval, feedback, identity, self-esteem and getting results become important for the first child.

Having breathed the atmosphere without other peers, the eldest child is alert to social customs, rules, regulations and authority figures in general. When the next sibling arrives, the competitive and aggressive instincts are catalysed and drawn out into the open. The eldest experiences what Freud and Adler refer to as the sense of dethronement and this promotes feelings of rage and jealousy. Competitive instincts are visible and the urge to maintain first place is a priority. Sulloway describes the first born this way:

> Like the alpha males of primate societies, firstborns covet status and power. They specialise in strategies designed to subordinate rivals. Firstborns tend to be *dominant, aggressive, ambitious, jealous and conservative.* At these five levels of behaviour, the influence of birth order is consistent and unmistakable.[27]

This position encourages a sense of responsibility and relationship to authority; therefore first borns are highly susceptible to rules, keeping 'the letter of the law', and seeing what is obvious but not always what is underneath. Since their position has been usurped, they may continue to feel vulnerable and fear being dethroned once again in adult relationships.

The middle child

During the class on siblings in our 'family development programme', I break the group up into the four categories we are now examining. The first borns gather together quickly, follow the instructions and ask how long the exercise will be. They go off to find a place to meet – usually *my* consulting room. The youngest ones usually end up outside, laughing, swapping stories of who was the most brutalized and how they managed to rebel and annoy their sibs. Ironically, there is often one only child in the class, so they join the eldest group. But the middle children remain in the seminar room and keep wondering what is happening with the other groups. 'I bet the youngest ones are having lots of fun', someone inevitably says. Middle children identify themselves through the eyes of their older and younger sibs. On one side they see the elder's need to perform well, on the other side they see the younger sib rebelling. The eldest and youngest are more vocal and demanding when asserting their needs, which often leaves the middle feeling withdrawn or solemn. Parents frequently mistake their quietness or self-absorption for their ability to take care of themselves, when in actuality they may be feeling withdrawn or depressed. The middle child feels left out, suspicious of what they have been missing. They often describe the sense of not knowing where they stand, being invisible or caught in the middle.

The middle child is in the position of the peacemaker and mediator. They are younger than the eldest sib whom they want to emulate yet older than their younger sibs for whom they may feel responsible. They are able to see both sides of the argument and have a difficult time choosing either side. Conflict and confrontation may seem difficult and they are compelled to try to avert confrontation, not only with themselves but between others. They may appear as if they are getting on with the task or amusing themselves, but this may be more a sense of resignation. Often middles will describe a sense of confusion as to their role and direction in life, and envy of those who seem to be more sure of themselves. This envy may be a remnant of their childhood feelings for the elder who appeared to have more resources and parental support and guidance.

Like the second child, the middle can often identify with the feeling life that is flowing underneath the family. In this way they become the emotional caretakers of the family, highly sensitized to someone feeling left out or something amiss in the family atmosphere. They may tend to instinctively act out these feelings or spontaneously respond to someone's needs. The second and middle child are both at risk of fulfilling the unspoken needs of others at the expense of their own and becoming enmeshed in the hidden agendas of their other sibs.

Here the Lunar temperament may be emphasized, as well as a stronger identification to mother. The second and middle child are also attuned to the energies of Venus, as ruler of Libra, in the capacity of mediator and relationship counsellor for the family. Mercurial energies are called forth in the second and the middle child. These are needed to outwit and trick the elder. A sense of humour and a resignation as to the way life *is* often accompanies this position.

The middle child may also forge a unique intellect out of this role. I have often found it is the middle child who has constructed a potent learning tool, a programme or an explanation through the distillation of familial experience. They are able to articulate the complexity of human relationship and interaction.

The youngest child

The youngest child in the family is in last position and is the only sibling in the system who will not experience younger sibs. The arrival of a sibling is a jolt to consciousness, bringing recognition of differences and separateness. The youngest does not have this experience and is often typecast as the 'baby' of the family, which has both its privileges and its burdens.

The youngest is pampered with a ready-made support system. By the arrival of the youngest, family members have begun to find their niches and there may be a more relaxed atmosphere to child rearing, so the youngest is often less supervised or less bound by parental rules and expectations. This greater freedom is often a contentious issue for the other siblings. However, the youngest child can also be the one who is ridiculed, bullied and scapegoated by older siblings. Their size and low status through the earlier years may be the brunt of the elders' jokes. The youngest may be the common shadow figure for their older undifferentiated siblings. This is a common theme in fairy tales: the youngest son is the simpleton who is able to perform what his older brothers cannot; the youngest sister is tormented by her elder sisters, but then released from her suffering and transformed into a beauty. The elder shadow siblings are the agents of individuation for the younger child. Youngest children carry the archetypal role of being challenged by tasks and trials, and struggling to individuate, which will encourage them to move farther afield than the others.

Myths also portray the youngest child as the carrier of the new order, confirming the old adage 'the last shall be first'. Both Chronus and Zeus were the last children in their sibling system, and they led the coup against the old order, establishing the new. Youngest children press to extend themselves beyond the familial horizon. Through education, experimentation and travel, they reach beyond the family beliefs, values and customs. Their quest beyond the familial limits often leaves them confused as to where they belong. They challenge the status quo and rebel, bringing something new back into the family. This revolutionizes, or at least challenges, the family beliefs and traditions. Youngest children struggle against their siblings' and parents' resistance in order to achieve their independence.

Having had no followers, the youngest may compensate for this with their friends and in social situations. They are sensitive to the 'underdog' and the 'have nots', befriending the powerless, and encouraging and supporting the underprivileged. This overcompensation as leader or saviour contributes to their vulnerability and being taken advantage of. They know what it feels like to be last and smallest, often overcompensating by becoming extroverted. Within the family, the last child can also side with the sibling or parent he sees as powerless or oppressed, supporting the one he identifies as the victim or disadvantaged one. Birth order theory suggests that the third child is sensitive to the parental marriage and responds to any tension or discord between the parents. A youngest will also be at risk of being triangulated in an unhappy marriage, easily enmeshed in the parental battles, championing the underdog, especially if cast as mother's son or daddy's daughter or one of the parent's favourites and allies. The last child left at home is in danger of feeling he has to protect and rescue a parent if there is marital discord, or in a single-parent family, or when a parent is ill or unable to cope. In a family where the power imbalance between the parents has created an unhealthy situation, the youngest may have been parented by older sibs making separation from them difficult.

In childhood the sibs always appear bigger, more capable and better adjusted. This attitude is often internalized in the youngest child. They can see the elders' attributes yet not their own. They are often surprised in adult years to find out that their sibs admired their personality and achievements when they were younger. Youngest children are the last to arrive, the last to take or find their place, and this may be a recurring theme throughout their lives. Often they are confronted with having to fight for their space or claim their place.

Youngest children have more access to the archetypes of Jupiter and Uranus. In a system where everyone is older, more established and have more resources than they do, the youngest feel the need to venture into other worlds to explore how others live. The urge to move farther afield brings them in contact with their spirit of revolution and rebellion and their fate of founding the new order.

The only child

Only children are similar to eldest in that they share parental attention and adoration exclusively without the interruption of another sibling. Unlike the eldest they do not experience being replaced or dethroned or the potent confusing feelings that accompany the arrival of a younger sibling. Winnicott suggests that an only child misses the experience of mother going through the stages of pregnancy and the mysteries and secrets of child bearing. But even more importantly, an only child does not feel the powerful emotions evoked when a new sib enters the family.

> It is so usual as to be called normal when a child is upset at the birth of a new one . . . For all children a big difficulty is the legitimate expression of hate, and the only child's relative lack of opportunity for expressing the aggressive side of his nature is a serious thing.[28]

Siblings draw out powerful feelings of love and hate. The only child does not have the sibling system to experience the ambivalence and polarity of feelings – to be able to experience powerful negative feelings that do not destroy relationship. This could contribute to the fear of expressing negative feelings, being confronting or angry in later relationships. As Winnicott suggests, the competitive and aggressive instincts do not have the safe container of the family and may spill out into the school yard. Observers studying the ramifications of China's one-child policy suggest an increase in aggression and bullying and a difficulty in sharing. It seems that the only child must find avenues to express aggressive instincts and power with peers. A younger schoolmate may have to become the surrogate sibling. Growing up without siblings also suggests that only children do not have to share toys, clothes, valuables and especially parents. Therefore the issue of sharing and ownership may become a pattern throughout their adult relationships. There is also no division of labour or tasks that are often shared with a sibling in family life.

The sibling is an archetypal image and a part of each individual's psyche. We need a caretaker to survive physically, not necessarily a sibling. However, to survive psychically, we need a sibling as a primary agent of socialization. This image in an only child moves to compensate for the loss of a sibling with the friend as a replacement sib. Friends become ultimately very important for an only child and it is the friends from childhood who became the surrogate siblings. In many cases of only children, I have seen fate arrange it so there is a replacement sibling: a cousin, a lodger, a neighbour. The inner image of a sibling is activated towards breaking the isolation the only child feels. With the increase in the number of only children and day care for working parents, siblings are the surrogates at the day care centre. Friendship is the sphere in which the only child will most likely find a surrogate sib, therefore the attachment to friends is strong. Near the end of the natural life cycle, there may be no original family members, stressing the importance of friends as familial substitutes.

An only child may have difficulty in separation and leaving home. There has been no opportunity to separate from a sibling and still experience the continuity of life. Siblings help mark important separations and transitions in the earlier years. Separating from a parent is much more difficult and threatening for the only child, and often results in the initiatory phases of late adolescence and 'leaving home' being traumatic. In adult relationships I often find only children have difficulty leaving relationships that are unhealthy, since there are few images to trust that life goes on after separation. An only child has no sibling allies to fight with against the tyranny of parental power or the oppression of the parental ruling class. The family atmosphere may also be ripe for triangulation. With an unhealthy marriage, the only child feels trapped and often responsible for taking care of the 'abandoned' parent. The only child also feels the full responsibility for an ageing parent's care, having no siblings to share this responsibility with. Nor are there siblings with whom to share the grief of parental loss. The only child may also be prone to wanting mother to be a sister, creating role confusion. With this high tendency towards enmeshment, separating is risky. Adler also echoed this when he suggested the only child was prone to a 'mother complex', for the only child has the exclusive focus of mother.

As parents to siblings, only children may experience difficulty in understanding their own children's relationships and unconsciously collude with keeping siblings separate from each other. They may also find conflict amongst their own children devastating since they have not had this sibling experience.

Some only children blossom under the spotlight of the parental focus, not having to share the attention, aware that they are the sole beneficiaries of the parental legacy. However, this rich legacy is a singular legacy, and sharing a life with a partner is often when the difficulties arise. This is suggested by Salvador Minuchin:

> The significance of the sibling system is seen most clearly in its absence. Only children develop an early pattern of accommodation to the adult world, which may be manifested in precocious development. At the same time, they may manifest difficulty in the development of autonomy and the ability to share, cooperate and compete with others.[29]

Only children grow up in a familial environment populated by adults and are prone to becoming strongly identified with the parent. They are conscious about rules and social customs. From an early age they are sensitized to Saturn. While this archetype may represent an only child's ability to perform well in the world, Saturn often symbolizes both the self-preservation and the loneliness of an only child. While only children may have access to all of the parents' resources, they may also wonder why there is no sibling to share this with. They may feel they have 'missed out'. This missing seems to be part of the sibling myth except the only child has the literal experience.

Adler drew our attention to the fated role that birth position plays in our lives. As parents we are prone to replicating our sibling experience with our own children, particularly sensitive to the child that mirrors our birth position. Our experience of position in the sibling system is taken into our adult relationships, friendships and marriage. Birth order is taken into the workplace – elders strive for recognition, status and leadership positions, often becoming depressed when they realize what they have achieved does not feel authentic as it is motivated by the continual urge for parental approval. The middle child shapes the atmosphere of the organization, while the third or youngest often feels left out or marginalized yet injects revolutionary blood into the organization. Consciousness of our birth position and the arrangement of our sibling constellation may help us become aware of the roles and expectations assigned to us and the personality forged from this. We then may be more free to shift our perspective.

While Adler encouraged us to look at the arrangement of the family constellation, Jung inspired us to acknowledge the mythic and collective images that underpin the family.

Notes

All references to *The Collected Works of C. G. Jung* will be abbreviated as *CW*, followed by the volume and paragraph number.

1. Adler, *What Life Could Mean to You*, 133.
2. Ibid., 128.
3. Lois Rodden in *The American Book of Charts* (Astro Computing Services, San Diego, CA: 1980), 260, lists Adler's birth time under DD: Dirty Data, the category containing rectified and speculative times. She quotes a time of 00.15 a.m., which was published in the magazine *Mercury Hour* (July 1976) by Dewey, quoting Ebertin. Rodden lists other speculations.
4. Henri Ellenberger, *The Discovery of the Unconscious*, 649. Details of Adler's siblings and their birth dates are given on 577–9.
5. Ibid., 577, quoting Phyllis Bottome.
6. Ibid., 578, quoting Phyllis Bottome.
7. Phyllis Bottome, *From the Life* (Faber & Faber, London: nd), 16.
8. Adler, *The Practice and Theory of Individual Psychology* (Kegan Paul, London: 1945), 10.
9. Bottome, *From the Life*, 21.
10. Bottome, *Alfred Adler, Apostle of Freedom* (Faber & Faber, London: 1939), 30.
11. Adler, *The Neurotic Constitution*, trans. Bernard Glueck and John Lind (Kegan Paul, London: 1921), 1.
12. Adler, *What Life Could Mean to You*, 24.
13. Ellenberger, *The Discovery of the Unconscious*, 592.
14. *The Correspondence of Sigmund Freud and Sanador Ferenczi* (vol. 1; Belknap Press of Harvard University, Cambridge, MA, and London: 1993). In a footnote to letter 13, there is a reference to a letter dated 27 February 1899. When speaking of Adler, the footnote suggests, he was 'in contact with Freud since at least 1899'.
15. William McGuire (ed.), *The Freud/Jung Letters*, Freud letter 147F, 18 June 1909.
16. Ibid., Jung letter 217J, 29 October 1910.
17. Jung, 'Problems of Modern Psychotherapy', *CW* 16§150.
18. Heinz L. and Rowena R. Ansbacher, *The Individual Psychology of Alfred Adler*, 382.
19. Alfred Adler, *Social Interest: A Challenge to Mankind*, trans. John Linton and Richard Vaughan (Capricorn Books, New York: 1964), 41.
20. Harold H. and Birdie Thosak, *A Bibliography for Adlerian Psychology* (Hemisphere Publishing, Washington, DC: 1975).

21. Because of its vigorous attempts to link the pattern of the sibling constellation with human behaviour, birth order research is often compared to astrology. Reviews of Frank Sulloway's book *Born to Rebel* used the astrological comparison, and Walter Toman's article on birth order research in *Psychology Today* 4 (12/70) was titled: 'Never Mind your Horoscope, Birth Order Rules All'.

22. Cecile Ernst and Jules Angst, *Birth Order: Its Influence on Personality*.

23. Louis H. Stewart, *Changemakers: a Jungian Perspective on Sibling Position and the Family Atmosphere*, 44.

24. John Bradshaw, *The Family*, 33–6, summarizes the fourfold approach to birth order based on the research done by Dr Jerome Bach at the University of Minnesota.

25. Karl Konig, *Brothers and Sisters: The Order of Birth in the Family* (4th edn; Floris Books, Edinburgh: 1984).

26. Sulloway, *Born to Rebel*, xv. 'Historically, first borns have tended to have more offspring.'

27. Ibid., 79.

28. D. W. Winnicott, *The Child, the Family and the Outside World*, 133. Winnicott often speaks eloquently of the only child. He was a youngest with two older sisters but has suggested he grew up as 'an only child with multiple mothers' (see *Winnicott* by Adam Phillips, Harvard University Press, Cambridge, MA: 1988).

29. Salvador Minuchin, *Families and Family Therapy*, 60.

5

Shadow Figures and Sacred Partners

Jung's Inner Siblings

We are that pair of Dioscuri, one of whom is mortal and the other immortal, and who, though always together, can never be made completely one. Carl Jung[1]

The inner sibling

Jung infrequently wrote of the impact of siblings on personal development, yet his charting of the psyche was influenced by two sibling themes. These themes were not explored as familial patterns but as collective imprints inherent within the human psyche. Throughout his collected works Jung refers many times to 'the motif of the hostile brothers' and the 'royal brother–sister pair'. Jung cites the hostile brother motif as an instinctive inherited tendency.[2] He had no surviving brothers, so as the only son he often constellated this theme in his male friendships.

Inspired by mythological themes and alchemical imagery he frequently referred to the brother–sister motif as a pair of opposites, that in *antiquity* were married, and in the present time seek union and reconciliation. The royal brother–sister pair represented the conjunction of the opposites, Sol and Luna, the polarity that was of great importance in alchemy. This pair of opposites would sometimes take the form of the *hiero gamos* or 'sacred marriage'.[3] Antiquity refers to a deeper, more inaccessible and universal layer of the unconscious, the level that captivated Jung. These themes helped give form to two of his psychic archetypes: the shadow, a partial representation of the theme of the hostile brothers, and the 'anima', inspired not only by the mother–son union, but by the royal marriage of the brother–sister opposites.

The shadow is the psychic depository for rejected qualities that the ego disowns. Shadow stands as a counterpoint to the ego, like the other side of a coin. Ego and shadow are both born out of the same complexes, and like hostile brothers, the ego disinherits its shadow sibling. Jung usually saw this archetype represented as a same-sex figure in dreams, a figure who exemplified qualities scorned by the ego. The shadow can serve as a bridging figure between the dark, repressed and frightening qualities within the unconscious and ego consciousness. The shadow contains the very qualities that are often needed by the ego to feel fulfilled. This dark and foreign aspect of our self is well represented by the hostile sibling or the dark twin as it is the part of self we may try to 'kill off'. The archetype of the shadow therefore could be easily roused by our sibs.

The anima is the inner contra-sexual image for a man: his innate feminine figure, shaped by mother, sisters and female others. The anima is rooted in the first female experience of mother, but sister becomes an intermediary figure that facilitates the partial withdrawal of the anima from mother and out into the world of sister's friends and other women. She is his 'other' for a time, not his mother nor his wife, but none the less a special partner. Anima is the feeling, intuitive and receptive guide that accompanies the male on his descent into his unknown. This archetype was discovered and defined through Jung's personal experiences with his inner feminine voice. During a period of reflection when writing down some of his fantasies, Jung experienced an inner female voice. He became greatly 'intrigued by the fact a woman should interfere with me from within'. He concluded that this inner female must be the 'soul' in an archaic sense. Since anima means soul, he gave this name to the inner feminine figure he felt played an archetypal role in the unconscious of man.[4] Logically Jung deduced that the counterpart, an inner masculine, must be part of the woman's interior landscape. This was named 'animus'. These interior contra-sexual opposites when represented by the brother–sister pair are often seen as the sacred marriage of Sun and Moon (Osiris and Isis, Apollo and Artemis), the unity of the divine sibling pair; images Jung thought were satisfying representations of individuation. This relationship was amongst equals: the inner relationship between the *adept* (the alchemist) and his *soror mystica* (soul sister).

Jung's contributions suggest the sibling is an imago already inherent within the psyche, shaped by our experiences. The motif of the hostile brother and the opposite-sex sibling marriage are in some form innately part of the landscape of the soul. Jung's ideas remind us that the sibling is also an internal figure, like the archetypal parent, that is shaped throughout life. Unlike parents, siblings may offer more accessible images of partners as they are equals. The external sibling becomes a possible screen on to which to project these innate internal images of 'other'. From a Jungian perspective we could postulate that same-sex siblings may constellate the projection of the shadow whereas opposite-sex siblings would invite the anima/animus projections. Projection, as Jung pointed out, is an unconscious mechanism and not a wilful one. The qualities that are externalized through projection range between the dark, negative pole through to a more idealized positive pole. The horoscope yields a way to explore an individual's personal relationship to these archetypes.

Imagining

Jung's specific references to sibling interactions were made earlier in his career while he was still in association with Freud. Like Freud, Jung alludes to the sibling birth as awakening a spirit of inquiry, honing a sense of curiosity and observation and opening up a new sense of exploration. He also suggests the sibling's birth stirs the imagination.

Jung confirms some of Freud's observations on siblings and draws a comparison with Freud's case of 'Little Hans'.[5] Freud had successfully psychoanalysed the five-year-old boy known as Little Hans. Many of his phobias had begun at the birth of his sister. Jung, in 'Psychic Conflicts in a Child',[6] refers to a similar case of a four-year-old girl in quite some detail. Both these cases concern first-born children (like Freud and Jung), and therefore the potent feelings unleashed at the birth of a younger sibling: in these cases opposite-sex siblings.[7] From Jung's correspondence with Freud we know that the case he is describing is his own four-year-old daughter, whom he observed and wrote to Freud about. Jung confirms that the birth of her younger brother led Anna (the pseudonym for his daughter Agathli) to a more vigorous questioning of her own and others' origins.

The birth of the baby brother was a stimulus for the four year old's fantasy life: 'reveries, the first stirrings of poetry, moods of an elegiac strain'. Jung explains that the new sibling is experienced as an obstacle to mother, and the child can no longer freely express her love in the usual way. Libido is suspended, directed internally, and becomes more introverted, resulting in an increase of fantasy and imagination. Jung reiterates Freud's idea that at the birth of a sibling, the elder child turns away from mother, separating out from her and awakening the spirit of inquiry. Jung stresses the awakening of the imagination.

On the eve of the baby's birth, Jung asked his daughter, Agathli, what she would feel if a brother arrived tonight. She responded: 'I would kill him.' Jung suggests that the response to remove the sibling is instinctual, yet initiates the process of reflection and questioning. Agathli began to question life and death vigorously. Her brother's birth prompted a separateness, but also awoke the urge to 'kill off' the brother–other. In the separation from mother there is more access to the child's own inner world. It is an inner world now filled with conflicted feelings and imaginings.

Brother–sister–other

Jung was a pioneering clinician with over eight years' clinical experience at the famous Burghölzli Institute. He rarely wrote of the family atmosphere and its influence on the individual. Jung preferred internal images, excavating archetypal symbols of the family – the Great Mother, the Wise Old Man, etc. Earlier in his career, Jung did study the family, drawn to research word associations amongst family members. He was fascinated by parental and ancestral complexes that were part of the family atmosphere. These complexes contained the unlived lives of both parents and ancestors which lurked below the horizon of family life, permeating the unconscious of the child. Jung himself felt influenced by what his ancestors left incomplete:

> I feel very strongly that I am under the influence of things or questions which were left incomplete and unanswered by my parents and grandparents and more distant ancestors. It often seems as if there were an impersonal karma within a family, which is passed on from parents to children. It has always seemed to me that I had to answer questions which fate had posed to my forefathers, and which had not yet been answered, or as if I had to complete, or perhaps continue, things which previous ages had left unfinished.[8]

However, Jung's interests led him to new terrain, and his research on the family atmosphere was not as developed as he would have liked it to have been.

In his 1909 lectures at Clark University on word association, one of his papers was entitled 'The Family Constellation'. Jung speaks of the potent influence of the family:

> The first moves towards friendship and love are constellated in the strongest possible manner by the nature of the relationships with our parents, and here as a rule one can see how powerful is the influence of the family constellation.[9]

He describes an interesting case of a twenty-six-year-old woman who consulted him for an odd symptom. She complained that periodically her eyes felt strange and was certain her stare stimulated erotic thoughts in men. Jung found it difficult to dissuade the patient from her way of thinking. Unravelling her story, he found she had recently been jilted by a man who was mentally ill. In her isolation and abandonment, her repressed erotic wishes were cast on to other men. Jung was curious why she had never suspected mental illness in her partner, wondering if she had a pattern of attracting unstable men. This suggestion was vehemently denied by the patient. However, in further exploration, she revealed her desertion on a previous occasion by a man who had spent a year in a mental hospital. Jung then traced the pattern back to her relationship with her brother. He discovered that after her father had alienated himself from the family, she transferred her love on to her brother, eight years her senior. When he was fourteen he became 'hopelessly insane', a pattern to which she was still unconsciously bound, choosing unstable men like her brother.

While this case points to the potent impact of the family on our unconscious patterning, it also begins to support Jung's theory that the opposite-sex sibling is a likely candidate for the projection of the anima or animus. The sister was six when her brother had his breakdown. This is Freud's Oedipal phase when the budding Eros is attached to the opposite-sex parent. The opposite-sex sibling is an intermediary figure that can carry the erotic projection, enabling its withdrawal from the parent before it is transferred on to a partner. Without the initial anchor of the father relationship, the animus may have become dangerously aligned with brother. The animus development could potentially become static, or fixed, on brother. In the case Jung described, the brother/animus figure continued to be projected on to partners that replicated the unholy fixation with her brother. Her experiences continued to confirm her loss and inability to release her brother.

It is possible for the anima/animus projection to become fixated upon the opposite-sex sibling when the parent is weakened, unavailable or missing during the development of the child. When the security and safety of the family is under threat by unresolved conflicts between the parents, the sibling system may feel a safer place to experiment with the erotic projections. The sibling becomes not only a replacement for the parent, but a more accessible love image. The natural transfer from the parent to the opposite-sex sibling and then out on to the world becomes more difficult. The projection becomes frozen on to the sibling, without the continuity of movement out into the world of others.

Jung suggested the flow of libidinal energies for a male (in his terms, the anima) were first directed on to mother, then to sister and finally on to sister's friends, or other significant females, and out into the world. This was consistent with psychoanalytic thought which also suggested the female's energies (the animus) took the same route into the world via father then brother. In Jung's words:

> The anima is an archetype that is always present. The mother is the first bearer of the anima image which gives her a fascinating quality in the eyes of the son. It is then transferred, via the sister and similar figures, to the beloved.[10]

Other Jungian analysts have explored the fixation of the opposite-sex sibling in developmental terms as the image of the 'ghostly lover'. Esther Harding introduces the figure of the ghostly lover in *The Way of All Women*: '. . . he is her soul mate, her "other half", the invisible companion who accompanies her throughout life.'[11] When the animus is fixated on brother, this image may be fused with the ghostly lover. More recently, Linda Leonard has also drawn on this theme in her book *On the Way to the Wedding*. She suggests that the brother–sister relationship is often the source of fixation which stifles the flow of creative energy. The internal grip of the opposite-sex sibling acts as a ghost that hovers over the formation of adult relationships. Inevitably, it is the necessity of severing this possession that restores creative potential. She also agrees that when the father is weakened or wounded, the older brother is ripe for idolizing, affecting the sister's later choice of mate.

> Frequently the older brother is idolised, particularly when the father is absent, passive or wounded himself. If the idolised brother plays a positive paternal role toward the sister, her choice of mate or inability to find one may be a direct result of his influence.[12]

While an older brother may be idolized, a younger brother may be protected. In protecting a brother against the wounded father, the sister may unconsciously represent herself as the victim. The introjected animus image then exerts the power of the wounded other which would continue to haunt successive relationships. This was the case for Susan.

Susan was thirty-three when she came for an astrological consultation.

She was concerned about her inability to form and sustain relationships. She was unable to 'consolidate her relationships' as she put it. Susan had the Sun in Libra in the eighth house which was relatively unaspected except for a semi-sextile to Jupiter and a wide conjunction (10 degrees) to Neptune. The Solar image in the horoscope was not well supported. The other personal masculine planet, Mars, ruled the third house of siblings, and was in Pisces opposite Venus. Gemini was on the fourth house cusp. Saturn culminated on the MC conjunct the North Node. During that year, transiting Saturn was squaring the Sun three times and in discussing the theme of 'consolidating' the masculine, Susan recounted a dream she had had recently, which still disturbed her:

> I am drunk and my brother is making advances at me. Incest. I reject him and push him away but he gets louder and louder and keeps demanding more attention. I am afraid and call out. All the time my parents' backs are turned.

Susan's father was an alcoholic and she experienced him as abusive. Her mother was described as disassociated and unavailable (Moon in Aquarius conjunct Chiron on the twelfth house cusp opposite Uranus). She protected her younger brother from father's rages and became his parent (Gemini on the fourth) and surrogate mother (Chiron/Moon). Unbeknown to Susan, she also became his saviour/lover (Mars in Pisces opposite Venus), offering him protection and love. Susan turned her back on her own negative feelings towards both her parents and the family atmosphere. These dark and difficult feelings were dissipated by parenting her brother and aligning herself with his victimization, not her own. She became identified with her role as saviour. Unconsciously, the animus formed the image of the victim/brother. This image of victim/other, she agreed, now haunted her adult relationships. Her beloved brother, to whom she was so bonded, was trying to rape her in her dream. His ghostly presence was forcing himself upon her.

Susan had not yet managed her negative feelings towards father. These feelings were converted into a sacrificial marriage with her brother, leaving her bereft of any supportive relationship to her own masculine. The inner masculine figure was still fixed to brother whom she must protect and support. While Susan was focused on the need to save brother, she was unaware of her victimization that occurred through the abusive scenario in the family. The transit seemed to be the beginning of awakening the rage that had blocked her journey towards an authentic relationship with the inner masculine. No longer able to protect her brother, who now turned on her, she was left to address her own feelings.

The progressed Moon was just beginning its second cycle through the third house, excavating the feelings of anger and rage that lay beneath her protection of brother. She continued to protect these feelings in adult relationships, perpetuating her sacrifice of self by repeatedly protecting men she saw as weak. Moving beyond the image of her brother/animus would risk exposure of the enraged feelings. The Moon's second passage through the third house would loosen some of her earlier experiences that contributed to shaping her relationship patterns. Susan was progressing through the sphere where she could once again experience these earlier feelings. As an adult her task was to begin to manage them. The dream replayed a scenario she was now emotionally ready to see and feel. While her eighth house Sun was strongly identified with an urge for intimacy, it also consciously avoided feelings of grief and rage awoken with authentic intimate encounters. The transit of Saturn was beginning to crystallize images of how Susan formed relationships. Her dream image of brother alerted her to her ghostly brother–lover.

The dream also contains the word 'incest'. Jung suggested that the incest taboo was inherently part of the landscape of the soul that prevented a retrogressive movement back to the womb of childhood.

> Incest is the urge to get back to childhood. For the child, of course, this cannot be called incest; it is only for an adult with a fully developed sexuality that this backward striving becomes incest, because he is no longer a child but possesses a sexuality which cannot be allowed a regressive outlet.[13]

The taboo directs the energy away from a fantasized union with the parent, out into the world. The urge for paradise and longing for unity within the circle of the family is prohibited, propelling one outside the sacred circle of kinship. In this way the taboo operates as an initiation into separation, activating the heroic aspect that seeks actualization and individuation outside the perimeter of the family. The sin of incest binds children to the complexes of the family, not allowing them to leave the enmeshed family experience. The taboo is the sacred line drawn between family members that allows each the sanctity and privacy of honouring themselves within the unit of the family. It encourages separation and the spirit of individuality.

As the taboo was about to be violated in the dream, Susan awakens to the realization of her inability to leave the family complex and be separate from it. Her protection of brother was, in a sense, psychological incest. Breaking the taboo kept her bound to the family complexes. Incest, as Jung said, symbolizes a 'union with one's own being'.

> Although the union of close blood relatives is everywhere taboo, it is yet the prerogative of Kings (witness the incestuous marriage of the Pharoahs, etc.). Incest symbolises union with one's own being, it means individuation, or becoming a self, and because this is so vitally important, it exerts an unholy fascination – not, perhaps, as a crude reality, but certainly as a psychic process controlled by the unconscious, a fact well known to anybody who is familiar with psychopathology.[14]

As an archaic taboo within the psyche, the image of incest alerts us to the premature intrusion of passions and power upon our own feelings. The taboo helps delineate the boundary between the spiritual union and the union consummated through the body before ego is strong enough to discern this in its own way.

Brother–sister incest, as Jung said, symbolized the union of opposites. It represents the union of two equals on the same kinship level unlike mother/son or father/daughter. As equals, each may facilitate the Eros in the other, the urge to relate on a deeper soul level. The opposite-sex sibling may constellate the images of union, relationship and intimacy in the other. The taboo allows these images to be internalized in a safe and sacred place until the libido can be withdrawn from brother or sister as the spiritual partner and directed towards a lover where union of spirit and body is possible. Alchemically, brother–sister incest was contained. The alchemical alembic serves as a potent image for the container of the family atmosphere. Bound within the alembic of a strong family (which at its heart is the parental marriage), the brother and sister may submerge themselves in their own unconscious processes without fear of violation.

'Incest' is a problematic word as its connotation is no longer symbolic. Jung and later Jungians explored the inner dimension to the incest taboo. Jung's animus imagery with its need for union with father–brother–son supposes that the animus has been contained within a functional family unit and that it was held by a strong, perceptive and loving father and brother. However, family containers have been smashed and incest is no longer always an inner experience but often a frightening reality. When incest has really occurred, the spiritual core of the individual has been violated. The reality now is that a 'real' individual needs attention, not the archetypal world.

Jung's exploration of the archetypal world left a rich and profound legacy that contributed to our understanding of a vast and deep inner world. This invisible world connected us back through time to the collective, restoring images of an association with a greater whole. However, the individual can disappear with this imaginative exploration. To grip and balance the personal with the archetypal, to not lose sight of the person in the archetypal realm, was a dilemma for Jung, and hence Jungians. Jung wrote eloquently of the feminine, yet his relationships with women were problematic. His theories acknowledge the necessity of the feminine as guide and muse to the man's inner world of soul, but Toni Wolff, his mistress and the embodiment of this, is left unacknowledged in Jung's autobiography. And while he wrote about the necessity of the *soror mystica* in the alchemical work, his biological sister remains virtually unknown. This powerful urge to know the feminine and her archetypal faces, yet personally split off from her, is reflected in Jung's horoscope.

Jung's Sun is exactly conjunct the descendant and squares Neptune (which is approaching the third house cusp). With Neptune in aspect to the Sun its effect would be to flood the personal realm with collective images, often perfected or idealized, which may have accounted for some of the ambiguity between his relationships in the personal sphere (Sun on the descendant) versus the archetypal realm (Neptune square the Sun). The descendant can often symbolize the meeting place of the anima/animus and the shadow. While the contra-sexual images can be constellated at this descending angle, their ascension into consciousness can also drag shadow qualities to the surface. This chasm between the personal and archetypal realm was evident in his relationship to his sister.

Jung and his sister/s

Jung's only surviving sibling, a sister, Johanna Gertrud, was born on 17 July 1884,[15] a week before Jung's ninth birthday. Little is mentioned of her in Jung's autobiography *Memories, Dreams, Reflections*, or in biographies about him. She is summed up by Henri Ellenberger: 'She never married, does not seem to have had a professional occupation, remained in the shadow of her brother, who she greatly admired, and died in Zurich on May 30, 1935.'[16] A footnote to one of Jung's letters tells us Gertrud worked as a nurse at the

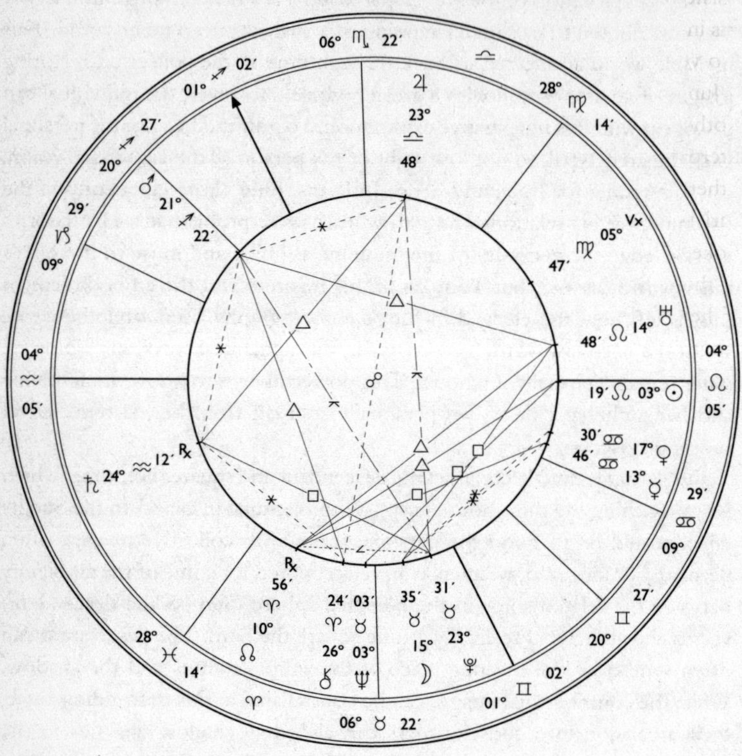

Figure 6: Carl Jung's horoscope, 26 July 1875, 7.32 p.m., Kesswil, Switzerland. Jung's daughter, Gret Baumann-Jung, was an astrologer who used the birth time of 7.32 p.m.[17] *This is the chart Jung himself possibly used. Given his penchant for symbolism and mysticism, he has been quoted as saying he was born 'when the last rays of the setting sun lit the room'.*[18]

Burghölzli Institute from 1906 to 1908 during the period her brother was there, then moved to Kusnacht in 1909 to live with her mother.[19] She also assisted her brother as a secretary until 1925.[20] Barbara Hannah confirms this in her biography on Jung, also in a footnote: 'Jung's sister, Gertrud, was also very helpful, mostly, I believe, in typing his manuscripts.'[21]

Jung was ambivalent to Gertrud's birth: 'when I was nine years old my mother had a little girl'. The birth came as a surprise to Carl who had interpreted his mother's confinement as an 'inexcusable weakness'. Jung's father, who was excited and joyful at the arrival of his daughter, brought Carl to his mother's bedside. His mother 'held out a little creature that looked dreadfully disappointing'. Later Jung also refers to his newborn sister as 'the thing'.[22] He describes himself as shocked and numbed by the reality of her birth. At the birth of his sister, Jung had the same astrological progression as Freud had at the birth of his first sibling, Julius. Jung's secondary progressed Moon was squaring his natal Mars in the eleventh house. The Lunar nature, symbolized by the progressed Moon, is at a developmental point where it is aware of a competitor (Mars). It also suggests an emotional reaction or shock has been recorded. The secondary progressed Moon (22° Virgo 21) was also trine his third house Pluto, activating the natal quincunx between Pluto and Mars.[23] The family matrix is interrupted and themes of rivalry and jealousy are awoken. The powerful feelings at this time, described by the Lunar progression, are synchronous with the birth of his sister. For Carl she may easily be the outer symbol of these feelings.

The first cycle of the progressed Moon (27.3 years) records the totality of the individual's feeling experiences. The second cycle of the progressed Moon often stirs the primary memory through dreams, somatic images, feelings, senses, etc. The same Lunar progression occurred twenty-seven and a third years later, repeating the square to Mars and the trine to Pluto. During this second cycle Jung wrote to Freud (14 November 1911; progressed Moon at 21° Virgo 43), citing him as a 'dangerous rival' with reference to their mutual interest in the psychology of religion. The synchronicity of the cycle suggests that sibling rivalry, accompanied by overwhelming feelings, may be the recurrent theme peaked at each of these times.[24]

Pluto is conjunct the Moon in the third house of Jung's natal horoscope. The transits this day, thus also his sister's horoscope, are revealing. Jung's Lunar return occurred just after midday in his third house of siblings. His sister was born under his Lunar return, hence their natal Moons were conjunct within six degrees.[25] Venus, too, had just returned and was in its retrograde cycle, and therefore would return once again within that cycle. Jung and his sister had Venus at the same degree: Jung's Venus was direct while his sister's Venus was retrograde.[26] With the Moon returning to its third house position, and Venus which rules the third, also returning on the day of his sister's birth, the sister relationship is prominent. Gertrud is not acknowledged as an important figure in Jung's life. Because the two personal feminine astrological archetypes are conjunct each other in the siblings' charts, the composite Moon and Venus would also be in the same positions. In Jung's chart they are both associated with the third house of siblings. Astrologically, the symbol of the sister is important to Jung. Why then is Gertrud missing from the picture of Jung's life?

With the Pluto–Moon in the third house, the dark feminine experienced through mother may now be assigned to sister. Venus, ruling the third house of sister, is in Cancer, the Lunar sign of mother. With the Moon in the third, the theme of the composite mother/sister is reiterated. In literal ways they were aligned, as Gertrud lived with her mother throughout her adult life.

	Gertrud	*Aspects to Carl*
Sun	*25° Cancer 13*	
Moon	15° Taurus 54	conjunct CGJ's Moon
Mercury	0° Leo 09	
Venus	16° Cancer 48	
	retrograde	conjunct CGJ's Venus
Mars	23° Virgo 43	square CGJ's Mars
Jupiter	10° Leo 56	
Saturn	19° Gemini 02	opposite CGJ's Mars
Chiron	7° Gemini 48	conjunct CGJ's IC
Uranus	24° Virgo 57	square CGJ's Mars
Neptune	22° Taurus 55	conjunct CGJ's 3rd house Pluto
Pluto	1° Gemini 49	conjunct CGJ's IC

Figure 7: Gertrud Jung's planetary placements (transits also for 17 July 1884, midday, Basel).

On her day of birth Mars was in Virgo squaring Saturn in Gemini both aspecting Jung's Mars: the midpoint of the transiting square was in exact aspect to Jung's natal Mars within one minute of arc. His urge for the freedom and spontaneous spirit of his Mars in Sagittarius was now being shaped by a sense of responsibility. Pluto, in Gemini, transiting the IC suggested his sister's birth altered the safety of the family atmosphere. A duality had been reawakened, a duality he would first recognize in his mother's twofold personality and later in his relationships with women. Gertrud's birth repeats the theme of aspects to Mars, hence an awakening in Jung of a sense of separateness. While the age gap of nearly nine years would contribute to each growing up as an only child, it is curious that Jung and his biographers rarely refer to Gertrud. Frank McLynn postulates that perhaps it was she who carried the family madness that Jung always feared:

> There is a suspicion – and lacking the documentary evidence which has never been released it can only be a suspicion – that some of the weakness Jung feared might overtake him had settled instead on his sister. It is distinctly odd that Jung never refers to his sister except on one occasion, and then in such a Delphic manner that one immediately senses that something is being hidden. He says that Johanna Gertrud, who died at fifty, was home loving, conventional, physically delicate, sickly and virtually sexless and in every respect different from him. A spinster, she went into hospital in 1935 for a simple operation but did not survive it. At root she had always been a stranger to Jung.[27]

Odd, indeed, that Jung who spoke of the sacred marriage of the brother–sister and the alchemical adept–*soror mystica* pair would be estranged from his literal sister. Jung may have been able to disassociate himself from fears of inheriting mother's madness by projecting the third house Moon–Pluto conjunction on to his sister, Gertrud. He may have abandoned the literal sister for the archetypal one.

Uranus in the seventh house is squaring the Moon in the third. Uranus–Moon is asphyxiated by demanding emotional encounters or relationships that curtail the sense of space, freedom and individuality. The individual with this aspect instinctively constructs a way to disengage from the oppression of feelings. Splitting off from the overwhelming feelings, symbolized by the Pluto–Moon, into the seventh house Uranus may have left Jung feeling distant and comfortably separated from the powerful internal feminine figure that underpins a Pluto–Moon conjunction. Splitting off from the third house Pluto–Moon would encourage the projection on to his sister. Gertrud could then easily be crowned with Pluto's helmet of invisibility. Jung's literal sister is lost to the archetypal sister, the *soror mystica*. Without the anchor of experiencing an equal relationship to his sister, his Pluto–Moon in the third may be the conduit through which the archetypal feminine speaks.

Jung inherited his mother's dual personality. Safely detached from the personal undertow of the Pluto–Moon, he would discover the chaos surfacing in his analysands, the seventh house others. Sabina Spielrein and Toni Wolff were examples of patients/analysands where Jung's Pluto–Moon transference was activated, blurring his detachment and separateness. While consciously feeling detached in his Uranian observer role, his seventh house clients' obsessions would constellate his Pluto–Moon. The feminine voice within Jung that inspired the anima was that of an analysand:

I know for certain that the voice had come from a woman. I recognised it as the voice of a patient, a talented psychopath who had a strong transference to me. She had become a living figure within my mind.[28]

Jung's inner feminine voice was 'a talented psychopath'. While she was an analysand, he would be able to separate from her but when he entered into his own feminine she was part of him. We can amplify Pluto's placement in the horoscope to include the symbolic entrances to our own underworld, like the cave at Avernus where Aeneas descended. For Jung, Pluto was in the third house conjunct the Moon; perhaps he found his underworld in the sphere of his sister/s and other female analysands, friends and colleagues. Pluto–Moon also suggests the potential atmosphere of loss and grief that he may have unconsciously absorbed from his mother.

Pluto in the third may literally suggest a sibling lost through death. Both Jung and his biographers have not clearly defined his sibling constellation, and perhaps with Pluto in the third it will remain a mystery. Jung's daughter, Gret Baumann-Jung, was an astrologer. In her article 'Some Reflections on the Horoscope of C. G. Jung', when referring to her father's third house Pluto, she says, in parentheses: 'three or four of his brothers and sisters died soon after birth'.[29] E. A. Bennet in an early biography of Jung states that 'Before his birth there had been two children, boys, who died as infants.'[30] However, none of the numerous biographies, or the Jungian literature I have researched, refer to the two stillborn girls that were first born. A private letter from the Jung Trust confirms that Jung's mother had given birth to two stillborn girls: the first on 19 July 1870 and the second on 3 April 1872. A son, Paul, was born 18 August 1873 and died five days later.[31] These two sisters, like Gertrud, are invisible. They are not within the main text of Jung's life and when mentioned are also in parentheses. Perhaps they are the images of the unknown feminine.[32] Jung refers many times to the motif of the unknown woman in dreams. He also associated this figure of the unknown

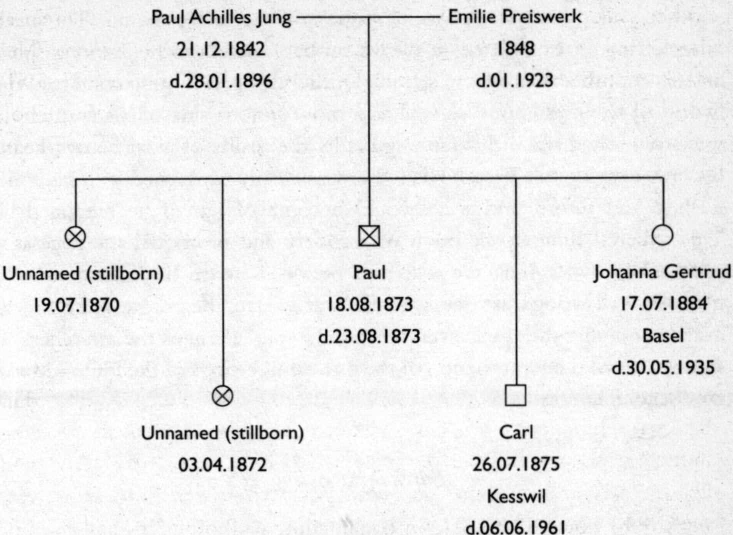

Figure 8: Jung's sibling constellation.

woman with the 'dual motif',[33] a motif that was apparent in Jung's own life. Venus, ruler of the third, is conjunct Mercury, an aspect which align sister/s to the image of the *psychopomp*.

In reflecting on the effect of his sister's birth Jung says:

> The sudden appearance of my sister left me with a vague sense of distrust which sharpened my curiosity and observation. Subsequent odd reactions on the part of my mother confirmed my suspicions that something regrettable was connected with this birth. Otherwise this event did not bother me very much, though it probably contributed to intensifying an experience I had when I was twelve.[34]

What Jung is referring to here is not clear. His mother's 'odd reactions' are later discussed as the split between her two very distinct personalities, part of the Pluto–Moon–Uranus constellation of his horoscope.

However, odd reactions would be consistent with a woman who had previously lost two (perhaps three) stillborn children, as well as another child after only a few days. Anxiety and grief may have been constellated in his mother at the birth of his sister: anxiety born from the fear of losing another child, grief from the memories of the lost children. The birth 'intensifying an experience' at twelve probably refers to his fainting spells and six-month absence from school. During this period Jung contacted the 'world of the mysterious' as well as a more serious side of his nature. He was soon jolted out of his fainting fits by the reality of what he overheard his father saying to a friend. His father was clearly concerned with his son's welfare and future, and what would become of him if he remained ill. This sobered Jung to the point of recovery and promoted the necessary self-healing. Later Jung refers to this period as when he learned 'what a neurosis is'. During this time, when he was twelve, the progressed Sun was exactly conjunct the natal seventh house Uranus. Perhaps the awareness to separate from the asphyxiation of the powerful feelings of the Pluto–Moon was becoming conscious.

Surviving a sibling

Jung's third house Pluto–Moon conjunction symbolizes his siblings who died. Wherever we find Pluto in the horoscope we also find that which is buried, occulted or repressed. Pluto's realm is the cavernous landscape of the underworld and his astrological legacy is often represented by secrets, grief that has been suppressed, incomplete mourning, or losses that have been buried to 'protect' the family. In antiquity one could not legitimately enter the realm of the dead without a proper burial. The river Styx was the boundary that could not be crossed without this ritual. Lacking this ceremony of completion, the unburied were condemned to wander aimlessly along its banks, hovering as a shade on the periphery of the Underworld.

Psychologically, that which has not been completed haunts us like an unburied shade. Jung was conscious of part of his inheritance from mother: the dark occult side that was part of her ancestry as well as her dominant and powerful personality. Pluto–Moon could be part of his inheritance that he was not conscious of. This may symbolize a deep sense of grief and loss passed on through the mother, an ancestral shade still hovering on the threshold of Jung's underworld. In the third it suggests the sphere of loss may be connected to a sibling.

Before Carl's birth there had been three deaths, maybe four. These contributed to the dark feelings he associated with his mother and her family. The psychological impact of the loss of a child, certainly in the late 1800s, was not known or yet of psychological concern. The mother's grief would normally be diagnosed as depression or hysteria.[35] Today we are more aware of the profound effect the loss of a child has on the family unit and the siblings to come. The dead child takes his place in the family. When the loss of the child has not been grieved or when his place in the family has not been acknowledged, his spirit becomes a shade which haunts the family and the ancestral line. Well-meaning parents often protect the surviving children by covering the loss and the grief under a veil of secrecy. The denial, while well intended, becomes toxic as the truth felt by surviving children is misshaped. A child born after the loss of a sibling is often a replacement child. In fact, a replacement child was frequently prescribed to cure parental grief. The replacement child struggles against the shadow of the dead sibling to find his own place in the family.

How was Jung psychically affected by the double loss of his older sisters? The Pluto–Moon has a powerful sense of the feminine which may have wielded its power from an archaic level of the unconscious. This unknown feminine may have coloured more of his thinking (third house) than we will ever know. Certainly it represented the fusion between the feminine and the mysterious, women and the unknown, that was thematic throughout Jung's life. Helene Preiswerk was one of the first to constellate this aspect of his fate. She was his mediumistic cousin and his first guide into the mysterious world beyond death. Jung participated in many seances with Helene who stimulated his lifelong reverence and fascination for the occult.

Jung tells of his trip to America with Freud in 1909. According to his biography he had begun to doubt Freud's ability to reveal the meaning of his dreams. Jung wanted to see meaning in dreams in a more symbolic way. One dream was particularly significant, for, as he said, 'it led me for the first time to the concept of the collective unconscious'. In the dream, Jung was in a house he did not know (Pluto–Moon). He descended from the upper to the main floor which was older and dated perhaps from medieval times. Then he discovered a stone stairway that led into the cellar. As he descended the stairs, he found a beautiful room that he felt was Roman. On the floor he saw a ring which he pulled on. The stone slab lifted from the floor to reveal a second stairway of stone leading further down to another level. Finally

I descended, and entered a low cave cut into the rock. Thick dust lay on the floor, and in the dust were scattered bones and broken pottery, like remains of a primitive culture. I discovered two human skulls, obviously very old and half disintegrated. Then I awoke.[36]

Freud was chiefly interested in examining the two skulls, whereas Jung was fascinated with the levels within the house that represented the layers of the psyche – the conscious state and its unconscious additions. Freud urged Jung to find a wish connected with these skulls; who did they belong to? Jung suspected Freud of steering him in the direction of acknowledging secret death wishes. Jung vehemently resisted this idea. This was not the first time these secret death wishes entered their conversation. Before setting sail from Bremen, Jung's interest in the 'peat-bog corpses' of prehistoric men found in Northern Germany convinced Freud that Jung harboured death wishes towards him.

Jung was interested in Freud's interpretation and therefore told a conscious lie, suggesting the skulls were those of his wife and her sister. 'After all,' Jung said, 'I had to name someone whose death was worth the wishing.' Jung chose sisters. Was this an unconscious reference to his two dead sisters? Interestingly, Freud, with the Moon in Gemini, lived with two sisters. Jung's choice of two sisters may have been a more conscious reflection of Martha and Minna Bernays. Jung had always suggested that Minna had told him of the affair she was having with her sister's husband, Sigmund Freud. Both men were enmeshed with their sisters, no doubt colouring their relationships to their female analysands, students and colleagues. Jung, with the Moon in the third (the natural house of Gemini), had two missing sisters.[37] The feminine was often twofold for Jung, which first manifested in his mother's two personalities, then as his penchant for 'pairing' women. Esther Harding and Eleanor Bertine were paired together, and as a couple moved to the USA and founded the Jung Institute in New York.[38] After his wife, Emma, died, Ruth Bailey and Aniela Jaffe combined to care for Jung. But the pair of women who shared his adult life were his wife, Emma, and his mistress, Toni Wolff. He analysed both, encouraged both to become analysts and together they held the split in Jung's feminine side. With Gemini on the IC, this duality was part of the family atmosphere which contributed to Jung's emotional makeup.

When Toni Wolff died in 1953, Jung did not attend her funeral. Later he carved a stone for her: 'She was the fragrance of the house.' Two years later Emma Jung died. He also carved a stone for her: 'She was the foundation of my house.' Jung acknowledged that Emma and Toni had been 'mystical sisters'.[39] Could his grief for Toni and Emma be entwined with his unknown sisters? His unknown sisters could be part 'of things or questions which were left incomplete and unanswered by my parents' (see page 67). I suggest they left a powerful mark on Jung's psychology.

Sibling shadows

In another of Jung's cases, he uses a hostile brother theme to show unconscious compensation in relationships. We now enter the territory of shadow. Jung describes his patient, a businessman, as 'somewhat arrogant', suggesting the essential cause of his neurosis was the unresolved jealousy towards his younger brother. The patient constantly criticized and denigrated his brother. The brother was a powerful figure in his unconscious life, apparent from the prominent role brother played in the businessman's dreams. He was often cast as a historical figure, such as Julius Caesar or Napoleon, in a grand setting like the Vatican. Jung concluded that the businessman inflated himself at the expense of his brother and since his extreme arrogance affected a wide social group, the compensatory figures in the dream were collective.[40] The unresolved feelings of hostility and jealousy towards the brother were woven into a shadow figure, compensating for consciously held attitudes.

The shadow is not simply an alter ego composed of rejected ego qualities, but is necessary for survival. The hostile brother theme is a mythic motif where one brother often dies so the other may live. The shadow brother, twin or double, is the story of Gemini. This double is also the numinous and vital aspects represented by the other brother or sister as shadow. Competitive and hostile feelings towards the same-sex sibling when transmuted into love often awaken the self, another of Jung's archetypes expressed as a same-sex figure.

Cain kills his brother Abel just as Romulus kills his twin brother Remus. Cain built the first city, Enoch, after his brother's murder, while Romulus founded Rome, giving it his name after his brother's murder. In 'killing off' the brother–other, the pathway to civilization (ego consciousness) is laid down. Shadow, then, is formed around what we have 'killed off'. Cain and Romulus are the faces of ego progress that must subdue the brother; aspects of themselves that they fear will hold them back. Hostile brothers are encountered again when building adult ego structures and founding their 'cities'. Jung and Freud virtually lived out this theme, 'killing off' each other in order to found their own psychoanalytic 'cities'. Freud's Sun was exactly conjunct Jung's Moon in the third, highlighting their sibling relationship. Each had their stationary Mars in the eleventh house, constellating the shadow brother figure in the sphere of colleagues.

Sisters also serve each other as shadow-doubles; in fact research has often suggested that sisters are more aggressive to each other than brothers. However, it is also suggested that sisters form more permanent bonds which endure throughout their lives. Brothers cooperate on activities and therefore battle over achievement; sisters share their feeling life and therefore are shadows in the realms of love, relationships and passion. The theme of the sister as carrying shadow was a theme that emerged in my consultation with Catherine.

Catherine is the second child, whose sibling constellation includes two other sisters. Catherine was born fifteen months after her older sister and seventeen months before her younger sister. Being close in age, the three sisters shared what Catherine thought was a loving and close sisterly bond throughout their lives, which drew their adult families together. When Catherine came for a consultation, her grief and disbelief at the loss of this bond was apparent. Her younger sister had had an affair with their older sister's husband, which precipitated a separation between the older sister and her husband. However, the older sister and her husband had been reconciled and now Catherine's younger sister was furious. The scenario was fracturing the three families. Other secrets emerged, and Catherine was devastated to find the sister bond was not as strong as she had always imagined. Catherine, who always played the role of the peacemaker, was shattered. In the familial fracas, she felt unable to be with either sister as her attempts at trying to mediate had left her feeling torn between them.

In an ironic way, Catherine was freed by her sisters as she no longer carried the role of mediator, a role her middle position assigned to her. In the time usually spent with sisters, she rediscovered her passion for study and returned to university. Her marriage improved and honesty and openness were more apparent in the relationship. As well, she had just been promoted into a position that gave her financial freedom and time to devote to her studies. So it was interesting to hear Catherine describe her sisters in terms of them being more clever than her, more successful and more attractive than her!

For Catherine, her sisters carried many of her projections that kept her separate from her more independent and adventurous nature. This was her sisters' domain – they were daring, independent and forward thinking.

However, they could no longer be hooks for Catherine's projection, having transgressed what she held as sacred – sisterhood. The container had been smashed and their luminosity had darkened.

Catherine's natal horoscope had a Moon–Uranus conjunction in Gemini in the fourth house opposite Jupiter. Mercury, also in Gemini, was on the IC and transiting Pluto was culminating on the MC opposite Mercury. The secure base she associated with the sibling system (Gemini on the fourth) was being excavated. She was discovering another truth under the sibling system that had curtailed her freedom. Her Sun in the third house which squared the Saturn–Pluto conjunction was a powerful image of her identification with her sisters. The independence suggested by her Moon–Uranus–Jupiter configuration was more conscious, having been released from its projection on to the sisters. The situation forced Catherine to be honest with herself and also about her competition with her sisters.

When Catherine began to see the links between her and her sister 'double', the pain of its recognition was deep. Her attachment to her sisters had eclipsed some of her own urges and development. Catherine suggested her unfulfilled creativity was due, in part, to the idealization of her sisters and the time wasted searching for their acknowledgement. She felt able to fulfil her creative urges but still mourned the loss of the idealized sister bond. Catherine's third house Sun also suggested the potent projections she cast upon her sisters, losing connection with her own identity. Transiting Pluto opposing Mercury was destroying the sibling myth that she had kept alive, releasing her. Like Psyche's sisters, they helped to awaken her to a more conscious journey.

The ancient Greeks saw the shadow-double as *psyche*. At death the spiritual double hovered over the body, then was guided into the Underworld after its body-double had been buried. Jung also suggested that when the body or ego was asleep, the shadow-double appeared through the individual's dreams. He often saw this figure represented or associated with a brother or sister. The same-sex sibling figure came through the dream representing the shadow or 'double' that was vital to the dreamer. Here the sibling acts as the *psychopomp*, the Hermetic figure.

Stan died on 24 June 1991. Ten days before he died he dreamt:

I am on a large boat filled with women. I am the only man on the boat which is about to be attacked and destroyed by the Japanese. A Japanese general comes aboard to tell me if we want to be saved I must swallow all the pictures of my family that I have in the room.

Stan was my father-in-law and had been diagnosed with terminal cancer three months previously, nine months after his wife had died. He came to live with us and this is how I know this dream that seemed to prepare him in some way for his passing.

Certainly we can set the dream in the realm of the anima – a boat, often a symbol of men's undifferentiated feminine – a vessel to sail over the water of feeling and filled with women. Boats were part of Stan's life; his parents migrated on one to Australia. On that voyage his older sister died and was buried at sea. He never knew her as he was born after his parents arrived in Australia. His brother was a naval officer in the Second World War and on duty in the South Pacific when his ship was sunk by the Japanese. For Australians, the Japanese were the enemy, a threat more real than the Germans, and for Stan, an enemy personally connected to his brother. Stan's brother had died previously, but his spirit was still part of the dream aligned with the Japanese officer, his shadow. Yet it is this shadowy figure that comes aboard to advise Stan and the others how to be saved. The shadow-double instructs him to swallow the pictures of his life, memories of those he loved while in body and those whom he would leave behind. The pictures of the ones he loved were now to be inner pictures, inner images carried by the soul that can free itself from the body. The shadow figure, perhaps inspired by his own brother, prepares Stan to ingest the pictures, the images and feelings to become part of the soul that could be carried with him across the Styx, in another boat!

Stan was shaken by the dream. His conscious world had been suspicious of the inner world of dreams and images. Yet a tranquillity appeared on his face in death. The internal world had become real to him and his last dream, at least the one he told us, helped him slip out of his body as easily as he slipped into the world of dreams. And instruction by a sibling-inspired shadow-double seemed appropriate.

Jung and astrology

Jung's interest in astrology spanned most of his lifetime. On 12 June 1911, he wrote enthusiastically to Sigmund Freud about the revelations of astrology:

> My evenings are taken up largely with astrology. I make horoscopic calculations in order to find a clue to the core of psychological truth. Some remarkable things have turned up which will certainly appear incredible to you . . . I dare say that we shall one day discover in astrology a good deal of knowledge that has been intuitively projected into the heavens. For instance it appears the signs of the zodiac are character pictures, in other words libido symbols which depict the typical qualities of the libido at a given moment.[41]

Jung continued to view astrology as a 'projected psychology' and used astrological research as an experiment into synchronicity. He referred to this experiment in an interview he gave shortly before his eighty-fifth birthday. The interview was published the week before his birthday and less than a year before his death. In responding to a question on astrology, Jung suggested: 'We are passing out of the period of the Fishes just now and into the sign of Aquarius, which may well bring some new values with it.'[42]

Jung spoke of the Astrological Ages in his lectures on dreams.[43] The timing of the change of the ages is uncertain and various times for the beginning of the Age of Aquarius extend well into the new millennium. Jung was aware of this, but what is of interest is that he relates the theme of the hostile brothers with the duality of the fish symbol. Hence the mutable and dual zodiacal constellation of Pisces, according to Jung, also represents another pair of twins or hostile brothers. As we know, the bright, spiritual and transcendent side of Pisces is often twinned with a dark, raging and dismembering side.

At one point in the examination of the fish symbol Jung is prophetic:

> If, as seems probable, the aeon of the fishes is ruled by the archetypal motif of the hostile brothers, then the approach of the next Platonic month, namely Aquarius, will constellate the problem of the union of the opposites.[44]

Certainly, at the end of the present millennium approaching the Age of Aquarius with the specific transits of Uranus and Neptune passing through Aquarius, the opposites as carried by males and females are seeking equality and union. It is in the earliest system, the sibling system, that we first learn how to relate, brother to brother, sister to sister and brother to sister. After all, brotherhood and sisterhood is what Aquarius is all about. Appropriately, Aquarius was rising over the horizon when Jung was born.

Notes

1. Jung, 'The Archetypes and the Collective Unconscious', *CW* 9.I§235.
2. Jung, 'The Symbolic Life', *CW* 18§523.
3. Jung, 'The Practice of Psychotherapy', *CW* 16§401.
4. Jung, *Memories, Dreams, Reflections*, 186.
5. Freud, 'Analysis of a Phobia in a Five-Year-Old Boy', *SE* 10.5 ff.
6. Jung, in 'The Development of the Personality', *CW* 17§§1–79.
7. Both Freud and Jung's next surviving sibling was a sister. Both these cases deal with the elder child and the younger opposite-sex sibling similar to Freud and Jung.
8. Jung, *Memories, Dreams, Reflections*, 233.
9. Jung, 'Experimental Researches', *CW* 2§1008.
10. Jung, 'Civilisation in Transition', *CW* 12§92 footnote.
11. Esther Harding, *The Way of All Women*, 38: for the full discussion of the 'ghostly lover', see Chapter 2 of this title.
12. Linda Schierse Leonard, *On the Way to the Wedding* (Shambhala, Boston, MA: 1987), 47.
13. Jung, 'Symbols of Transformation', *CW* 5§351 footnote.
14. Jung, 'The Practice of Psychotherapy', *CW* 16§419.
15. Henri Ellenberger, *The Discovery of the Unconscious*, 738, note 17, 'quoting Registry Office of the City of Basel'.
16. Ibid., 662.
17. Gret Baumann-Jung, 'Some Reflections on the Horoscope of C. G. Jung', *Spring* (1975). Besides the birth time, which is suspect, one other factor is important: the correct time zone. *The International Atlas* (ACS, San Diego, CA: 1988) reports Jung's birthplace, Kesswil (47N36, 9E20), in a time zone of 30 minutes for his birth date, a time zone started 12 September 1848. Contrary to this, many charts (including the one used by Gret Baumann-Jung) are calculated for LMT. This differential shifts the MC.
18. Lois Bodden quotes this in *The American Book of Charts* (Astro Computing Services, San Diego, CA: 1980), 321.
19. Carl Jung also lived in Kusnacht (228 Seestrasse), a house he had built on the shores of Lake Zurich.
20. William McGuire (ed.), *The Freud/Jung Letters*, Jung letter 217J, 29 October 1910.
21. Barbara Hannah, *Jung: his Life and his Work*, 205.
22. Jung, *Memories, Dreams, Reflections*, 25.
23. Freud's eleventh house Mars was stationary retrograde about to turn direct. Jung's Mars was also stationary, having turned direct the day before his birth.

24. During this period progressed Mars had entered Capricorn and was sesqui-square to his third house Moon. Therefore during the month the progressed Moon mirrored the progression to Mars.
25. The Moon averages 13 degrees movement a day.
26. Freud also had a direct Venus while his sister Anna had Venus retrograde.
27. Frank McLynn, *Carl Gustav Jung*, 49. When this book came out, the transits to Jung's chart were remarkable. Uranus was transiting the ascendant while Pluto was transiting the MC.
28. Jung, *Memories, Dreams, Reflections*, 185.
29. Baumann-Jung, 'Some Reflections on the Horoscope of C. G. Jung', 47.
30. E. A. Bennet, *C. G. Jung* (University Press, Aberdeen: 1961), 9.
31. From a private letter from Ulrich Hoerni of the Jung Trust, 13 August 1996.
32. For a perceptive critique on Jung and the feminine, see Claire Douglas, *The Woman in the Mirror.*
33. Jung, 'The Practice of Psychotherapy', *CW* 16§§16–17.
34. Jung, *Memories, Dreams, Reflections*, 25.
35. Jung's mother was hospitalized when Jung was three years old. This seems to have been a mental collapse and one wonders what impact these losses had upon her mental health.
36. Jung, *Memories, Dreams, Reflections*, 183.
37. Both Freud and Jung had Venus in the sixth house. Freud's Venus ruled the seventh house Taurus cusp, while Jung's Venus ruled the third house Taurus cusp. Jung's third house cusp was Freud's seventh house.
38. Frank McLynn, *Carl Gustav Jung*, 328.
39. Ibid., 520–22.
40. Jung, 'Two Essays on Analytical Psychology', *CW* 7§§279–83.
41. *The Freud/Jung Letters*, 427.
42. William McGuire and R. F. C. Hull (eds), *C. G. Jung Speaking: Interviews and Encounters* (Princeton University Press, Princeton, NJ: 1977), 444.
43. For Jung's amplification on the Astrological Ages, see the privately printed *Dream Analysis*, vol. 2, from notes of the seminars in 'Analytic Psychology' given by him.
44. Jung, 'Aion', *CW* 9.II§142.

6

The Sibling and the Family Life Cycle

Once therapists started to see the whole family together, other aspects of family life which produced symptoms were revealed, aspects which had been largely overlooked.

Virginia Satir[1]

Family Systems

Once the helping professions began to view the individual in the context of the family and as a member of a larger group, psychology became more cognizant of the sibling. Psychological literature on the sibling started to appear from the 1970s. Brian Sutton-Smith and B. G. Rosenburg wrote *The Sibling* (1970), and Stephen Bank and Michael Kahn published a thorough examination of siblings in *The Sibling Bond* (1982). While there is a growing awareness amongst psychological circles, sibling research and examination has been mainly initiated from the areas of sociology or family therapy.

Family therapy's systemic approach views the sibling as belonging to a sub-system within the greater organization of the family. Family therapy realized the lost sibling of the early psychoanalytic movement was important in shaping and influencing the personality. In 'systemic' or group work, each member of the organism becomes a vital part of the system's life force. This systemic approach is an important model for astrological counsellors as the horoscope contains images of the family and their ancestors. These images are encoded into the horoscope's symbols. An astrologer examining the horoscope has ample imagery to enhance the understanding of the ancestral legacy, the family of origin, the parental dynamics and the sibling system. The family is already inherent in each individual's horoscope, therefore family therapy offers the astrological practitioner insights that are valuable for amplification of familial images. Family therapy looks at the family as a system moving through time with definable life stages.

Like any organism, the family has a natural life cycle. The members of the family move through various stages and rites of passage as they mature.[2] This life cycle corresponds with the natural astrological cycles of the transiting and progressed planets, nodes and other celestial bodies. The family carries its own life force and momentum which extends across generations both living and deceased. There are many differing versions of the family life cycle which is understandably more complex than an individual's life cycle. The eight-stage model of sociologist E. M. Duvall is the one most widely used.[3] These eight stages span the life of the family:

1) the courtship of the primary couple,
2) their marriage,
3) child-rearing years,
4) their children's adolescence,
5) leaving home,
6) the readjustment of the primary couple,
7) old age,
8) death.

Other models include as many as twenty-four stages in the family life cycle, encompassing the nodal events, the entrances and exits of family members at each stage of family life. Entrances and exits of family members also correspond to stages of the life cycle that are the highest in stress for all the members.

Transitional periods in the family life cycle are the times when people are most vulnerable. Transition is generally critical, and awareness of these turning points in family life helps members make the transition more consciously and functionally. For example, the first child leaving home is a critical passage for the family and signals a crisis and change for each member. The younger sibling/s move forward accommodating the void created by the sibling who has left. Their roles, responsibilities and privileges will shift. The parents, who have launched their first child, will be more acutely aware of preparing for the readjustment phase of their lives when daily family life returns to them alone. This also applies in an astrological context. A major transit for one individual will affect all family members. If we view astrology systemically, we see transits to one individual's horoscope echoed by the other members of the same system. Major transits and life stages for one sibling directly impact on the others. Sibs share the formative years, so their experiences are impressed upon us. Their transits and progressions through the early life cycle are formative imprints on our own experience, influencing the way we relate to different astrological symbols and archetypes.

There are many variables to the family life cycle since traumatic events alter the course of the family. Divorce, remarriage, illness, relocation, retrenchment, untimely death, etc. will affect the course of the family life cycle. These variables are part of life and are symbolized astrologically by the transits to the horoscopes of the individual members of the family.[4] While planetary cycles will frame the life cycle for an individual and the family, personal transits create the interruptions and variations. For siblings there are important stages in their mutual relationship which is also a system moving through time. Family therapy no longer sees the sibling relationship confined to the 'nursery' as the early psychoanalytic fathers did, but as a developing relationship maturing throughout the course of individuals' lives. In many ways the sibling relationship is our first partnership, and we can acknowledge the important turning points that occur within it over the span of a lifetime.

There are many variants that could occur within the life of the sibling system that will dramatically alter its destiny. These would include things such as the death of a sibling, the birth of a handicapped or gifted sibling, separation through divorce, the imprisonment or disappearance of a sibling, etc. However, there are natural turning points which can be charted from the creation of the sibling system. These will be the initiatory phases in our life with our siblings. The possibilities are unique to each individual and therefore it is necessary to reflect on these changing times personally. The generic astrological cycles do not always correspond to the phases listed, but they are a guide to the important crisis points in our development with or without the sibling. The returns of the inner planets, Mercury, Venus, the Sun and Mars, occur within the first twenty-two months of life and are critical if a sibling was born during this time. The other planetary cycles occur throughout the rest of the life cycle and will signal important rites of passage in both our own and our siblings' experience. Figure 9 shows a sibling life cycle, tracking the eldest child throughout the life span.

Figure 9: Siblings in the family life cycle: important stages

Stages in the family life cycle	*Rite of passage*	*Key developments for siblings*	*Astrological life cycle*
Birth of the second child	Belongs to a system/group other than parental. Peer consciousness. Eldest – separation from mother. Younger – birth as the first separation experience.	Creation of the sibling system. For elder first conscious separation may occur via awareness of an intruder. Conflicting feelings – love, hate, jealousy, caring, indifference. Rivalry. Elder leaves exclusivity of adult world.	11–13 months: Mercury return. 10–14 months: Venus return. 12 months: Solar return. 17–23.5 months: Mars return.
Separation from sibling	Eldest – going to school, experience of life outside sibling system. Elder – Oedipal phase. Younger – first separation from sibling.	Eldest joins a new peer group, new adventures and definition of self outside siblings. Other playmates. Younger feels sense of separateness, loss of contact, more access to parent.	Age 6: Jupiter opposition. Age 7: progressed Moon waxing square. Age 7.5: Saturn waxing square.

Stages in the family life cycle	*Rite of passage*	*Key developments for siblings*	*Astrological life cycle*
Adolescence Early stage	Transition from childhood. Puberty. Younger – latency period.	Eldest – physical and hormonal changes, challenging of parental authority, boundaries and beliefs. Potential change of schools. Withdraws from younger sibs. Youngest – separation from older sibs, loss of the sibling as ally. Awareness of difference and different stages of development. Awareness of sibling roles.	Age 12: Jupiter return. Age 14: progressed Moon opposition.
Adolescence Middle stage	Autonomous experience. Liminality between childhood and adulthood.	Elder – rebellion, defiance of parental authority and rules. Defining self in opposition to family members *or* taking on the familial expectations and traditions. Younger – reaction, elder is the model for adolescent passage.	Age 15: Saturn opposition.

Stages in the family life cycle	*Rite of passage*	*Key developments for siblings*	*Astrological life cycle*
Adolescence Late stage	Transition to adulthood. 'Coming of Age'. Leaving home (see separate stage).	Elder – shifting focus beyond family. Changing priorities. Driving car, etc. Social life changes. Leaving school and entry into work force. Younger – separation from sib. Loss of contact with elder sibling. Different social circles and roles as now entering adolescence.	Age 18.6: Nodal return. Age 21: Neptune waxing semi-square. Uranus waxing square. Age 22: Saturn waning square. Age 24: second Jupiter return.
Leaving home	Adulthood. Launching of the young adult.	Elder – emotional and financial self-responsibility. Separation from family matrix. Younger – family roles and family dynamics altered. Younger moves to role of eldest child. More space and resources. Separation.	Age 18.6: Nodal return. Age 21: progressed Moon first waning square. Age 22: Saturn first waning square.

Stages in the family life cycle	*Rite of passage*	*Key developments for siblings*	*Astrological life cycle*
First sibling married or in committed relationship	Establishment of intimate bond with primary other outside family system to new system.	Shifting of primary loyalties. Focus of pairing shifts from sib to partner. Potential sibling jealousy and formation of a triangle between the sibling and the partner. Incomplete sibling feelings transferred to partner. Crisis of accession – new member of family and extended member of sibling system – sibling-in-law.	Age 24: second Jupiter return. Age 27.3: progressed Lunar return. Age 28: Nodal opposition. Age 29–30: Saturn return. Third Jupiter opposition. *Progressed Lunation phase return.
First child of a sibling	Establishing a new family system. Entry into parenthood.	Sibling now a parent. Other sibs have new roles – aunt/uncle. Welcoming a new member into the greater family system. Creation of new family unit.	Age 36: third Jupiter return. Age 37: second Nodal return. Saturn second waxing square.

* The progressed Lunation phase returns to the Lunar birth phase at age 29.5.

Stages in the family life cycle	*Rite of passage*	*Key developments for siblings*	*Astrological life cycle*
Parental old age and death	Mid-life. Confrontation with parental death as well as personal mortality.	Orphaned. Grief and loss. Hierarchy of family shifts so siblings are the elders and next in line. Sharing the family legacy – rivalry and incomplete sibling issues arise. Renegotiating the adult relationship between sibs. Sibling responsibilities for ageing parents.	Pluto squares itself (in Pluto in Virgo and Libra generation). Age 39–45: Uranus opposition. Progressed Moon opposition. Neptune waxing square. Jupiter opposition. Saturn opposition. Age 50: Chiron return.

Stages in the family life cycle	*Rite of passage*	*Key developments for siblings*	*Astrological life cycle*
			Age 55: second progressed Moon return. Age 56: third Nodal return.
Post parental death	Transition to old age.	Only siblings remain as original family members. Reconciliation or estrangement from adult siblings after parents' death.	Age 59–60: third Saturn return. Fifth Jupiter return. Progressed Lunation phase return. Age 72: sixth Jupiter return. Age 74: fourth Nodal cycle. Age 82: progressed Moon return. Age 84: seventh Jupiter return. Uranus return. Neptune opposition. Age 88: third Saturn return.

At the dawn of a new millennium the concept of family life is altering so rapidly it is difficult to speak of the 'average' family. It certainly is far removed from the family unit of Freud's time. While there still is an urge to regress to a nostalgic image of the family, we have turned a corner. All the outer planets are in the last four transpersonal signs of the zodiac which stress a more global family. Families are being liberated and becoming individualized. The family life cycle has needed to incorporate new rituals and rites of passage. The Pluto in Cancer model of family life is different from Pluto in Sagittarius familial experiences and values. I have summarized a few of the changes that are affecting the family life cycle, *especially for the sibling.*

- Family size has greatly declined, shifting the roles within families. With fewer members of a family, there are fewer members of the sibling system hence a greater intensity of interaction between siblings and all family members.
- The divorce and remarriage increase has created the 'blended' family. When families are blended the sibling order is disturbed.
- Unemployment rates are keeping children at home longer, deferring the stage of their 'leaving home'.
- Household roles are shifting due to both parents working.
- There are families with same-sex parents.
- The increasing use of day care is stimulating exchanges outside the family at an earlier age. The child's early playmates may now be 'siblings' from another family.
- The number of single-parent families has increased. This familial arrangement increases the likelihood of parentalization of a sibling and maximizes the risk for the last sibling at home to enter into the 'leaving home' phase.

Family therapy and systems theory are a valuable key to helping us amplify the astrological life cycle for both the individual and other family members. Family therapy has also helped to readdress the lost sibling from the early psychoanalytic movement. Pluto was in Gemini at the turn of the century when the psychoanalytic theories were becoming conscious. Now, at the end of the century, Pluto is in the opposing sign of Sagittarius. The opposition brings awareness and reflection; therefore the period with Pluto in Sagittarius will be indicative of changes that will emerge in psychoanalytic thought.

The natural astrological cycles and images remain as an important key to understanding the sibling relationship and its influence. In Chapter 7 I will examine the astrological images constellated in our relationships with sisters and brothers.

Notes

1. Virginia Satir, *Conjoint Family Therapy*, 4.
2. For a thorough investigation of the family life cycle, see *The Changing Family Life Cycle*, Betty Carter and Monica McGoldrick (eds).
3. E. M. Duvall, *Marriage and Family Development* (Lippincott, Philadelphia, PA: 1977).
4. To explore the transits to an individual's horoscope and how this affects the gestalt of the whole family, see Erin Sullivan, *Dynasty: the Astrology of Family Dynamics*, 195–223.

PART TWO

The Astrology of Siblings

Patterns established with brothers and sisters in early life may repeat themselves with husbands, wives, co-workers, bosses and friends at a later stage of development.

Howard Sasportas *The Twelve Houses*

7

Astrology and Sibling Dynamics

Saturn and the Sun indicate older brothers, Jupiter and Mars indicate middling ones, Mercury younger ones, the Moon older sisters, and Venus younger sisters.

Dorotheus of Sidon[1]

Traditionally, sibling territory is located in the third house. As first of the three houses of relationship, the third house underlies our earliest patterns of relationship, which in turn directly impacts the seventh and eleventh houses. All three houses are connected to sibling dynamics through this primary relationship to the third house. The sign Gemini, engraved upon the zodiac as the sibling sign, is of prime importance in the examination of sibling themes and dynamics. Mercury, patron of the sibling, is also a prominent indicator of the archetypal sibling relationship, especially in its aspects to other planets.

Siblings are a vital part of family life and the atmosphere and complexes of the family and ancestry greatly influence their development and relationship. As siblings are our earliest equals, companions, peers, partners, allies, comrades, associates, rivals and friends, their influence will permeate many other areas of the horoscope. One of the first experiences in our sibling system is sharing a common generation, one different from that of our parents.

Age spacing between siblings

Generally, siblings share the same generational influences. They are born into the same collective atmosphere, symbolized by the placement of the outer planets, Neptune and Pluto and often Uranus, in the same signs. If a sibling is born before the Mars return at twenty-two months, the two children may even share the same Saturn sign; the other possibility is the next sign. The shared placements of the outer planets, as well as their dynamic aspects to each other, recapitulates any aspect the other sibling has to the outer planet.

Jane was born with Pluto in Leo sextiling Neptune in Libra with both planets quincunx Mars in Pisces, at the midpoint of her Pluto–Neptune. Her sister was born a year later, within a day of her birthday. Pluto and Neptune were both within two degrees of Jane's. Her younger sister's horoscope reinforced the outer planets' quincunx aspects to her Mars. Jane not only experienced her own dynamic Mars aspects, but her younger sister's synastry aspects reinforced the pattern as well. Her sister became the constant reminder of Jane's difficult relationship to her own Martian qualities. Jane's peer group will also remind her of this aspect, but it was her sister who first stressed the pressure of the aspect. Jane was reminded constantly of being usurped by a sister during *her* birthday celebrations. With the added pressure of the synastry aspects to Mars, their relationship had been a battleground for as long as Jane could remember. Born close together, sharing the same larger influences, siblings struggle for identity in close proximity with one another. Identification with the sibling can range from a strong enmeshment and fusion, copying one another, through to competition and de-identification, choosing the opposite of what the other chooses.

Siblings born after the first Saturn square (seven and a half years later) may feel more separated and distant from their elder sib since they do not share or witness the same initiatory life passages. They may feel as if they are growing up alone or in a different group. Uranus will then be in a different sign making the individuation process of each child very different. These sibs need to claim their uniqueness and individuality in differing ways. Astrology offers us a way to define the generational ambience and ethos that the sibs participated in together through an analysis of the outer planetary statements.[2]

Neptune's transit through one sign is always fourteen years, whereas Pluto's transit varies owing to its elliptical orbit. Their last conjunction was in Gemini in 1892–3. In 1938 Pluto ingressed into Leo having begun its acceleration through the signs. Pluto's passage from mid-Leo to Capricorn averages the same duration as Neptune's – fourteen years per sign. Neptune ingressed into Libra in 1942 and both planets began their synchronous travel through the zodiac in sextile. This symmetry lasts throughout the latter half of this century and for the first four decades of the next. For most of this period Neptune and Pluto are within a five-degree orb and are exactly sextile each other nearly fifty times. Siblings born after the Second World War share this generational heritage. They will move through their lives touched, affected and changed by the same collective events and developments. Neptune represents collective ideals, dreams and visions while Pluto suggests the generation's intention, purpose and motivations. Sibling systems are microcosms of their generation. Siblings have the opportunity to participate in the emerging collective spirit that will express itself throughout their lifetime. With Pluto in Sagittarius and Neptune in Aquarius at the turn of the millennium, the elemental combination returns to fire–air. Siblings are likely to grow up in a more ideological atmosphere, where the vision and dreams they share are the ideals of humanitarianism and progress, motivated by a spirit of cross-cultural unity. Perhaps, once again, siblings may not be bound by familial or cultural ties. However, the shadow of prejudice, dogma and totalitarianism may also be part of the inheritance of this generation.

The first child, while born into a new generation, is more impacted by the generational values of her parents than those that will follow. There are no other members of her generation and the attitudes of her parents' generation dominate the familial atmosphere. It is a difficult task for the first borns to give up their identification to the parental world in order to join their peer group. A later-born child is able to discern more clearly the generational boundaries between parents and siblings. The eldest has been strongly indoctrinated into the traditions of the older order while the younger carries the new and different generational statements more readily.

Socialization outside the sibling system also occurs with others of the same generation. On our first day at school we share the classroom with others who have the same outer planetary placements, very often sharing Jupiter and Saturn. It is generally not until the Jupiter return (at age twelve) that we begin to socialize more frequently outside our age comfort zone. It is also with our brothers and sisters, if we have them, that we may first become aware of gender differences.

Gender, archetype and the sib

Archetypes are not gender specific; however, cultures, families and individuals are. Archetypes are amoral, without value judgement, unlike their human vessels. James Hillman succinctly noted that 'archetypes transcend both men and women and their biological differences and social roles'.[3] In current times there is a great uncertainty about the roles that gender assigns. Cultural constraints have become more relaxed towards stereotyping gender roles and psychological awareness of the internal contra-sexual nature has increased.

However, we are still perplexed by the difference between the archetype of masculinity and masculinity, the archetype of femininity and femininity. Yet with siblings there is a genderless and androgynous component, since equality and symmetry are primary to the relationship. Love between siblings is originally free of gender typecasting.

The symmetry of the sibling relationship may be more conducive to sexual exploration. As equals, sibs may more easily explore their sexual natures without the overwhelming fears of castration, rejection, domination or punishment from the parent. As more accessible agents for this contra-sexual side, androgyny is promoted through the relationship. The politics of gender enter our sibling system through the familial and cultural attitudes towards gender roles and expectations.

Researchers have suggested that the gender of our siblings impacts upon our own feminine or masculine development. A boy raised only with sisters may develop exaggerated masculine traits to compensate for his fear of becoming over-feminized. As a result, his undeveloped feminine side remains infantile and attached to the very sisters he is trying to de-identify with. Equally, he may identify strongly with the feminine, more so than his male friends who do not have sisters. A younger sister of a brother will be prone to developing more masculine traits than a younger sister of a sister, or conversely, learn to be coy and seductive. Same-sex siblings can also contribute to our definition of masculinity or femininity. A younger brother of a macho brother may be very reactionary to his brother's extreme definition of masculinity and compensate by developing more feminine traits. The ego's embrace of masculine and feminine traits is greatly influenced by the gender experience with our siblings.

Myth and psychology continually demonstrate that the sibling is an archetypal reality. Therefore what representatives does this sibling archetype have on the planetary pantheon? Traditional astrology grants Mercury the role of rulership over the sibling, and, in my own experience, Mercury's domains of Gemini and the third house are clearly sibling territory. Interestingly, Mercury is often described as asexual or bisexual, linking the sibling world and androgyny. Siblings are equals and we may strongly identify with an opposite-sex sibling, helping us feel more comfortable with our contra-sexual side. My experience is that Mercury is not embodied by a sibling but describes more a sibling theme, issue or story. Major aspects to Mercury resonate with sibling roles, themes, stories and complexes. The planet that aspects Mercury provides an image of an archetypal presence that may have greatly influenced our primary relationship to the sibling and therefore later relationships. When there are transits or progressions to Mercury, the sibling story is highlighted in some way, as we saw with Alfred Adler. Progressions of Mercury carry the developing and evolving sibling themes of our lives.

Venus and Mars are the archetypes that a sibling would most likely embody. Because Venus and Mars are equal archetypes that inspire relationship they are prone to being projected or transferred on to the sibling. Venus not only represents the sister archetype, but also carries the familial attitudes towards the feminine. Venus will be experienced in our relationship with siblings of either sex, however it is more likely to be embodied by or projected upon a sister. Similarly, Mars is an archetypal brother figure representing the masculine attitudes of the family and more likely to be projected on to a brother. Besides the obvious indicators of the sibling, I look to Venus as a sister image and Mars as a brother image. Aspects to both Venus and Mars, as well as their placement in the horoscope, may tell a powerful sister or brother story with the attitudes of the family impressed upon their experiences.

Sally has Venus in Scorpio in the twelfth house squaring Pluto on the MC. This became a snapshot we could use in the consultation to explore the powerful dynamics that permeated Sally's relationship with her sister. She described her sister as dark, underhanded, dominating and obsessive: a powerful shadow image for Sally who could never forgive her sister for coming between her and her idealized father.

Angela has a Chiron–Venus conjunction in the third house and is the youngest of three sisters. During adolescence, her sisters taunted and teased her about her weight, the size of her breasts and how she dressed. Angela became convinced she was as her sisters described – ugly. The family atmosphere also supported this wounded image of the feminine. For instance, when Angela started menstruating, her mother's advice about sex and men was the proverbial message: 'men only want one thing'! The feminine experience of the celebration of womanhood and sexuality was severely damaged, not only by her mother, but confirmed by her own generation of sisters. As Angela told of these experiences, I was aware how striking and well presented she was, which seemed to be the opposite of how she felt. Her damaged self-image and fear of sex continued to be a wound in her relationships. Her sisters' voices were still audible in every relationship. Like Psyche, Angela suffered at the hands of her shadow sisters and, like the mythic heroine, she was about to embark on a conscious journey towards her own self-esteem, somewhere still intact underneath the familial attitudes.

In Homeric tradition, Venus and Mars were half-siblings, both children of Jupiter. As constant companions, lovers and siblings they are often powerful representatives of our sibs or an indication of a passionate relationship to them. Another mythic brother–sister pair, Apollo and Artemis, are also important in honouring the sibling bond.

Brother Sun and Sister Moon

Artemis and her twin brother Apollo were loyal and devoted to each other since their birth. Apollo is 'the brother she loves'.[4] 'The Second Hymn to Artemis' tells us that when Artemis had satisfied her urge for hunting in the wild, she went to her brother's temple in Delphi, hung up her tunic and arrows and changed into a beautiful dress. Here she joined her brother, the Muses and the Graces in song and dance.

Artemis and Apollo first bonded in the womb of their mother, Leto. During her pregnancy, Leto was refused refuge in every place to which she went. Finally, the rocky, abandoned island of Delos offered her sanctuary in exchange for the promise that the son to be born would first build a temple on the island, before he became too famous. The abandoned island of Delos was now guaranteed to become an honoured centre in antiquity. Myth suggests that Artemis was born nine days earlier on a neighbouring island, Ortygia, and then helped her mother deliver her twin, Apollo. The twins had become bonded, even before they were born, through their shared gestation in the womb of their troubled mother. Artemis, the midwife for her twin brother, became his feminine guide and companion in the world. Apollo and Artemis were close allies, mates, and together they protected their mother, Leto, and her honour.

By the later classical period, Apollo and Artemis became associated with the two great luminaries, the Sun and the Moon, fostering their relationship as a powerful couple. Artemis' association with the Moon may have come as late as the second century BCE by which time she had been Latinized to Diana.[5] By the period when astrology became of interest to the Greeks, Apollo and Artemis were firmly aligned with the Sun and Moon. Our primary astrological pair of luminaries have a sibling derivation which the alchemists knew and we have forgotten.

Ptolemy, writing in the second century CE, suggested that we first look to the opposite-gender luminaries when considering marriage in the horoscopes of men and women.

> With regard to men, it is to be observed in what manner the Moon may be disposed . . .
>
> But, in the case of women, the Sun must be observed, instead of the Moon.[6]

In a modern context we translate this to mean using the woman's Sun and the man's Moon to delineate some of the characteristics of the inner partner. Contemporary astrology continues to look at the powerful union of the Sun and Moon as an image of the *conjunctio* or *hiero gamos*, forgetting the sibling story that underlies the luminaries. Apollo and Artemis are now part of the template of the Sun–Moon couple, and their relationship is an important reminder of the layer of the sibling bond that underlies adult relationship.

The traditional astrological statement that Sun/Moon combinations were indicators of marriage inspired Jung to conduct his synchronicity experiment that compared the aspects between the Sun and Moon in couples' horoscopes. Jung said: 'Ptolemy regards the conjunction of a masculine Moon with a feminine Sun as particularly favourable for marriage.'[7] Did Jung know he had this aspect with his colleague and rival Sigmund Freud? Or that his sister's Moon was also exactly aligned with his Moon in Taurus? With couples, my experience of the synastry aspect of the Sun–Moon is powerful in two ways: firstly it constellates their parental marriages and revisits their parents' issues and patterns. Secondly, it magnetizes their sibling experiences: their sense of equality, the ability to be an individual and be identified. Two layers of relationship exist and what often goes unnoticed in the 'marriage' is the sibling patterns that are affecting the partnership.

In their own way Apollo and Artemis were married. Artemis had already chosen to be a virgin and therefore remained true to her brother. Apollo's adult heterosexual relationships were also reflective of his powerful union with his sister. His most successful relationship was with Cyrene, a replica of his sister: a huntress, independent, strong, from the wild. The Solar–Lunar dyad as represented by Apollo and Artemis is companionship, friendship and sibling loyalty. Apollo was primarily bound to his sister, claiming substitutes for her as his partners. Unlike Zeus and Hera, who had a difficult time returning to their sibling marriage, Apollo and Artemis have a difficult time leaving it. This theme enters into adult relationships when separation between the siblings has not taken place. Perhaps, as in the case of Artemis and Apollo, the separation is difficult because of their mutual enmeshment in supporting and protecting their mother. The unbreakable attachment may be born out of a toxic family atmosphere drawing the siblings into a union that permits no other relationship to exist. Apollo and Artemis remind us of the powerful sibling level that is part of the landscape of our relationships.

In opposite-sex siblings, the Sun and Moon may be of interest in assessing sibling dynamics especially when the relationship has been symbiotic or fused. Either Sun or Moon could also be cast on to a sibling when a parent is absent or disengaged. If father is missing there is a strong tendency for a son to become parentalized in the family, taking on the role of father and attracting the other siblings' Solar projections. Likewise, if mother is missing psychologically or physically, the daughter may be drawn into the vacuum of her absence, becoming the replacement Moon in the family. These situations will be clear through the examination of the family history and dynamics, and will resonate with themes in the chart that confuse the role of the sibling with that of the parent. Freud's example showed this confusion between hierarchical and equal roles. Astrologically, this is apparent when the parental and authoritative indicators are placed in the realms of equality in the horoscope or vice versa. For instance, when the parental archetypes of the Sun or Moon are placed in the third house or Gemini, or in aspect to Mercury, there may be a lack of boundary between the roles of sibling and parent. When an authoritative archetype such as Saturn is placed in equal territory, like one of the three houses of relationship, then the quest for an equal relationship may be complicated with an authoritarian approach. The following list details the differences between the two systems.

Parental system	*Sibling system*
Hierarchy	Equality
Vertical	Horizontal
Meridian	Horizon
Houses of endings	Houses of relationship
Matriarchy	Sisterhood
Patriarchy	Brotherhood
Mentor	Friend
Boss	Colleague
Parent	Partner
Dependent	Independent
Power imbalance	Power shared
Therapist	*Psychopomp*
Symbiosis	Separation
Regression	Progression

Sibling synastry

My only sibling, an elder brother, left home to get married when I was fifteen. For most of these years we shared a bedroom. Sometime later I constructed the horoscopes of my family members and was stunned and perplexed when I calculated one for my sister-in-law. It was the same as mine! We are both Librans, although she is two years older than me. However, we share the same angles: Venus is in the same degree in Scorpio squaring Mars in Leo which is conjunct Pluto, and so on. My first narcissistic thought was that he had married me. My brother, the eldest, is appropriately a Capricorn with Saturn opposite the Sun. His traditional values allowed me to rebel, and so it was many years later that I 'settled down'. My wife was born three weeks before my brother, sharing his planetary placements from Mars out – maybe my brother and I were tied together in some mysterious way!

Today, while I find this synchronicity amazing, I do not find it uncommon. Sibling dynamics are replayed in our relationships with our partners, friends and colleagues, who, as surrogate siblings, repeat similar patterns. This is one area of chart comparison that astounds students – a sibling's planetary placements, aspects and patterns are often replicated in the partner's charts. Sibling transference is more common than we care to admit, especially when we are estranged, angry or when there is unresolved grief or other incomplete issues.

Sibling synastry can be very revealing and informative as to the formation of early patterns of relating and attitudes towards the same or opposite sex. Freud's sister Anna had a retrograde Venus in Sagittarius exactly opposite her brother's Moon in Gemini, which may have contributed to the polarization and confusion around the feminine roles of mother, sister, wife and daughter. Adler had his Mars in Aquarius opposite his elder brother's Sun in Leo, which contributed to his brother becoming a competitive image in Adler's psyche. In some of the cases described in the following chapters we will recognize the importance of the inter-aspects between two siblings' charts.

Generally, siblings have their choice of differing zodiacal signs for the planets Sun through to Jupiter. If these planets are in the same sign as the sibling, or are strongly aspected to the sibling's inner planets, this will be an indicator of an important theme in relationship. Alfred Adler's exact Solar opposition with his brother became his 'masculine protest', while Jung shared both the Lunar and Venusian placements with his sister, influencing his relationship to the feminine. These aspects may also be an inherited motif in the family history, and verifying the family's astrological ancestry often reveals the same planetary contacts between other family members. Synastry aspects between siblings may crystallize into a relationship pattern which exerts its influence on later relationships. Siblings belong to their own system which is part of the family system and its ancestral legacy. The drama played out in the sibling synastry may also extend back through the family history. The individual and the family also move through time, and any similar aspects shared between siblings will receive the same transits during similar passages of time. The sibling relationship is continually developing and maturing.

For the most part the siblings will share the same outer planetary combinations, therefore the inner planets and angles are the most important in chart comparisons between siblings. As mentioned previously, if one of the siblings has an outer planet aspecting an inner one, then the sibling born in the same generation stresses that particular planetary combination. Because the relationship is on a more equal level, the possible outcomes of the planetary aspects between the charts have more scope and latitude.

I use the same rules for sibling chart comparisons as I do when working with other couples. Planets still have their traditional meanings and the inter-aspects symbolize how successfully we interacted with our siblings. When we have more than one sib we experience a multiplicity of relationships, therefore different parts of ourselves may be drawn out with each sibling depending on the synastry aspects. With a multiplicity of relationships we may not feel as intensely about relationship as people do from a two-sibling system. The size of the sibling group defines whether our early access to relating was limited or varied. An only child may lack these early experiences in relating that help mould and define who we are in the context of another.

Notes

1. From a text by ancient astrologer Dorotheus of Sidon, article by David McCann, *The Traditional Astrologer* 8 (spring 1995).
2. For a detailed description of the generational influences of Neptune and Pluto on the family, see Erin Sullivan, *Dynasty: the Astrology of Family Dynamics*, 11–27.
3. James Hillman, *The Myth of Analysis*, 50.
4. 'The Second Hymn to Artemis', from *The Homeric Hymns.*
5. Sarah Iles Johnston, *Hekate Soteira: a Study of Hekate's Roles in the Chaldean Oracles*

and Related Literature (Scholar's Press, Atlanta, GA: 1990). Johnston says: 'Artemis' identification with the Moon precedes that of Hekate with the Moon; the first certain evidence for the idea is found in the second century BC', 31 note 8. Artemis' association with the Moon may also have been a logical derivation from Apollo's link to the Sun. Johnston also suggests that by the time of Plutarch (AD *c.* 46–*c.* 120), the identification of Artemis with the Moon was common.

6. J. M. Ashmand, *Ptolemy's Tetrabiblos* (Symbols and Signs, North Hollywood, CA: 1976), 124.

7. Jung, 'Synchronicity: an Acausal Connecting Principle', *CW* 88§69 footnote.

8

The Astrology of Gemini
Recognizing the Missing Other

. . . college years; years of apprenticeship, of wanderings into new worlds, of being drawn and repelled by touch and smiles, deeply uncertain yet aggressively sure, the more set the less the flow of life seems seizable by hands and brains, projecting symbols, images, words to reassure oneself that one is knower and master – such is the Gemini phase: the entrance into the wide world of human society, the gates to the great experience of union with the Beloved. Dane Rudhyar[1]

Mythic siblings

Castor and Pollux, the two bright stars in the constellation of Gemini, are an eternal reminder of the sibling bond, a relationship so important to the ancients that their story was written into the heavens.[2]

The twins, Castor and Pollux, were also known as the Dioscuri, sons of Zeus. This paternity refers to the earlier mythic version where both brothers were the divine heroic sons of Zeus. By classical times, the twins were known to have originated from a much more complex family atmosphere. This account of the myth became the popular version, originating from the epic poem the *Kypria*.[3]

Their parents were a royal couple, Leda and Tyndareus, the Queen and King of Sparta. Zeus desired Leda and in order to seduce her, he changed into a swan. He was then pursued by Hermes, in the shape of an eagle. Trickster Hermes colluded with Zeus to drive the swan into the safety of the Queen's embrace where Zeus ravaged her. Leda then bore two giant eggs as a consequence of having been impregnated by both Zeus and her husband. From one egg emerged the divine progeny of Zeus, Helen and Pollux; from the other, the human offspring of Tyndareus, Castor and Clytemnestra. The duplicity of twinship offers various possibilities: one set of twins is divine, the other is mortal; one set is male, the other is female; and yet another combination arranges each set of twins as divine male/mortal female and divine female/mortal male.

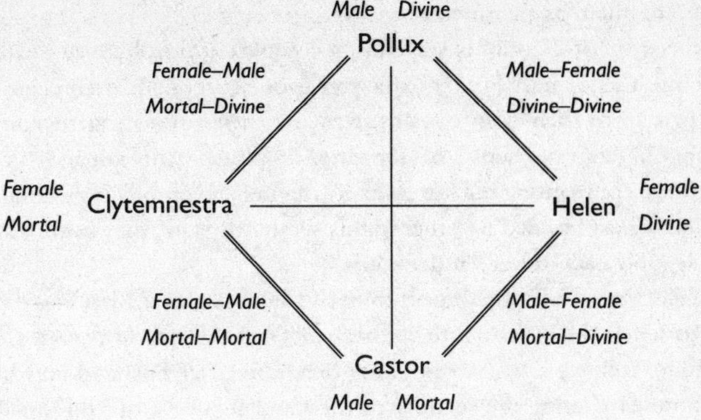

Figure 10: The duplicity and symmetry of sibship.

Their duplicated and symmetrical fourfold sibling constellation is an integral part of the Gemini myth. This complex constellation of 'others' at birth and the ultimate loss of this connection is often the fate that underlies the experience of Gemini.[4] Both sets of twins carry the complexity of the sibling enmeshment into their adult relationships. Helen and Clytemnestra marry the brothers, Menelaus and Agamemnon, while Castor and Pollux also marry a sibling pair of sisters, their twin cousins. Early imprints and patterns from our sibling relationships are often recreated with adult partners.

Both Castor and Pollux were known as great warriors and honoured heroes in their homeland of Sparta. They were skilled in sport and both were successful in the Olympic games. Depictions of the twins often show them wearing the *pilos*, an egg-shaped helmet. With similar head gear they appear symmetrical. But the egg shell reminds us that although they were born to the same mother, each had a different father. They appear equal, yet their fate is different. Even though they are nurtured in a similar familial atmosphere by the same mother, their destiny is not the same.

Paris, following the instructions of Aphrodite, arrived in Sparta to seduce the twins' sister, Helen, and carry her back to Troy. Unaware of his intent, the twin brothers graciously welcomed him. Soon after Paris' arrival, the twins left to attend the marriages of another pair of twins, their cousins Idas and Lynceus. However, before the wedding had even taken place, Castor and Pollux abducted their cousins' prospective brides, yet another set of twins, claiming them as their own.

Again the story of Gemini is staged in a complex atmosphere of duality and twinning. Castor and Pollux, as a pair, not yet individuated, claim a feminine pair from their twin cousins, weaving their stories together in a way which obliterates a sense of separateness. Each twin engages in a similar pattern, confronting the same shadow figure and embracing a similar relationship. Whilst bonded together in this symbiotic state, they cannot see anyone else, only each other's reflection.

Meanwhile, Paris took the opportunity of the absence of Menelaus and the twins to seduce Helen and lure her back to Troy.[5] Helen, now possessed by Aphrodite, follows Paris, abandoning her home, her husband and her brothers, forever altering the security of the familial lineage of both Sparta and Troy. (Ironically, while Castor and Pollux are abducting the betrothed sisters of their cousins, their own sister is being taken away from them.) Leaving the sibling system in pursuit of an external relationship creates a potential schism in the familial dynamic. The family is forever altered when a sibling takes a partner, for now the sibling and family constellations are joined with another ancestral line. All of the siblings in the system are confronted with the change in their relationship, the transfer of loyalties, and the reality of the sibling leaving home and entering the world of adult relationship. The family as it *was* can never be so again. One way to deal with the emergent shadow and unresolved feelings is to cast them on to the sibling's partner and family, in this myth on Paris and the House of Troy.

Another variation of the story suggests that Castor and Pollux were in conflict with Idas and Lynceus over the division of a large herd of cattle. All four had successfully raided a neighbouring territory and returned with the cattle. Conflict arose over possession which precipitated Pollux's separation from Castor, a powerful Geminian theme. Both sets of twins battle with each other and during the conflict Castor, the mortal twin, is killed by a spear. The opposites are no longer fused but torn apart. Their destinies are now revealed: Castor must die as a mortal whereas Pollux, who has the gift of immortality, must live. They are to be separated.

Pollux is now alone. Seeing his brother killed in battle and separated from him evokes an unbearable grief. Ultimately, Castor completes what is missing in Pollux and with his loss, Pollux feels empty and incomplete. His grief at the loss of his brother–other is so intense he cannot bear to be separated from him. In his despair, he petitions Zeus to allow him to relinquish his immortality and join his brother in death. In a rare bequest, Zeus grants Pollux, his divine son, this wish.

Geminian behaviour is typified as scattered, nervous and non-committal. Often what underlies this behaviour is a frantic search for something that we feel separated from. In essence, all Gemini placements contain an image of a birth twin that feels missing. What is missing is often unconscious, but none the less drives the individual forward to quest and question for the lost other. In this myth, it is the severed connection to the twin/sibling that allows the other to cross the threshold to the Underworld. Castor, the mortal, becomes a *psychopomp* leading his brother across the liminal of death. In Gemini, the experiences of separation awaken the Mercurial functions. Separation begets consciousness, and the consciousness of being separate is painful. Gemini in the horoscope may carry the first experiences of consciousness, therefore the earliest images of separateness.

Gemini is an early experience in the zodiac – it is the first sign in the trinity of air, and the first mutable and dual sign. It is the first representation in the zodiac of the consciousness of duality, separation and opposition. Gemini, occurring early in the zodiac, is a metaphor for a primal stage in psychological development. The ability to understand, reflect or analyse has not yet been developed and a secure sense of emotional attachment has not yet been internalized. Gemini, as a symbol of the developmental process, is too young consciously to hold the impact of Pollux's profound loss. Hence the impact and feeling of the loss is repressed, forgotten in the underworld realm. Potent feelings of grief, abandonment and separation are interred and rendered unconscious. These feelings surface as restlessness and emptiness, anxiety that something is missing or lost, and an incompleteness that beckons us to continue searching. Quite commonly this 'missing' feeling is projected out on to the world, especially the compatible world of equal others. This feeling of connection to the missing half is often idealized as the soul mate (Libra) or the bonds of fraternal or sororal love (Aquarius). Underlying many Geminian placements is a feeling of profound loss which cannot be explained rationally; it becomes embodied in the nervous system, stimulating anxiety and lack of focus. The unconscious memory of a primal separation is awoken in the closeness of an adult partnership or intimate friendship.

There are many differing versions as to how the twins were reunited. While most references suggest the twins alternate between the two worlds of Heaven and the Underworld, how this occurs is depicted differently in various sources.[6] The Spartans saw Pollux, the immortal half, as the morning star while Castor, the mortal twin, was the evening star. While one rose out of the dark and ascended towards Heaven, the other descended into the twilight of the nether world, forever separated by the horizon. In a similar version, Castor spends one day in Heaven while his brother passes the same time in the Underworld. They follow each other between Olympus and Erebos but never meet. Another version locates them together, one day in the Underworld and the next day in Heaven. These similar motifs have the twins swinging in a manic-depressive cycle between the highs of Heaven and the lows of the Underworld, a common motif underlying Gemini.

The twins' afterlife has numerous possible interpretations. One suggests the constant search for the missing other which seems to be part of Gemini's fate. The twins, once fused and bonded together, are now eternally separated, which describes the essence of Gemini. However, we can also 'read' into the myth another suggestion. With the consciousness of their differences now apparent, it is more possible for the twins to experience both opposites within themselves. Both are variants on the archetype of Gemini. Castor and Pollux remind us of the eternal quest for the missing other and the life journey of reconciliation and relationship with our sibling/s.

The twinship of Castor and Pollux differs from other myths of twins in that their story aspires towards the achievement of affinity. As youths they are bound to each other, yet they are inherently unequal as one is divine, the other mortal. In death they achieve equality. Other stories more often reflect oppositional elements through a bright twin and a dark twin, casting the two siblings as rivals. Another pair of twins, Zethus and Amphion, has also been associated with the sign of Gemini.[7] They were also sons of Zeus, known as the Theban Dioscuri, but their personalities were much more differentiated. The management of their rivalry and awareness of each other's differences encouraged individuation and separateness. These differences became important in their life task of constructing the Theban walls. Gemini is the eternal story of the sibling bond and the image of the quest for our reconnection to this *a priori* figure. The sign, Gemini, weaves the sibling story into our own horoscopes.

Gemini on the house cusps

Whichever house Gemini rules is a sphere of our lives where the sibling story may be located. Each of the four angles and the eight intermediary house cusps of the horoscope is a demarcation of a new, yet unfamiliar, terrain of life experience. Like gates, house cusps suggest a division of territory and are markers between these territories. Each house is governed differently from the preceding territory and therefore there are different procedures, customs and rules for each one. In Greek antiquity, gates and doors were common symbols of threshold, especially for entrances to the Underworld. For each individual the horoscope reveals their personal image of the dweller on the threshold, or the gate keeper, symbolized by the sign on the cusp and its ruling planet.

As a symbol of threshold, the house cusp alerts us to the entrance into a state of liminality as we cross from one realm into another. Liminality is the experience of being between two fixed points of reference and is a time of reorientation. Therefore, the sign on the cusp of a house is a potent symbol of initiation into this new sphere of life. The essence of the sign colours the experience of the house and may be the first image that we meet as we enter this territory. The sign and its ruling planet are the gods waiting to be honoured in this area. Gemini and its ruler, Mercury, are honoured through the sibling bond and its consciousness of separation. Gemini's nature describes an area where a dawning of consciousness, or a separation, may take place. It is an area where we struggle with the tension of polar opposites, moving back and forth between two extremes, caught in Gemini's duality. It is an area where a sense of primal learning starts, the beginning of individuating and perhaps even a restless search for something that feels missing. The house that Gemini rules will also bring some of the sibling issues into its domicile. It is here we may need to excavate some of the sibling story, perhaps not just from our own history, but the familial and ancestral history as well.

The environmental atmosphere described by the house is multi-dimensional. Firstly, the house can often describe the literal and manifest environment. Secondly, the house can describe the psychic layer – the psychological landscape and atmosphere underpinning this terrain. As well there is a teleological level to any house: what is the meaning of this area of my life and how may this sphere be integrated into the whole of my life? In examining the astrological statements of the house position, the astrologer can suggest the potential meaning or purpose behind the experiences of this environment.

Houses are complex, and when excavated reveal potent symbols and images of importance to the individual for quickening the understanding of patterns in one's life. We will concentrate on Gemini and its symbol of the sibling relationship to further our exploration into sibling patterns. Simply, when Gemini is on the cusp of a house it may symbolize an important sibling pattern in this area of one's life, a pattern that could ultimately continue to be lived out in this sphere of life.

When the natural wheel is referred to, it is assumed there are no intercepted signs in the horoscope. If there is an intercepted polarity, the order of signs on house cusps is disturbed and the ascendant may not be the one that is suggested. In these cases, contrast the house position of Gemini with the sign on the ascendant to see how the description could alter. If Gemini itself is intercepted then this could suggest that the sibling story or the siblings themselves are not as easily accessible. The following descriptions are only a way to muse over the sibling images in our life. If the theme they suggest is repeated by another statement in the chart then the possibility described is heightened; if there are two or more statements confirming this theme then the possibility is much more a probability. I have also listed other astrological combinations that may be similar to the following themes. The sophistication of the astrological model contributes to these themes being seen in various ways.

With **Gemini on the fourth house cusp** (natural wheel, Pisces rising), the sibling story may be an important aspect of the parental story. Either or both parents may carry a potent image of his or her own sibling constellation into their families of creation.

At the heart of the family of origin may be a sibling story unconsciously carried by the parent that permeates the family atmosphere. It could be one of loss, separation, estrangement or a pattern of enmeshment or fusion that affects the individual's sense of security. Often, the parent's sibling story is important to understand as it has played a direct part in the early atmosphere of the home. The parent may have tried to compensate for his or her own sibling experiences, affecting the family atmosphere.

The Gemini experience of the lost sibling may be part of the family history, a feeling that something is missing. This may be the story of a lost child in the family, a potential sibling relationship never experienced or, for an only child, the experience of having the parent as both a parent and a sib. The consciousness of separation is part of the familial atmosphere, and this could range from a healthy experience of seeing both parents equal and separate to a more insecure experience of having the family separated and even the siblings divided up amongst the parents. The parents may be highly attached to their children, forming a close relationship since any dissension within the sibling system could constellate feelings of loss. These feelings would confront the parent/s with the incomplete relationship to their own siblings. Having a close bond with one's children may help defend the feelings of loss that may have been part of the parental sibling system.

In our younger years, the sibling relationship may have offered more emotional security than the parental relationship, as it may have provided more of the nurturing and sense of belonging. The individual's family atmosphere may have been complicated with the confusion of roles: the sibling acting in a parental way while the parent could have been more comfortable being one of the siblings. Mother may have preferred the role of a sister, father the role of a brother, rather than that of a parent. Here the hierarchical structure of the parental system tries to be equal to the sibling system. The parents themselves could be engaged in the struggle to be equal to each other, manifesting as sibling rivalry and competition. We could have experienced the parents fused together like twins, unable to separate, reminding us of the relationship between Apollo and Artemis.

The *puer* side of Gemini, which searches for eternal youthfulness, may be carried by one or both of the parents, disturbing the hierarchy of the family. Roles of authority may be confused, and the sibling system may have gained a sense of autonomy too early. Hence the atmosphere of the early home could have spawned anxiety about emotional security, contributing to a confusion about who was or was not dependable. If the individual transferred a parental figure on to one of the siblings then this parentalized sibling's separation from the home would have been traumatic. This would also contribute to a later sense of confusion between dependency and equality in adult relationships, or an inability to draw boundaries between the relationship to our siblings and the relationship to our partners and family.

The fourth house not only speaks of the family of origin but of our families of choice and creation. Therefore we may bring the Gemini influence into our adult homes, looking for brotherly or sisterly contacts with our partners and children. Our siblings' families are also important and they may be absorbed into our family, bringing their conflicts and complexes into the family atmosphere. It is in our own home and family that we seek to find the missing other. In order to provide a secure base we need to honour the Geminian processes that were part of our family of origin. This may entail a conscious descent into the annals of the familial history to link together the severed threads of the sibling story within the family. Mercury needs to be honoured in the home through an active inquisitive atmosphere, permeated with learning, conversation and travel. Ultimately the secure base that we provide for ourselves is a home filled with enough physical space to house our multiplicity of interests, enough emotional space to allow comfortable 'breathing space' and enough psychological space to nurture the severed links inherited from our family of origin.

Similar astrological statements: Mercury in the fourth house or Cancer, the Moon in Gemini or the third house, Moon in aspect to Mercury, Cancer on the third house cusp, the ruler of the third house (in the natural wheel, Venus) in the fourth or Cancer.

Gemini on the fifth house cusp (natural wheel, Aquarius rising) locates the sibling at the threshold of our personal creativity.

The fifth house cusp draws a clear boundary between the family of origin and what lies beyond it. It is the cusp we cross to 'leave home' and venture into the heroic world of creating our own life external to the family. The fifth house, being the second from the fourth, could also represent the resources of the family that are available to us for this journey. These resources need not be seen as financial but perhaps relate more to the sense of worth and emotional security we ingested from the experiences within the family. Hopefully, we enter the fifth house experience of encountering that which lay beyond the family with a sense of self-worth, faith in ourselves, a secure foundation and knowing the experience of being loved. With this solid foundation, the only risk the fifth house implies is in risking our vulnerable ego and pride in expressing who we are to others. Without this secure base that the family provides, we are at risk ourselves, for we lack the innate resources to deal with the response that the world has to our sense of self. Being at risk to another's response suggests that we are prone to inflation if the feedback is positive and depression if the reviews are negative, constantly losing our sense of who we are in the reaction of the other.

With Gemini on the cusp, an older sibling may be a role model whose image provides a passage into the external world; or if there is a younger sibling, we may be the role model. The sibling's feedback when growing up is vital as it may directly influence our sense of ego strength in the world. It is to siblings that we may look to find the personal creativity that helps define who we are. They may act as the reflecting pool for our developing sense of self. With Gemini on the fifth we may seek a sense of mirroring from our siblings.

The fifth house is the arena of experimentation in relationships where we look for a partner to reflect back our sense of self-worth. In the fifth we engage in the joy and creativity of self-discovery, hence this statement may also suggest that the sibling is important here as a playmate and co-creator for our sense of personal creativity. However, the sibling could also be the person on to whom we project our creativity, echoing back her emerging ego, while ours remains unacknowledged. We may see her as the heroic one, able to manage the dragons of the external world; the sibling becomes the hook for our projection of the creative self. Therefore this combination could also speak of the possibility of adoration of the sibling. The fifth often talks of unrequited love or a broken heart. The heart may be broken by a sibling who does not return the love. The sibling may be an image of the lover whom we are seeking and it is through the pain of a broken heart that we are able to break the attachment to her.

With Gemini on the fifth, the issue of separating from the sibling is important as the bond may interfere with the early process of forming relationships external to the family. We may always expect an idealized sense of fraternal or sororial love to be part of any relationship, disappointed when love does not return to us the image that we wanted. Certainly, with Gemini here, we look for the heroic in the sibling, but could also experience the painful realization of separateness and disconnection. In our journey to move away from the family, it is the siblings we may need to separate from, or remove ourselves from their shadow. With this placement we may feel eclipsed by siblings, or abandoned as older sibs leave home on their process of self-discovery. Or we unwittingly abandon a younger one for our own heroic quest.

We may also see our creativity reflected back to us in the mirror of the sibling. Here the consciousness of separation occurs when we experience that we are not the reflection we see in the mirror of our sibs, and later, others. We may often see the reflection of the sibling in our own children, or a reflection of ourselves in the face of our sibling's children. We instinctively bring our own sibling issues and experiences into the interrelationships between our children, and are vulnerable to favouring the child who recreates our own sibling position and/or role.

Similar astrological statements: Mercury in the fifth house or Leo, Sun in Gemini or the third house, Leo on the third house cusp, ruler of the third house (in the natural wheel, Mars) in the fifth or Leo.

*

Gemini on the sixth house cusp (natural wheel, Capricorn rising) brings the sibling story into our daily lives.

The sixth house cusp suggests ways in which we may maintain a sense of well-being by creating daily rituals that evoke this energy. In a sense, the sixth house is our daily housekeeping rituals that provide a sense of order and cohesion to our lives. These rituals help us to focus on the tasks of daily life and maintain a sense of centre. Hence, without this anchor into the hearth of self, stress accumulates and becomes somatic. The cusp of the sixth house points to the part of the body system that is the most vulnerable to this stress. With Gemini on the cusp, it may be through the nervous system that the stress of what feels lost or missing may be embodied. This could manifest as biting nails, nervous twitches, an early smoking addiction, etc. Breathing and the respiratory system are vulnerable as well, shortness of breath perhaps defending the grief of the lost other.

For Gemini, the rituals of daily life would include the image of sharing the daily tasks and intimate space with a sibling. For an only child this would be experienced as a great loss. Often with this placement I have seen a sibling missing from the daily routines of life – away at boarding school, siblings split through divorce, half-siblings from a parent's remarriage – retelling the Gemini myth of the missing sibling, this time from daily contact.

This may suggest that unresolved issues are brought into our sphere of work, with fate supplying a figure who draws the sibling issue to the surface. Hence sibling rivalries may enter the workplace. Equally, we may find a brother or sister amongst our work colleagues to share the daily life, to conspire together against other workmates and join forces to rebel against the parental boss. Here in the sphere of work we may instinctively replicate the sibling system, placing ourselves in the same position as in the earlier system, repeating the roles that we were comfortable playing. Equally, the workmate may constellate the lost sibling and we could find ourselves enmeshed or symbiotic with those that we work with. No clear boundary is established between the rituals of work and the rest of our life.

The need to share with an equal on a daily basis, yet still retain a sense of our own centre, is imperative. Therefore having variety at work, a social atmosphere and the possibility for daily contact with others is important. Yet focusing on our own interests, irrespective of the sibling–other, is also part of the sixth house. It is through the relationship with the sibling that we discover our own innate rhythms and what serves us best.

With Gemini on the cusp of the house of health, the health of the sibling may have been an issue in the early years. Daily life may have focused on the well-being of the sibling and we may have been involved in some of the administering to the sib. At a young age this may have been confusing and overwhelming, constellating the duality of the healthy–unhealthy twin. It is the well-being of the sibling that may have unconsciously moulded our attitudes towards our own health and daily maintenance. If the pattern of health was an issue in the early sibling environment, we may unconsciously carry this pattern into the adult sphere of relating once again, interacting with partners whose health may be an issue.

Similar astrological statements: Mercury in Virgo or the sixth house, Virgo on the third house cusp, ruler of the third house (in the natural wheel, Neptune) in the sixth house or Virgo.

Gemini on the seventh house cusp (Sagittarius rising) combines two spheres of equality and is a reminder of the archetype of the sibling marriage. This could suggest that we unconsciously model our primary adult relationships on the experience from our sibling system, expecting the same responses and outcomes. If we were the eldest child we may take this experience into our adult relationships, expecting the partner to follow our leads. We naturally assume first place. Or if we were an only child we may find the adult relationship where we have to compromise and share the same space is too difficult a task. While sibling themes are always a part of our adult relationships, this statement addresses the issue head on. It suggests the duality or ambivalence of feelings experienced earlier in the sibling system are once again brought into consciousness in the present relationship.

Relationships become the focus for the underlying mythic theme of the lost twin. We may unconsciously expect the partner to fill the empty void, to replace what is missing. Hence, there is a lot of psychic attention focused on keeping the partner as the complement to what feels missing inside. The descendant, representing the Hesperides of the horoscope, is on the western polarity of our visible horizon in life. To place Gemini here could suggest that the partner may become the projection for the lost other, the Castor to our Pollux. One of the patterns that could emerge is that of creating a relationship where each reflects the other's missing half. The descendant sign is so often literally recreated in the partner's horoscope that the probability of a Geminian statement in the other's horoscope is quite high, adding to the collusion that is taking place. The partners become the twins that are eternally bound together, not able to separate. The symbiosis of the partnership is often mistaken for a close relationship; however, under the surface there is a fear of independence, individuality and separation. The other extreme, of course, in this sphere of adult relationship is to project the 'dark twin' on to the partner, playing out the shadow to such a degree that we strike to kill it off. Both sibling patterns may arise here – the missing other that we merge into or the dangerous side that needs to be wiped out.

Gemini on the seventh suggests that complexes or incomplete issues with the siblings or the partner's siblings are ripe for emergence in adult relationships, and with Gemini here may be transferred on to our 'significant others'. The partner may trigger some of the earlier feelings of rivalry and competition, being overly sensitive to anything that seems unequal or not fairly shared. The partner's siblings may literally appear upon the scene constellating feelings of rivalry and competition.

With Gemini here, our partner becomes our sibling substitute, the soul mate. We share everything with the partner, often against an innate need to have our own space. Hence, when it comes to the emotional and sexual level of the relationship, the sibling taboo on incest may appear. This may feel as if the relationship is more comfortable on the level of the equal or the friend, but too risky or even taboo on the level of intimate other. This level of intimacy becomes what is missing in the relationship and often the partners must experience the grief of the loss of relationship in order to be together.

The seventh house can describe all one-to-one relationships, and with Gemini here we may bring our unresolved sibling issues into our close partnerships with friends and colleagues, competing for our place against them. With Mercury as the guardian of this threshold, he may overshadow our partner who then becomes the *psychopomp*, leading us into the unknown terrain of our own shadow substance.

Similar astrological statements: Mercury in Libra or the seventh house, Venus in Gemini, Libra on the third house cusp, ruler of the third house (in the natural wheel, Uranus) in the seventh house or Libra.

Gemini on the eighth house cusp (natural wheel, Scorpio rising) brings an encounter with the sibling over shared and sacred territory – the parents and their resources. This encounter can either contribute to a sense of intimacy or create an estrangement with the sibling. With Gemini guarding the threshold to the ancestral legacy, the sibling relationship is tested in this area, often evoking a sense of betrayal by the brother or sister. Gemini on the eighth house suggests that what we have inherited from the family needs to be shared with the sibling–others. But the eighth house territory, unlike the essence of Gemini, is not an equal territory, and it is through the guise of a sibling that we often face the painful realization that the parents' resources, be they love, money, power or emotional support, were not divided equally amongst the siblings. This betrayal, catalysed by the sibling who may have seemingly gained more from the parent, brings the painful consciousness of separation. Equally, we may have been fated to betray our sibling in order to remain true to what the parent wanted. It is in this realm that we are called to be brutally honest with our own self in the face of opposition from the sibling. It is when this risk is taken that the sibling relationship can be authentic. Sometimes this can recreate itself in a new and open relationship, but more often the relationship becomes estranged when the truth is revealed. Siblings may still engage in power and control issues rather than face the truth that they are equal to the others. There could be a secret that has been kept from the sibling, or a familial secret that has been inappropriately kept by the siblings. At some point the secret may be revealed (Gemini brings this to consciousness) and the siblings are asked to face each other in a moment of truth. This astrological statement seems to demand an intimate honesty with the sib which may feel impossible yet ultimately is important.

Gemini on the eighth could also suggest a sibling story that may be part of the parental marriage. I have seen an estrangement or death as part of the sibling experience of one or both of the parents that the child is unconsciously influenced by. One of the parents or grandparents may have been a twin, and the grief over the other twin's death or estrangement has become part of the ancestral legacy. An emotional separation may have taken place with one of the parents' siblings or grandparents' siblings, that was never resolved, lying as unresolved grief that the child absorbs from the parent. It is with the pain from the death of an intimate relationship that the ancestral grief could be awoken.

Since the eighth is the domain of death, the death of a sibling, either literally or through estrangement, may be part of the initiation. Equally there could be a sense of depth of intimacy with the sibling that interferes with the process of forming another intimate relationship. Here we could have an image of the sibling marriage, so closely fused, that emotional bonding to others is difficult. Part of intimate relating could also be to the partner's siblings. They certainly are likely to enter the marriage either physically or psychically with this statement. Hence a sibling or partner's sibling (or ghost of the sibling) may be triangulated within the individual's adult relationships.

Crossing this Geminian threshold suggests a confrontation with the issues of siblings on the deepest levels. It is in this area that we may feel the deepest love or the greatest betrayal. Fate may continue to present others in our lives on to whom we unconsciously transfer the sibling. These others, usually intimate friends, constellate the primal issues of separation and betrayal, yet also union and intimacy.

Similar astrological statements: Mercury in the eighth house or Scorpio, Pluto in the third house, Pluto in aspect to Mercury, Scorpio on the third house cusp, ruler of the third house (in the natural wheel, Saturn) in the eighth house or Scorpio.

Gemini on the ninth house cusp (natural wheel, Libra rising) is an image that the sibling relationship may be a key to a broader horizon. The siblings may venture farther afield and break with some of the family's traditions. The sibling system challenges the beliefs, morals and philosophical attitudes that were part of the familial atmosphere.

The cusp of the ninth house is the gateway to the collective realm of what lies beyond our familial and cultural inheritance. The ninth is a sphere beyond what we have known or experienced to date, new cultures and new attitudes of life. Following the eighth house initiation, which connects us to our sense of loss, is the spirited vision of what lay beyond death and what can be resurrected. With Gemini on the ninth, it may be the sibling who helps initiate us into the vast world that lies beyond the immediate experience of our family and our community.

The sibling may be the voyager, the traveller into the higher realms, asking questions we hadn't thought of asking, going where we hadn't dreamt of going and exposing us to a world beyond the picket fence that holds the family's morals intact. It is siblings who may awaken our search for the truth or inspire us to forge our own beliefs. They appear fluent in the ways of the world and may be influential in forging our beliefs and values in life. We have the image of the sibling bringing back a sense of adventure into the sibling system, acting as a *psychopomp* that guides us into new territory. At least this is our expectation. We may become disappointed when we find that our sibs are not the worldly-wise gurus we had wanted them to be. We search for an equal that can share our wonder of the world about us, explore what lies beyond the neighbourhood and discuss the meaning of life together. So with Gemini on the ninth, the sibling may be the inspiration behind our choice of travel destination, our course of university study, our interest in an alternative religion or our fascination with a particular author.

Equally, we may bring back our wanderlust into the sibling system and try to inspire one of the sibs to be our companion on the journey. The ninth house is also connected to our siblings-in-law and with Gemini here we may find a new culture open up to us via our partner's sibs. It may be through them that we are exposed to a larger world, foreign to the one we grew up in. We are in-laws to a new set of values, customs and beliefs. We have also entered the collective terrain of sisterhood and brotherhood and we may find surrogate siblings in our pursuit of wisdom. Our new sisters and brothers may be part of the young liberals, part of the ashram community or fellow travellers exploring the same terrain that we are. We meet our sibs once again as we branch out to explore the world around us.

Similar astrological statements: Mercury in the ninth house or Sagittarius, Jupiter in Gemini or the third house, Jupiter in aspect to Mercury, Sagittarius on the cusp of the third house, the ruler of the third house (in the natural wheel, Jupiter) in the ninth or Sagittarius.

Gemini on the tenth house cusp (natural wheel, Virgo rising) suggests the sibling story may be an overt part of the parental story. The parental attitudes and expectations have been influenced by the parents' experiences within their sibling systems.

The Midheaven is the highest point on the ecliptic at our moment of birth. As such it represents a pinnacle or a goal we reach for. With Gemini on the MC, the sibling may have been an earlier image of someone we looked up to or who played an authoritative role in our lives. His choices in life may have directly impacted on ours. The MC is the parental axis of the horoscope, representing their expectations for the child in the world. This could also include the expectation to fulfil the unlived life of the parent. The parent's experience in his sibling system will directly influence the child. If the parent's experience of his siblings is estranged, then there may be an expectation that his children will compensate for this lack by forming a close bond with each other. Individuals with Gemini on the MC may feel the pressure to relate to their siblings in a way that pleases the parent, thus fulfilling his expectations. The gulf between the idealism of how the parent views his children's sibling relationships and the reality of what takes place may be wide. Therefore the individual may also feel the necessity to maintain the relationship to the siblings.

Since the MC is so visible, what could be apparent is the great differences between the siblings. With Gemini on the tenth, we may have been conscious from a very early age of the differences between ourselves and our sibs, since this was continually being pointed out. This may have complicated the situation in the sibling system, as the differences may have led to favouritism with our parents.

Here the sibling issues are intermeshed with the domain of authority, control, tradition and responsibility. This may suggest that we may have had the experience of either an older authoritarian sib or, as an elder, felt responsible for the siblings. With Gemini on the MC, there is a strong impression of duty and responsibility for others, the role of looking out for others. This starts early in the sibling system, and then may become political as we mature. We have the ability to be very conscious of the dynamics of this primal relationship which contributes to our later vocations as parents, teachers, counsellors, etc.

From the individual's experience, authority and equality are often confused and we may find the authority figure who tries to be the equal, or an equal who takes an authoritative role. Part of our early experiences in the sibling system prepare us for the life experience of trying to balance both authority and equality.

Similar astrological statements: Mercury in the tenth house or Capricorn, Saturn in the third house or Gemini, Saturn in aspect to Mercury, Capricorn on the cusp of the third house, the ruler of the third house (in the natural wheel, Pluto) in the tenth.

Gemini on the eleventh house cusp (natural wheel, Leo rising) suggests that the sibling story is encountered in the sphere of friends, associates and in the community at large.

The eleventh is the house of community, the groups we encounter and belong to outside the family: groups that we belong to because of our interests, our passions or our professional affiliations. This is also a house of kin, not bound by blood, but by a similar spirit of interest. Eleventh house experiences include our first class photo, our circle of friends, girl guides, the school council; groups where we were part of the community without other family members. But with Gemini on the threshold, we may have shared these experiences with our sibling/s; they may have been our companions, part of our circle of friends and part of our communal life. The sibling could be the guide to a new world of interests, away from the family. Separation from the sibling may have been difficult because of the spirited connection and may only be realized through a physical separation, such as attending a different school, etc. This could become a pattern in adult groups, where differentiation from the other members is difficult as we continue to identify with the others in the group. Gemini on the eleventh suggests we find our separateness through our participation in the larger community.

Gemini on the eleventh could also suggest that we approach our friendships and colleagueships based on the sibling model. Friends are brothers and sisters, unconsciously recreating patterns of sibship with us – sibling rivalry, loyalty, etc. Sometimes we may nickname a friend 'Brother John', or use expressions such as 'she is like a sister to me'. We may feel the close bonds with friends that we were not able to feel with our literal brothers and sisters, our substitutes for the lost or idealized sibling. Since the eleventh house is also a house of relationship, we all are susceptible to recreating unfinished sibling business with our friends and colleagues. However, Gemini on the eleventh house suggests that we may encounter these incomplete sibling issues in the organizations and groups we join. People should be alerted to the potentiality of recreating their ordinal position or completing the left-over sibling rivalry. While this may be a necessary task within the group, the consciousness of their actions helps ease the tension created by the distortion of the sibling material.

Many community programmes recognize the universality of the close bond underlying the sibling archetype. Organizations that use volunteers to help the disenfranchised and underprivileged often model their names on the sibling bond, for example 'Big Brothers', 'Brothers and Sisters'. When we connect on this level of interchange, we empower the terms sister and brother with communal meaning. With Gemini on the eleventh, our brothers and sisters are sought in the greater community. Through like-minded pursuits we rediscover the sibling.

Similar astrological statements: Mercury in the eleventh house or Aquarius, Uranus in the third house, Uranus in aspect to Mercury, Aquarius on the cusp of the third house, the ruler of the third house (in the natural wheel, Venus) in the eleventh house or Aquarius.

Gemini on the twelfth house cusp (natural wheel, Cancer rising) weaves the twins' story with our ancestral lineage. Here we have an image of the lost twin, deeply rooted in the annals of the ancestors, which is impressed upon the psyche at an early stage.

Individuals carrying this image often feel they have literally lost a twin. The imaginative process conjures up a lost twin: a sense that some part of the self has not be born and that something is missing. The image suggests a primal memory of sharing the womb, as well as a loss of this. Gemini suggests consciousness, but the twelfth represents pre-conscious, collective and deeply unconscious states. An image of separation is registered deep within the psyche, inaccessible to daily consciousness but apparent in the imaginal life through dreams, irrational thoughts or feelings, visions and creative endeavours. Modern science confirms that the loss of a twin *in utero* may not be solely fantasy. Many foetuses start off as one of a pair, but struggle for life with the other absorbing them, or overpowering them. The struggle takes place at the beginning of life before any consciousness of this is even detectable. Another factor may be that a parent or ancestor's memory of sharing the womb with a twin could be passed to a child through the psychic atmosphere of the family. Frequently with this placement there is a 'twin' in the family ancestry, or the story of a pair of estranged siblings.

This placement suggests we may be vulnerable to our sibling's unconscious life, perhaps living out some of her fantasies or becoming the scapegoat for them. There may be a deep-seated impulse to sacrifice ourselves for the sibling, giving up our sense of identity to liberate a brother or sister. Certainly in the sibling system this placement would most easily constellate the one who is sacrificed. There could be a sense of not being seen or acknowledged by the siblings.

This placement also lends itself to a symbiotic relationship with the sibling, idealization and identification, perhaps living out her depression or despair. It can also manifest in the sibling who is ill, directing the attention away from the others. This sense of merger with the sibling has a painful other side: separation and even estrangement. No matter how close the bond, the consciousness awoken with the sense of separation is acute. We may feel isolated and alone, cast out by our sibling/s. While we may have used the sibling system as a safe retreat from the harsher realities of relationships, we are forced at some point to retreat from this system ourselves. The opus feels as if we need to learn to draw more distinct boundaries between ourselves and our siblings to ensure that we are not drawn into imprisoning ourselves in the role of muse or helper for them.

The facility to articulate another's feeling life or recognize the depth of another's pain begins in the sibling system. The role of the listener, the messenger, the guide, the attendant is developed at the expense of personal visibility. Later, these roles may be taken into the adult world of equal relationships, the person becoming entangled and enmeshed with others. The urge to surrender oneself to the sibling, to lose oneself in his addictions, but eventually claim one's sense of separateness in relation to him, is all part of the process.

Similar astrological statements: Mercury in the twelfth house or Pisces, Neptune in the third house, Neptune in aspect to Mercury, Pisces on the cusp of the third house, the ruler of the third house (in the natural wheel, Mercury) in the twelfth house or Pisces.

With **Gemini rising** the sibling story is on the horizon of the individual's life.

The ascendant marks our entry into the world, from the womb of the twelfth house into the spirit of incarnation. Like the Underworld river, the Lethe, we cross this boundary into incarnation forgetting our past and what came before. The ascendant symbolizes what we first encounter in the world, and with Gemini on the horizon of our life, we could enter into a world already defined by the sibling. Sibling/s may have already set a precedent with the niche they have created in the family.

With Gemini on the ascendant, we need to identify ourselves with those in our immediate environment. Younger siblings would be very alert to modelling themselves on older ones, mimicking their identity, presenting themselves in similar fashion. Gemini mimics, and a model for Gemini to copy would be a sibling.

The ascendant is a bridging mechanism between the inner life and the external world and of great importance in protecting private aspects of the self beneath the surface of the personality. Therefore with Gemini on the ascendant, there may be a close tie with the sibling/s in younger years when the interior self is still dormant and the persona is important. As the years progress, it may be painfully clear that there is little connection with the sibling/s beneath the surface. Now on the horizon is the Geminian experience of the lost twin, the painful realization of being separate and dissimilar. Often this experience may be quite unconscious – the individual is perplexed as to how the relationship with a brother or sister became estranged. As adults we may live in different worlds and a conscious attempt to bridge these worlds is needed to cross the gulf between them. This may manifest later in a similar pattern of identifying quickly with others, only to find out subsequently there is not that much in common. For Gemini rising, the opus may be learning to sustain relationships and how to navigate in relationship when the initial identification wanes and separateness and differences appear.

Another aspect of this placement could suggest that there is a strong competitive streak with the sibling. The sibling is used not only as a role model but a goal post. The sibling is visible and his successes and/or failures are watermarks for our own progress. Here is the individual who may also develop a personality that is in complete contrast to his sibling. He may have played the family role of the one that is different from his siblings, and in this way managed once again to define himself in reference to the sibling.

The individual is born with the urge to relate and to share, yet is also susceptible to becoming the twin/shadow to what is lacking in the other. While there may be an initial urge to mimic the sibling–other, we often become identified with what the other is not. With Gemini rising we are susceptible to being the hook in the family for the shadow of our sibling.

Similar astrological statements: Mercury in the first house or Aries, Mars in Gemini or the third house, Mars in aspect to Mercury, Aries on the cusp of the third house, the ruler of the third house (in the natural wheel, the Sun) in the first house or Aries.

Gemini on the second house cusp (natural wheel, Taurus rising) links the sibling theme with the issues of value, worth and possessions. Our experience of sibling relationships may have contributed to the way we define our sense of values, what we appreciate and like. Within the sibling system we could have defined our values in contrast to our siblings. The sibling may have been a model for developing our sense of taste and appreciation for what we find worthy and valuable. The helpful sibling could also play the role of guide to our acquisition of resources, contributing to our sense of comfort and security. This could also imply that the sibling may have been supportive in helping us feel more comfortable with our body and its functioning. However, on the other side, we may have felt ripped off or cheated out of our resources by the 'dark twin' who may have stolen what we felt belonged to us. As either ally or enemy, the sibling helps or hinders our orientation to the physical world.

With this statement we are also called upon to share our resources with the sibling. The second house represents the sphere of where we begin to define ourselves and find security through what is ours. The 'me' of the first house soon develops into the 'mine' of the second house, and with Gemini here, we may be aware of our resources through either sharing them with sibling/s or claiming ownership of them. Here we enter the territory of staking claim on what is ours in reference to our siblings, learning to share with them as well as clearly defining our own territory. Younger siblings may feel that what they own is not really theirs, but belongs to the elder sibling since it was handed down, while elder ones may feel resentful having to pass on what was once theirs. Gemini on the second is acutely sensitive to any inequality of resources amongst the siblings, and may feel the need to have what the others have in order to feel equal. The early experience of how we shared our resources – toys, clothes, and even affection – may be a forerunner for how comfortable we feel sharing these later with adult partners.

Our sense of self-worth and self-esteem may be directly influenced through our relationships with our sibs and how we were valued by them. We may search for a reflection of self-worth from the sibling who becomes an important primary figure for the development of personal worth and value. The urge to possess what we find as valuable is also part of this territory. We could feel either possessive of our sibling or possessed by him or her. This could become more acute in adolescence, when we may feel possessive of our friends, not wanting to share them with our siblings, or vice versa. This intensifies our early relationships and can make separation from the sibling a difficult task.

It is in the sibling system where we may first learn what is of value and worth to us, then continue to seek these values in our adult relationship. We may unconsciously expect our adult friends and partners to carry the same attitudes towards sharing their resources as our siblings. Perhaps in the search to value our siblings we inadvertently begin to value ourselves.

Similar astrological statements: Mercury in the second house or Taurus, Venus in Gemini or the third house, Taurus on the cusp of the third house, the ruler of the third house (in the natural wheel, the Moon) in the second house or in Taurus.

Gemini on the third house cusp (natural wheel, Aries rising) locates the sign on its natural house. This placement suggests the sibling would be a major influence in the formative years while we are learning to crawl, walk and speak. Both Gemini and the third house are about early consciousness, curiosity and the wonder of new discoveries. Therefore the sibling may be a great object of curiosity and wonder. By the developmental stage represented by the third house, we are free of the constraints of the crib and stroller. With this new mobility, the search for what lay behind, above, over and beyond is under way. Here we may find an older sibling as a guide, challenging us to move farther afield. Similarly, this could represent the older sibling's discovery of the freedom and space that lies beyond the sibling system. We may feel twinned to one of our siblings and together enter into the world beyond family – the neighbourhood, the classroom and the school yard. No doubt the sibling system is our first social system and within this system we look for our friends and confidantes.

This image suggests that siblings may learn from each other or that learning is an important statement amongst them. The development of language and ideas as a third-house task is important to siblings. Projecting our ideas or abilities on to a sibling could create the role of 'the bright one', the 'clever one'. In later years we may find our siblings having learned and studied what we now are drawn towards. The sibling as *psychopomp* may lead us into interesting areas of learning, study and education. The need for conversation and communication with our siblings is very important and necessary in the development of a healthy relationship to learning, communicating and expressing our ideas. Both physical and mental activity with siblings are important to satisfy the need for interchange and relationship. Without these there would be a great sense of loss. Hence an only child might need to create a twin, playmate or a double to converse with.

Part of the natural sibling interchange is gossiping, name calling, lying and cheating – all images that are alive with this placement. Depending on other aspects of the horoscope, this may have been wounding, as the third house is our first experience of the power of the word and negative name calling may have been damaging. We may also have had nicknames for our sibs and remember vivid images of teasing and playing with them. On the brighter side, this could suggest learning early with our sibs to deflect and lighten criticism or verbal abuse. With our siblings we may have learned to be the trickster ourselves, outwitting them as Hermes so cleverly did. No doubt the link to the sibling is strong and underlies a quest to find an equal other in relationship.

Similar astrological statements: Mercury in the third house or Gemini, the ruler of the third house (in the natural wheel, Mercury) in the third house.

*

Mercury will be the ruler of the house where Gemini is on the cusp. The sign and house position of Mercury, and especially aspects to Mercury, will also be brought into this sphere. Therefore Mercury's placement will temper and refine these scenarios.

Personal planets in Gemini

THE MOON IN GEMINI

The Moon in Gemini as with the other airy Moons – Moon in Libra and Aquarius – has a complex and difficult psychological task. Having the Moon in an air sign implies that the drive for emotional security is constantly filtered through an experience of disconnection. The earliest feelings, recorded by the Moon, include an innate sense of separateness, space and distance. Hence there may be a strange sense of dislocation: a feeling of being disconnected from where one is or where one settles. The gulf between the sense of closeness and separateness propels the Moon in air to swing back and forth between extremes.

In adult life, forming a separate identity to those close to us is a healthy task, yet it is a frightening one for a child in the early developmental stages. The primary need in early life is attachment and bonding which promotes a sense of security and feeling of safety in the world for a child. Having a sense of secure attachment promotes an easier transition into the world beyond parent and family. When we are emotionally secure and connected, the process of separation is easier and less frightening. Moon in air signs suggests that the sense of early attachment is permeated with images of separateness and distance. The Moon, carrier of pre-verbal and *in utero* imagery, reaches back to the primal feelings of disconnection. While these feelings may not be apparent in the family atmosphere, these powerful images have none the less permeated our feeling life. Hence the rituals of bonding would constellate these earlier feelings, inducing anxiety. Even in adult life, the airy Moon feels the anxiety that comes with the experience of closeness. Conversely, the Moon in air feels bonded and connected when distanced from the love object. When there is a sense of separation, enough space and distance between us and our loved one, the Moon in air responds with feelings of closeness, attachment and love. Through the loss of connection, we become conscious of the bond of love. For an air Moon, *loss* also contains the painful realization of the depth of connection. Grief and loss are often the catalysts for encountering the feeling life.

In the space between secure attachment and functional separateness is the fear of being separated from those that provide life. While this may be a common fear for all children, for an air Moon, especially a Moon in Gemini, it is experienced too early. Gemini, as an early experience, does not yet have the ego strength to contain the dichotomy between attachment and loss. Perhaps, to defend this insecurity, the Moon in Gemini attaches itself to an idea or an other to complete the missing feeling. However, the fate of such a placement is to have the loss eventually erupt into consciousness, often triggered by a literal loss in the external world. For instance, Barbara's husband announced he was leaving her for another woman, synchronous to transiting Pluto opposing Barbara's Moon in Gemini. To Barbara's surprise, the loss of her husband awoke the painful grief for her older brother who had died when she was seven. She believed she had mourned for her brother, yet what passed for mourning was a distancing of herself from the overwhelming feelings of loss she could not contain. The Pluto transit in her adult life forced her into an authentic connection to her feelings and allowed her to mourn the death of her first love.

I am always surprised at how often the Moon in Gemini corresponds to the actual loss of a sibling. Why the astrological symbols sometimes literalize, and at other times are purely psyche's images, is an engaging mystery. As fate unfolds it seems the Moon in Gemini struggles with a profound loss of 'the other', be it the sibling, the partner, a friend, a parent or a child. This loss stems from a deep-seated sense of the missing half of self. The earlier loss of a sibling is not always literal but is none the less a powerful image which is part of the unconscious landscape. It could be experienced as the sense of searching for the lost other, either through our adult relationships or through a child. With the Moon in Gemini, loss could also be reflected through *not* mothering or fathering a child.

Bringing together the two astrological symbols of the Moon and Gemini suggests that the unconditional and hierarchical system of the Moon is filtered through the experience of equal relationship. Mother, as part of the hierarchical system, may be experienced as a sister. An experience of Moon in Gemini may be the experience of mother as a young girl, not a woman, who urges to befriend rather than mother the child. In this scenario the child would be obliged to change roles for her own safety and therefore become a sister to her own mother. The family structure may try to operate along lines of equality, leaving a girl child confused as to her roles and expectations. Feeling the void of leadership, the young girl may assume the role of mother to her own siblings. The invisible, yet sacred, lines that are the boundaries between the family members are transgressed, leaving the child vulnerable to becoming parentalized too early.

The Lunar temperament, with its proclivity for symbiosis, may feel the sense of merger with the sibling when the Moon is in Gemini. The Moon is the primary planet of love, and this unconditional love and acceptance may have been experienced with a sibling. Hence, the conscious experience of separateness with the sib may be painful. A sibling may receive the projection of the unconditional one and a fusion and dependency upon a sister or brother may be created. Sometimes the individual, if the older sibling, feels he or she must perform the role of parent, as Freud did, or conversely be the child to the older sibling 'parent', making separation and independence from the system difficult. The fusion of parent/child/sibling roles within the family may be recreated if we become parents and expect an equal relationship with our children.

VENUS IN GEMINI

Venus in Gemini feels more akin to this sign than her feminine colleague, the Moon. Venus is a multifaceted goddess, imported from the Near East where her eastern counterparts included the Phoenician Astarte, known as an androgynous and bisexual goddess. In esoteric astrology, Venus rules Gemini which repeats the theme of the sibling as our first representative of equal relationship. With Venus in this sign we are alerted to the importance of a sibling bond, and how this relationship may have contributed to our sense of feeling loved, valued and appreciated.

The affinity of Venus for the airy trinity is also seen by her rulership of Libra and her epithet 'Urania', being the daughter of Uranus, Aquarius' ruler, in Hesiod's cosmogony. She is also the sensual, earthy and erotic goddess in her rulership of Taurus, but in air she finds her ethereal nature and is concerned about equality in her eternal quest for the soul mate. In air, Venus is searching for the perfect love, the idealization defending the natural pain and loss experienced through the actual process of loving. If Venus is in Gemini, the first powerful love experience, other than mother, may have been a sibling. Gemini is dualistic, therefore this is accompanied by a dark side: loss, rejection or pain. Perhaps like Pollux we must petition the god to avoid the pain of separation from the loved one.

Venus in Gemini may carry conflicted and contradictory feelings about love for a sibling, swinging between idealization and denigration. However, there also may be a symmetry in the sibling relationship. With Venus in Gemini, the opposite-sex siblings may feel comfortable being partners and companions to their siblings. Like Artemis, the sister may feel able to identify with her brother's masculinity, and like Apollo, the brother may feel able to identify with his sister's femininity. The sibling relationship can provide the space for each to identify safely with the mirror image of themselves. Same-sex pairs may also polarize in their relationship. For example, while one brother may identify more with the masculine, the other may turn towards the feminine. The urge to be what the other is not will be strong. In a healthy sibling relationship this would mean a flexibility of roles; however, in a dysfunctional family atmosphere these roles are likely to become fixed: 'she's the sportswoman', 'he's the artist'; 'he's the bright one', 'she's the pretty one'. Venus in Gemini, while offering great fluidity of role change with our siblings, can also become fixed in a role of constantly searching for its other side.

Venus in Gemini suggests an urge to form harmonious bonds with our sib/s. However, in an ancestral context, Venus (as carrier of the feminine) in Gemini would also suggest that sister relationships in the family are important. What is the inherited sibling situation: mother's relationship as a sister, father's relationship to his sister? What are the attitudes in the family towards the feminine as an equal? With this placement, especially when Venus is aspected to an outer planet, there is often a feminine legacy influencing the well-being of the individual's sibling world.

Venus' penchant for triangles may continue throughout life, an indication that the sibling separation has not taken place. Sibling love is still being tested. In adolescence the triangle may occur with friends and the sibling, and later with our partners and the sibling. However, we may also move into a triangular relationship with our partner and his or her sibling. With Venus in Gemini, love is restless and changeable, and the triangulation may well be the mechanism to provide space and avoid commitment. With Venus in Gemini, the sibling–other could be part of our circle of peers, so there is a sharing of friends and companions, sometimes lovers. In this way Gemini remains unattached, bound to its first love, the sib.

The sibling can be an important mirror for our sense of values, how comfortable we feel with our own image, our tastes and what we appreciate. With Venus in Gemini, our siblings are an integral part of our formation of adult relationships. Aspects to Venus from other planets will help to form the pictures of the dynamics of the relationship.

THE SUN IN GEMINI

Although tabloid astrology has exclusively focused on the Sun sign, in actual practice the Sun is not as easy to typify or categorize as the columnists would have us believe. In astrological tradition, the Sun represents the archetype of the father, since patriarchal tradition places father at the centre of the family system, just as the Sun is the centre of its system. Similarly, the Sun is described as a source of life, vitality, energy and essence. It is purposeful and individual. However the Sun, as the focal point in the system, is not just father or the archetypal centre, but a psychological process that is the continually evolving relationship between the ego self, and the psyche self. The Greek myths of the hero portrayed this process in the stages of the heroic journey. Allegorically, the heroic trials and labours were accomplished through the ego in great feats of strength, will and intelligence; yet this process ceded to the descent and return of the hero where the ego skills were of little use. At this stage of the cycle, the hero would enter the realm of the gods and encounter the fabulous world beyond the rational bound of the ego, the territory we know as *psyche*. The Sun is difficult to typecast because it represents an archetypal process of fluid and dynamic interchange between the ego and the deeper self. The Sun symbolizes the hero who must face his trials and labours.

The process that the Sun in Gemini undergoes is the confrontation with the duality and complexity of human relationship. The family may have unconsciously identified the Sun in Gemini person as the 'carrier' of this duality and complexity. More than any other placement, I feel that the Sun in Gemini is aware and conscious of the duality of life, and its labours are to facilitate the integration of the opposites. For a fixed or rigid family, the Geminian duality is frightening and its defence is to identify the child with one side only, either the bright twin or her dark shadow. This exacerbates the split.

In myth, the heroic process includes a mentor, which is akin to the fostering and life-supporting energies of the Sun. For a person with the Sun in Gemini this may be a sibling or a sibling substitute, such as a friend or colleague, who facilitates an innate shamanistic ability to cross over to the other side, fosters her ideas, and supports her contradictory views of life. Without this support, Gemini is often condemned to swing uncontrollably back and forth between the extremes of life, and in the process burning out the nervous system. To be able to experience vitality and energy, and to shine in the world, it is necessary for the individual to be able to swing freely between the extremes.

The Sun in Gemini's process centres around the sibling archetype: equality, the exchange of ideas, symmetry in relating. Geminian Suns create sibling experiences in their friendships and in the bonds forged with like-minded equals. With colleagues they find brothers and sisters. But through these relationships, the complex mythic patterns of the siblings are constellated: rivalry, loyalty, indifference, solidarity, passion, support and love. The libido of the Sun is awoken through siblings and their substitutes. It is through these relationships, where both the brilliance and the humour of ideas can be explored, that they learn either to breathe or be suffocated in relationships. Equality is necessary. Elders may be seen as equals, threatening hierarchy and patriarchy with this focus on equality.

MARS IN GEMINI

The masculine archetype is seen more definitely in Mars. Its masculinity is more differentiated than the Sun; Mars is phallus and the head, two main centres of masculine identification. Mars in Gemini is a potent image of a brother. With or without a birth brother, a warrior figure is sought through the circle of peers early in life.

This placement immediately conjures up images of sibling rivalry and warfare with our sib/s. This is often the case; but Mars in Gemini could equally represent the sibling who is a champion, a role model and a heroic figure for the other sibs. The sibling becomes an important facilitator for the process of identification and separation. Notably, with Mars here, we will be acutely aware of our differences and conscious of our individuality. We may experience our initial separation anxiety with our sibling/s and use them as a goal post for our own achievements or as a benchmark for our own emergent identity. Through the sibling we may learn how to be comfortable with ourselves, to establish our boundaries, to fight for our rights, to feel independent and to forge a separate identity. With the sibs we may begin to feel secure in desiring different things and being different from them.

Competition with the sibs may be overt. Family attitudes are important in assessing how these competitive feelings are handled. If the Martian energy is denied or lacks an outlet of expression, then it is introjected back into the self. When Mars is forced back upon itself, it festers and becomes toxic. Symptoms of an unexpressed Mars are a lack of vitality, loss of enthusiasm, illness, being directionless and lacking goals. When the natural competitive streak with the sibling is punished or denigrated, then anger may be covertly expressed towards the sibling. As a result, anger may be triggered autonomously by competition with our workmates, associates, even partners. A repressed Mars also lacks the clarity to differentiate, or know what it wants. In Gemini, this type of Mars is injured from its inability to express its volatile feelings with the sibs, contributing to a lack of differentiation and discrimination with other peers.

Mars seeks role models. In the Greek myths, Hephaestus was the brother that Ares (Mars) de-identified with. Their family atmosphere was polluted by both parents' rejection of them, therefore Mars chose to identify himself in opposition to his brother. With a same-sex sibling, identification may be an issue. Mars in Gemini confronts its other half through the sibling. In a supportive familial environment, this will probably bring a healthy sense of competition. But in a disengaged family, Mars in Gemini will probably go to war with the sibling, competing and wanting to 'kill him off'. Mars in Gemini may be a literal brother with whom we are strongly identified, whether we can consciously accept that or not!

In Homeric genealogy, Aphrodite was Ares' half-sister. Ares and Aphrodite had a passionate relationship. With Mars in Gemini, the opposite-sex sibling may be an important symbol in the development and acceptance of our sexuality. The sibling image may still be an important aspect of our adult sexuality and relationships. In the positive sense, the opposite-sex sibling can help us feel confident and assertive in our sexuality, holding the projection of partner until we are ready to separate and move into another relationship. The darker side of this placement leaves us feeling jealous of our sibling's friends and partners, unable to separate successfully. For a woman, Mars in Gemini may be a powerful image of her internal brother figure who is part of her own contra-sexual self. The potentiality to experiment with our sexuality is present in all sibling relationships but with Mars in Gemini it is more conscious. Mars in Gemini continues its fight for equality amidst the conflict and duality of life.

MERCURY IN GEMINI

Unlike the other personal planets, Mercury does not easily accommodate gender stereotyping. Although Hermes was definitely masculine, the astrological Mercury has become less defined by gender and often is described as asexual, bisexual or androgynous, which is inherently part of Mercury's ability to embrace duality and opposition. Like a shaman, Hermes/Mercury crosses the liminal between life and death, given the role of the boundary crosser and guide.

Since Mercury is not identified through gender, the planetary energy is not as easy to ascribe to a sister or a brother, but suggests what qualities and themes are inherently important in our association first with siblings – then with peers. In Gemini, the importance of the sibling system is immediately recognizable. Within the system we find the doubles of our lives, a sibling becomes our surrogate twin. Within the sibling system the development of language, communicative and social skills may be honed. There is an emphasis on early learning and it may be from a sibling that we learn to copy or duplicate. Mannerisms, gestures and language may be mimicked in an attempt to learn and keep up. The relationship with our siblings influences our ability and urge to learn, study, communicate and inquire. With Mercury in Gemini the sibling is a guide to our process of discovery and learning, or conversely, our siblings may follow our leads throughout life. This may occur at various stages in the life cycle when one sibling ventures into new territory and the others follow. This theme could be replayed in our adult relationships with friends or partners.

Mercury was also the patron of thieves. In Gemini he is an image of the trickster sibling; he represents the lying and cheating that is part of the sibling system. It is with our sibs that we may have mastered the art of lying, thieving and trickery. There may be issues about this in our sibling system – feeling outwitted or unfairly punished due to a sibling's lies. Here we may also learn to gossip. The intervention of the parent is important to help form appropriate guidelines. Without this authority, Mercury may get lost in its own lies and tricks.

Similarly to the Sun in Gemini, there is a consciousness of duality and polarity. Experience is seen from both sides. In the sibling system, the role of the 'middle' child may be constellated, relaying messages back and forth, interpreting the moods of the system and trying to resolve tensions between the others. This facility to appreciate the whole picture allows them to identify with both sides, which may be interpreted as disloyalty. Therefore, the attempts of another sibling to tie them to an opinion or promise were probably unsatisfactory. The only way one may have felt able to give a commitment was after talking the issue through with the other, relinquishing the role of the middle child.

The power of communication and the power of the word may have first been experienced with a sib. For Mercury in Gemini there is often a sense of regret or loss over what was not said, what could have been said or what *was* said. Communicating effectively and openly with our siblings helps build the confidence to relate to others directly. Mercurial types are the storytellers and script writers of the system, often instinctively saying what needs to be said. With Mercury in Gemini our relationship to our friends and partners is like that with our siblings; what is of priority is the facility to share ideas and talk the process through.

Gemini's story is often more complex than we have acknowledged. It contains the template of a primal and primary relationship in our lives that we are continually searching for.

Notes

1. Dane Rudhyar, *The Pulse of Life: New Dynamics in Astrology*, 52.
2. Pollux is his Latinized name from the Greek, Polydeuces.
3. The different versions of the twins' birth suggest both are Zeus' sons, or both are sons of Tyndareus. The *Kypria* suggests Castor is mortal and Polydeuces immortal, indicating the dual parentage. No version ever suggested the reverse.
4. Gemini can symbolize the lost sibling. In popular myths of the twins' birth, some of Leda's other children, hence the Dioscuri's sisters, are not mentioned. The *Ehoisai* (Catalogue of Women, sixth century BCE), lists two other daughters of Leda: Timandra and Phylone. Euripides, in *Iphegenia at Aulis*, mentions another daughter, Phoebe. Gemini may represent the severed connections to kin, especially siblings, throughout the familial ancestry.
5. Helen's abduction from Sparta is made all the easier for Menelaus' departure for Crete.
6. For the various sources that describe the differing versions of the Dioscuri's afterlife, see Timothy Gantz, *Early Greek Myth*, 1.327.
7. Hugh Lloyd-Jones, *Myths of the Zodiac* (Duckworth, London: 1978), 51–3.

9
Hermes
Patron of the Sibling

The god Hermes' relationship to his older brother Apollo is a key to understanding a competitive and acquisitive aspect of the archetype. Jean Shinoda Bolen[1]

From envy to equality

Hermes was determined to claim a place amongst the Olympians. He was the son of Zeus, the god who was supreme ruler of the Olympian corporation, and in order for Hermes to gain his position he saw his older brother, Apollo, as the obstacle. After detailing to his mother his ambition to become one of the immortals, his sibling rivalry towards his half-brother becomes apparent:

> As for honours,
> I'm going to get in on the same ones
> that are sacred to Apollo.
> And if my father won't stand for it,
> I'll still try,
> I'm capable certainly,
> to be thief number one.[2]

At this point in the myth Hermes is not yet one day old and his intense competition with his brother is evident. This is a pattern that seems to be part of sibling fate – to struggle for equality with and against the sibling. Sharing the same god as parent, Hermes, an embodiment of the younger son, sets about to win an equal place with his brother and his other Olympian sibs, in the eyes of his father.

Hermes enters a family which already contains older sibs. This position is often likely to constellate envy, as the younger feels a power imbalance between himself and the elder sibling/s. An elder sibling may be more prone to jealousy, while the younger is prone to envy.[3] Jealousy results from love betrayed, when love is transferred to another or we suspect that we are being displaced by a rival who steals the love we have known. It is ignited when a younger sibling usurps our place and seduces our parents' love and affections away from us, placing us in a triangular relationship. But envy is didactic and power based. In the sibling system, it is the younger who is envious of the elder's position and possessions. Hermes is in an inferior position, while Apollo is in the position where he may feel betrayed by his father's new love for his clever new child.

Envy and jealousy are normal human emotions that find themselves constellated in the family. Certainly this would be true with the introduction of a new sibling into the system. But the extent to which the emotions are pathological or become complexes depends upon the atmosphere of the family, the parental maturity in identifying and deflecting the complex, as well as ancestors' unanswered questions that are now part of the familial fate.[4]

Hermes, the younger son, orients himself towards the sibling Apollo, not the father Zeus, in his quest for equality. It is by stealing the cattle sacred to Apollo that Hermes attempts to be noticed, envious perhaps of his brother's possessions and very aware of the possessions that are most important to Apollo. The images of cattle, cows and bulls are symbols woven throughout the myths of siblings. Cattle became the contentious issue between the two sets of twins in the Gemini myth. The symbol is multidimensional: here it could represent the envy of another's valuables and the sibling experiences of ownership and sharing of resources. Another time it could represent the primal feelings underlying the relationship, or the fertility inherent in it. For the sibling relationship is a fertile relationship, where creativity is sown and harvested, as well as a relationship that influences our values and self-esteem. Astrologically, we are in the sphere of Taurus, the sign preceding Gemini, which symbolizes ownership. As the sign that precedes Gemini, it could also speak of where the complexes of the sibling constellation are safely buried. What are the cattle that Hermes feels compelled to steal?

While these brothers did not share the same womb, they shared the same paternal seed. Neither brother is the exclusive creation of his father, therefore their father's realm is to be divided equally amongst the brethren. How this is accomplished is dependent on the sibling position; for Hermes as the younger feels he must steal from his brother, and Apollo, the elder, feels he must defend his territory from the usurper, furious that he has lost an exclusivity to his father and his resources. Apollo is now forced to share the familial resources.

The orientation of the sibling system to the hierarchy of the parent demands an equality with the other members of this system. What a task for the parent! – to ensure a sense of equality and fairness presides. Complicating this task, feelings of competition, rivalry, anger and outrage are awakened when we realize that we must share the greatest possession of all – our parents. Sharing with our siblings our parents' resources, in both their life and death, will constellate the feelings of jealousy and envy around them. And for Apollo, the Solar god, to share the father will not be easy.

Hermes' association with thievery and trickery are clearly illustrated in the 'Homeric Hymn to Hermes' with the abduction of his brother's prize possessions. This behaviour is inherent in the sibling system. Part of the Hermes/Mercury archetype and the third house is to experience lying, cheating, gossiping and teasing amongst the siblings in our search to be recognized and separate. To chastise these expressions would contribute to impeding a natural evolution and growth of equality amongst the sibs. Hermes and Apollo's father, Zeus, is not involved at this stage and, like many parents, oblivious to the machinations that are being played out amongst his children. But as a father his justice, fairness and insight will be called upon to resolve the squabble soon enough!

After Hermes absconds with his brother's herd of cattle and cleverly conceals it in a cave, he takes two of the cows and sacrifices them to the gods.[5] Interestingly, Hermes cut up twelve pieces to sacrifice to each god, perhaps as a self-motivated ritual of entry into the family. Once again it was two of his brother's cattle that were sacrificed in his invocation to belong. The older sibling often feels he has sacrificed something of value for a younger sibling. Apollo eventually finds out that his cattle are missing and tracks Hermes down. He is enraged at Hermes for the theft. Hermes, already a master thief, is now a master at lying, using all the innocence that a baby can in declaring that he is completely free of guilt – how could he possibly have committed the theft Apollo is accusing him of, he was born just *yesterday*! Name calling, lying, cheating, stealing and blaming are all part of sibling survival.

While it appears Hermes must take from the elder to feel equal, the story also tells us that the younger Hermes has a gift for his brother – a lyre. Before Hermes had set out to steal Apollo's cattle, he encountered a turtle outside the cave. Inspired by its fluorescent shell, he decided to fashion an instrument that would create a harmonious and beautiful sound. And so on the first day of his life, Hermes creates the lyre which is the instrument his brother Apollo becomes associated with in myth. It is the younger thieving brother who supplies this part of his integral identity.

Finally, Hermes shows Apollo where the cattle are. He has made his statement of equality. The brothers now have the potential to form a good relationship. On the sibling level, we learn to share power and resources. This is one of the initiations of the sibling system in that its members are called to belong in a communal way, sharing the familial resources and power. In functional sibling relationships, the power imbalance due to age, physical size, intelligence or parental influence is eventually replaced by a spirit of cooperation, exchange and fraternal love. The sibling system is a microcosm of social structures in life and it is here we learn for ourselves how to find an equal place in the world. Hermes, while he always will be in second position to his elder brother, none the less finds his place of equality. He is different from his brother but equal to him, unlike their relationship to Zeus, the parent, where there is power imbalance and inequality.

One of the roles Hermes is assigned is his role as *psychopomp*, the only recognized messenger to the realm of Hades. In becoming the messenger to Hades he also becomes the god who guides the soul across the boundary separating life from death. He becomes the god of liminal space. Hermes as guardian of the sibling sphere also brings the role of *psychopomp* to this realm. It is the sibling who often is the guide of souls in our early years. Older siblings help the younger ones across important thresholds. Younger sibs are influenced by the way the older sibs have crossed the thresholds of change in their lives. In our younger years it is our sibs who are witness to the rapid developments in our lives, and often among the first witnesses to important rites of passage in childhood.

Apollo and Hermes give us the archetypal story of brotherly rivalry transmuted into fraternal love. While they are both sons of a powerful father, Zeus assigns them enough autonomy to address one another as equals. He creates the atmosphere for the potential rivals to become equals. They commence their relationship with competition, rivalry, theft, rage and lies, but end up in an exchange of valuable aspects of themselves. Each adds to the other. While both Apollo and Hermes are often seen only as rational gods, they also share shamanistic roles. Hermes is the boundary crosser and the guide of souls into the Underworld. Apollo presides over the arenas of divination and healing. Together they share a similar direction in life, orientated towards the order of life that was so important to their father. They are now equals and custodians of their own private realms. Envy and jealousy have found their complementary sides of power and love through their sibling relationship.

Hermes, as the patron of the sibling, is most evident through the aspects to Mercury in the horoscope. Planets aspecting Mercury will bring their archetypal influence into the sphere of sibling relationship.

Mercurial aspects

The sibling experience is influenced by the planets that aspect Mercury. As a messenger, Mercury often allows full expression to the planet that it aspects. The aspecting planet's essence will colour the sibling relationship, often quite literally. Traditional astrology categorizes aspects by their degree of ease or difficulty. In reality this is not so easy, for the harmony or difficulty of an aspect is influenced by a disparate group of factors ranging from the family atmosphere to an individual's level of consciousness. Astrologically, the inherent nature of the planets involved in the aspect is important, whether they are antagonistic, supportive or ambivalent. Perhaps we could suggest that the traditionally 'easy' aspects of the trine and sextile offer us more choice of expression. The tension of the aspect is lowered and therefore there is less chance that the energy will become a complex. However, this is dependent on many variables. While more difficult aspects of the square and quincunx unite psychologically incompatible elements, their difficult union may have been eased in a supportive and understanding family atmosphere. Each aspect must be personalized.

In a geocentric horoscope Mercury can only be separated from the Sun by a maximum of 28 degrees, therefore its only major aspect to the Sun is a conjunction. There are two types of conjunction between Mercury and the Sun. The superior conjunction happens when Mercury is direct and on the far side of the Sun from the Earth's vantage point. The inferior conjunction occurs when Mercury is retrograde and closest to the Earth. Mercury in its retrograde phase suggests an intensification of the sibling issues. With Mercury and the Sun conjunct, a fusion or *con*fusion between the sibling, generally brother, and father may occur. There may be issues of favouritism or feeling overshadowed by the sibling. Like Hermes and Apollo, there may be a fraternal contest for father's approval and recognition.

Venus and Mercury are also contained within a confined arc of 76 degrees and their major aspects to each other are the conjunction and the sextile. These planets in aspect may point to feminine themes in the sibling system, and how the sibling was influenced by the feminine attitudes in the family, which may have been carried by a sister. Carl Jung had Mercury and Venus conjunct, and his sister became a representative of the familial attitudes towards the ancestral feminine. Themes of value, self-esteem, sharing and equality are also important.

Themes of caring and nurturing between siblings are important when Mercury aspects the Moon, often pointing to an older, protective sibling, or a younger sibling we took care of. There may be confusion or lack of boundary between the parenting and sibling roles. Communication of the feelings becomes important, and in the more positive aspects the siblings have been able to communicate their love and concern for each other. Patterns of communication, sharing ideas and learning are all influenced by our siblings. We may still remember the emotional impact of our siblings' lying, name calling or gossiping. With this aspect we would interpret the silence between our siblings to try to comprehend the feelings trapped beneath the lack of communication. This could crystallize into a pattern of articulating our friends' or partner's feelings. The ability to express feelings is an important aspect of relationship, first learned in association with our siblings.

Mercury's aspects to Mars suggest that independence, competition and adventure may have been experienced with our siblings. A model of a champion or someone to emulate could be projected on to a sibling. On the one hand, this aspect suggests an image of a supportive and encouraging brother figure; on the other, it could point to a bullying and dominating sibling. The more difficult aspects may stress rivalry, unhealthy competition and perhaps brutality. Power in the sibling system is phallic centred and the biggest and strongest may wield their power in an aggressive manner. Either way, the sibling plays the role of initiator, prompting independence and the pursuit of individual goals.

Jupiter–Mercury contacts suggest a broad exchange of ideas and ideals with a sister or brother who may have been our teacher or guide. The sibling is a socializing agent who may lead us beyond the family's beliefs and morals. We may have shared a variety of experiences with our siblings or been inspired by their quest for meaning in life. The dark face of this wiser sibling image could be an arrogant or inflated sibling who is prejudiced, dictatorial and overbearing. Within the sibling system we may have experienced a wide set of experiences that helped formulate our philosophy on life.

Saturn often symbolizes an older or only sibling. In aspect to Mercury it may speak of the duty and responsibility we associate with the sibling and therefore the other equals we relate to. Within the sibling system we may develop autonomy, setting appropriate boundaries between ourselves and our siblings. This aspect could lead to the formation of stable and enduring relationships. However, it also suggests that there may be feelings of aloneness or separateness from the other siblings, the boundaries now becoming barriers that separate us from the others. This aspect also suggests the sibling may have been in the role of teacher, authority figure or parent to the other sibs. Negatively, the image of the depressed, patronizing or rejecting sibling could be constellated.

Chiron in aspect to Mercury brings the themes of mentoring, wounding and healing into the realm of the sibling. This may imply that the sibling fostered our spiritual development, encouraging the heroic spirit. However, it equally suggests the sibling as an agent of wounding, perhaps through the medium of name calling, abandonment or rejection. With this aspect we may feel alienated or separated from our siblings, as if exiled from our community of peers. Literally, this image could suggest a sibling that is physically or mentally handicapped, an adopted sibling or the separation from the sibling through death or a schism in the family.

Uranus may bring its sense of individuality and freedom to the sibling system when it aspects Mercury. With siblings, and later friends and partners, we seek a sense of freedom, adventure and experimentation. The sibling may have been our first image of independence and individuality, acting as a freedom fighter and rebel. However, the sibling may also have been distant, aloof or cold. In its negative manifestation we have the image of the sibling who may have been disengaged from us, non-committal, even cruel. With these planets in aspect, we seek our individuality within the group and perhaps have to forge our own sense of independence first with the sibling.

Creativity, magic and enchantment are part of Neptune's domain. In aspect to Mercury we wanted to share this imaginal and fantastic realm with the sibling. However, we may also have idealized the sibling as a refuge from the difficulties of growing up, fusing together to avoid the pain. On the one hand, this aspect may suggest the compassionate and devoted sibling; on the other, it suggests the deceptive or addictive one. We may have first learned to sacrifice our sense of identity in our relationship with the sibling, surrendering our self in either the idealization or the protection of the sibling. This could suggest a sibling who was ill or troubled and rendered us invisible. We urged to be close and share the wonder of the internal world with the sibling but may, ironically, have felt estranged, so that the sibling relationship constantly carried an unlived potential.

Pluto's domain is the nether world and its aspects to Mercury imply that the sibling may be the vehicle that exposes this world to us. This could suggest the sharing of a deep and indelible bond with the sibling, a sense of intimacy and trust. However, the other polarity brings us in contact with feelings of betrayal and emotional control with the sibling. The sharing of resources, power and love are important issues in the sibling system which, when not exchanged equally, may ignite into an explosive situation. Secrets are part of Pluto's territory, and in aspect to Mercury these secrets involve the siblings. Pluto's encounter with death may also be part of this aspect, bringing a sense of loss or grief through the sibling. In the sibling system we first encounter the confrontation with honesty, trust and the powerful impact of feelings.

Notes

1. Jean Shinoda Bolen, *Gods In Everyman* (Harper & Row, San Fransisco, CA: 1989), 168.
2. 'The Hymn to Hermes', from *The Homeric Hymns.*
3. See Louis H. Stewart, *Changemakers: a Jungian Perspective on Sibling Position and the Family Atmosphere*, 97–8.
4. The 'ancestor's unanswered questions' is an image that Jung uses. For elaboration, see page 67.
5. This part of 'The Hymn to Hermes' suggests that it was Hermes who first invented fire, an interesting thought for the god who will develop into the god of the alchemical process. For an insightful and thorough diachronic study of Mercury/Hermes, see Freda Edis, *The God Between.*

10

The Houses of Relationship

Sibship, Partnership and Friendship

The sibling system is the first social laboratory in which children can experiment with peer relationships.

Salvador Minuchin[1]

Equality in relationship

An equalitarian relationship is conceived and constructed in the three houses, the third, seventh and eleventh, known as the houses of relationship. Experiencing equality in relationship is founded originally in our sibling experiences, symbolized by the third house, then transferred into relationships outside the family of origin. The third house of the horoscope is a template for our relationship patterns.

These houses symbolize the conscious attempt to establish peer or equal relationship, as well as the patterns formed by earlier sibling experiences. These territories do not model the parent–child relationship, which inclines towards unequal and dependent relationship, but equality and individuality, the level of relationship first encountered with the sibling. Through this trinity of houses, the theme of creating and sustaining equal relationships, as well as our urge for social intercourse, develops. The psychological landscape in each house is interconnected, therefore our sibling relationships will be recreated in our partnerships and friendships. Equally, the experiences with partners and friends facilitate change and healing with our siblings. Ultimately, the sibling relationship extends to all our other equal interactions, from our playmates to our co-workers.

In the horoscope, assuming no interceptions, the signs on the cusps of the houses of relationship are either sextile or opposite the ascendant, conjunct or trine the descendant, sympathetic to the horizon of our life. This trinity of houses supports our personal view of the world, our personality and our urge to strive forward. Conversely, these houses are 'at odds' with the meridian, the vertical angle which is ancestral and inherited. The signs on the cusps are either semi-sextile, quincunx or square the MC–IC axis. Perhaps these houses describe a sense of individuality forged independently of our heredity and ancestors' expectations. These houses describe relationships that are compatible with our sense of individuality and our urge to be equal, which clashes with parental and hierarchical expectations.

The third house symbolizes our inherent disposition to becoming an individual within a larger system, the sibling system. Within this system we develop our individuality in relationship to the sibling, learning to be independent yet part of a community. The other relationship houses have a similar task. In the seventh we strive to sustain our individuality within marriage, while in the eleventh we experience our independence within our social circles.

The element of air: the breath of relationship

In the natural zodiacal wheel, the houses of relationship are the air houses. On first reflection, air may not be the element we would ascribe to relationship as it is can be separate, non-attached and distant. Air is the spectator, not always the participant; the messenger but not necessarily the message. However, air encourages equality, individuality and consciousness which are necessary in relationship, permitting merger and union without the loss of self. Astrologically, this is represented by air preceding water in the zodiac, and the houses of relationship preceding the houses of endings. Air ensures we can lose ourselves in relationship and then find our way back to ego, the part of self that remains separate. If there is a healthy sense of separateness, then this safeguards regressing to a union of total merger or surrender where the self is lost. Air encourages enough separateness to relate to someone different from ourselves. The houses of relationship provide a venue for this task, so that the merger into relationship, implied in the following trinity of houses, can be conscious. Separateness and symbiosis, two polar instincts that underlie life, are continuously balanced by the element of air.

The defensive side of air uses detachment and separateness as a barrier against relationship, mobilizing the intellect to criticize the irrationality of emotional encounters. The analysis of relationship defends the uncertainty and lack of control that the actual experience of relating brings. The defence mechanism most easily employed by air would be projection and projective identification. Projection within the air houses is common, therefore siblings, partners and friends are available 'hooks' for the qualities we continue to repress as well as for our fear of involvement.

The ability to separate (*not* detach or split off) is influenced by our sibling experiences. The ability to leave unhealthy relationships or group situations could be anchored in our first experiences of separating from siblings. Only children have a difficult time separating from destructive relationships. The only child's sense of separating is aligned with separation from the parents which maximizes insecurity and loss; whereas in our sibling relationships we have learned to be both independent and part of a group. Throughout childhood we experience a series of separations with our siblings which do not damage or destroy the relationship. The only child, lacking a sibling relationship, may not have adequately internalized a sense of separateness.

Airy qualities of detachment, non-attachment and witnessing are all important in the participation of equal relationship. In these houses we meet the witnesses of our life. The third house sibling witnesses our childhood years, shares the same history, the same culture and is the touchstone of our early life experiences. The seventh house partner witnesses in us the process of maturation and discovery in the world beyond the family. The eleventh house colleague and friend witnesses both our personal and professional, individual and collective, experiences as we mature in the wider world. In these houses, the record of our personal developmental history is shared and witnessed by the significant others in our lives.

The air signs associated with these houses are Gemini, Libra and Aquarius. In the natural wheel, Gemini corresponds with the third house, Libra the seventh and Aquarius with the eleventh. The glyphs that represent these signs are dual, two lines detached from each other. Gemini and Aquarius are represented in human form while Libra is the only sign represented by an inanimate object – the scales. Duality, judging, weighing are all part of the process of relating.

The modern rulers of the air signs, Mercury, Venus and Uranus, as well as the classical ruler of Aquarius, Saturn, are the regents presiding over the territory of equal relationship. They are the deities we encounter in the archetypal process of individuation and relationship. Again, duality is important. Mercury in the role of *psychopomp* travels between the antithetical worlds of Hades and Olympus; Venus in her role as Venus Urania is the heavenly and spiritualized Venus, while Venus Pandemonia is her common, earthly side. Finally, Uranus shares the rulership of Aquarius with Saturn. Aquarius is split between the new order, ruled by Uranus of the heavens, and the old order, ruled by Saturn. Different forms of rulership also connect these signs together. Mercury rules Gemini and is also exalted in Aquarius or the eleventh house. Saturn, as the traditional ruler of Aquarius, is exalted in the sign of Libra. Venus rules Libra in traditional astrology and Gemini in esoteric astrology. Threads of amity run through these signs. Throughout the air signs and houses there are consistent symbols reminding us of the process of linking, connecting, bridging, as well as separation, duality and polarity.

On the cusp of relationship

The signs on the cusps of these houses in our personal horoscope are significant in delineating our approach to relating. With no interceptions in the horoscope, the same element will be on all three house cusps. If a sign polarity is intercepted, it increases the possibility of two different elements on these cusps, and the element is thematic of how we forge our individuality, separateness and equality.

An overview of the dominant element on these three house cusps will indicate how we instinctively approach relationship. With no interceptions in the horoscope, the element on the three house cusps is also compatible with the element on the ascendant. Figure 11 shows the combination of elements without intercepted signs in a horoscope.

Element on houses of relationship	*Element on ascendant*	*Element on MC*	*Element on IC*
Fire	Air	Water	Earth
Earth	Water	Fire	Air
Air	Fire	Earth	Water
Water	Earth	Air	Fire

Figure 11: Elemental combinations between angles and the cusps of the houses of relationship.

Assuming no interceptions, let us look at the element on the cusp of these houses to sketch an initial picture of our inclination to *approach* relationship. Planets in the houses and aspects to the house rulers will describe the attitudes the individual forms towards equal relationship.

*

The element of fire embraces Aries, Leo and Sagittarius on these three house cusps. Fire is a spirited element and the approach to life experience is generally highly instinctive, spontaneous, forthright and wilful. With this element guarding the threshold to the arenas of equal relationship we could suggest the individual may approach relationship in a courageous, competitive, challenging and inquisitive way, empowered with a sense of self-discovery and urge for excitement. The sphere of relationship is a vital area for investigation and experimentation of the self. Fire would desire that its partner share this sense of adventure, travel and wanderlust.

Fire is passionate and, like its element in nature, burns new ground and yearns to move farther afield. While there is passion and excitement, there is also restlessness and boredom. The natural tendency may be to enter relationship in a flash, with verve and dynamism, yet find the fires grows cold and the original passion wanes. Fire demands its freedom and needs to explore new territory, which often leads us away from relationship. In the early experience of relationship with siblings, fire needed to feel free to do its own thing, yet also wanted to compete and play with its sibs. In the sibling relationship we may have first experimented with abusive, combative and competitive behaviour. Fire also needs to inspire and empower and this could be an important aspect of relating both in primary and adult years. The necessity to be in relationship with those who are able to meet our need to adventure, quest, philosophize and discover the truth, is very important. We may have tried to share these ideas with our siblings. How disappointing if this was not reciprocated; perhaps we decided early that relationship may not be able to embrace our powerful needs for change and the eternal quest for truth.

Fire's burning spirit and quest for philosophical perfection and absolute truth meets its shadow in negative feeling, lethargy and criticism. Fire individuals are frustrated with their partners' inability to share their vision. Or worse, the partner may point out the potential pitfalls and problems with this vision. The fiery one may interpret this as criticism, whereas it is often a genuine attempt to help anchor the vision. Negative feelings are also denied by fire's need to be buoyant and feel the rush of life energy. Denying negativity or depression encourages projection of these feelings on to a partner. Negative feelings that are difficult for fiery individuals to accept are imported into their relationships by their partners. A more earthy or watery sibling may have been the first one to carry the projected negativity or depression for them.

What fire is first attracted to in others is their independent spirit, their vitality, their ability to take risks and their outlook on life. While we may attract these qualities in our quest for equal relationship, we will also attract the shadow of these qualities. The independent, courageous entrepreneur we admire is also wilful, non-committed and arrogant. With fire on this trinity of house cusps it would be within the sibling system that we may first have explored these volatile and competitive feelings that later surface in our quest for a mate.

With the earth signs, Taurus, Virgo and Capricorn, on these house cusps, we meet a very different approach to relating. Earth is more conservative and self-controlled, and has an appreciation of time. Unlike fire, the natural inclination is to move slowly and cautiously into relationship. Earth needs stability and security, and therefore it is important that relationships provide this ongoing structure. It is important too that our partners are committed, reliable and stable, serving the needs of the relationship. Relationships are nurtured through attention and work. Earth individuals are serious about relationships, as they represent an investment of emotional and material resources, as well as a commitment of time.

Earth on the cusp of the third house would value commitment, fidelity and devotion in sibling relations and would also feel responsible and protective towards siblings. Equally this may manifest as duty and obligation towards the sibling which could inhibit the formation of other relationships. These houses as spheres of equality, duality and consciousness are at odds with the element's natural inclinations. Therefore attitudes and relational patterns could become fixed or unchangeable as a means to control the emotional fluctuations in relationships. Hopefully, with earth on these cusps the earlier experience of rules, responsibilities and tasks of relationship helped forge an awareness of the need to provide a secure structure for the relationship. Earth partners can be appreciative of both their own and others' need for privacy and solace. When feeling insecure they can become possessive and controlling, inhibiting the other's freedom and privacy. With earth on the cusp of relationship, control, possession and the equal sharing of resources are important issues.

Earth is the element of incarnation and materiality. Resources and possessions are important with earth on these cusps. Earth's task is to learn to share and discriminate between what is mine and what is yours. With earth on the third, sharing with the sibling could have been an issue. In the sibling system we learned to claim what was ours and share our resources. In differentiating what was valuable to us, we could ascertain whether we were secure enough to share it. The contemporary symbols of values, money and possessions, enter the earthy sphere of equal relationships. How we manage to exchange these resources with our partners is directly proportional to how bonded and trusting we feel in the relationship. We may project our issues of value on to a partner who is unable to share his resources freely or who uses his resources to defend intimacy. With earth on these house cusps there is a connection between our ability to share what we have and our ability to be intimate. How we managed to share our possessions with our siblings is a major factor in how comfortable we are with sharing our resources with our adult partners.

Earth is the element of the five senses, and sharing the sensual world is important: looking at beautiful art, listening to an inspired piece of music, sharing a sumptuous meal, filling the space with fragrant essences or embracing and being affectionate with one another, are all images of the important world of earthy pleasure. With earth we are drawn to worldly, attractive, successful types who often become dull, patronizing and single-minded when we are projecting our own earthy needs. With earth here we want to define boundaries within our relationships without cutting off the life force, having a stable and committed relationship without it becoming fixed and bound to routines. Earth on these houses cusps strives to find the balance it needs in the constantly changing atmosphere of the relationship.

The air trinity includes Gemini, Libra and Aquarius on these house cusps. This triumvirate of signs is compatible, at least theoretically, with the area of relationship. It is natural for air to want to share its ideas and experiences. Air is constantly seeking its other half through the process of relating. However, air seeks a multiplicity of experiences and may share its ideas and experiences in many differing relationships, being indiscriminate about privacy and containment. Relationships may be an arena of curiosity and often air's inquiring and interactive manner is mistaken for a deeper emotional or more intimate interest.

Like all elements, air needs relationship. It is comfortable with the issues of equality, sharing and the theory of relatedness but has difficulty in the sphere of intimacy and emotional constancy. With air on these house cusps it is natural to experiment with a range of possibilities in relationship, satisfying the curiosity and inquisitive urges that are part of an airy type.

These types need a great amount of space, emotionally, physically and psychologically, before they are comfortable enough 'settling down'. Changeability is natural, and without enough space air feels stifled and unable to breathe, increasing the levels of anxiety. If the relationship feels stifling, the urge to separate is triggered. With air on these house cusps the need to experiment with relationship is necessary before an authentic commitment to a relationship can be given.

With air on the third, the sibling becomes important as the first equal with whom to share ideas, learning and the experiences of life. The sib is the partner with whom air can relate, gossip, experiment emotionally and satisfy its curiosity. Communication on all levels within relationship is important, and in the sibling system a lack of communication or sharing of ideas would have adversely affected later relationships. While air attempts to be clear and articulate, it is often emotionally very unclear and inarticulate, acting covertly rather than in an emotionally honest way.

Air on the cusp of these houses conjures up the image of a witty, gregarious, charming and insightful individual to whom we are immediately attracted. However, as the luminosity wears away we become aware of a flighty, aloof person who obscures our own ideas. When there is such a dramatic swing between the two faces of the archetype, we are in the grip of a projection. Air on these cusps needs the space to be able to experiment and without this permission is prone to projection, so that the sibling, the partner and the friends are the witty, intelligent, non-committed ones. With air here, we instinctively know our need to be separate and independent, requiring the space and versatility of differing relationships in order to come to terms with the issues of emotional commitment and dedication.

The water element contains the signs Cancer, Scorpio and Pisces, bringing a depth of feeling and love to the area of relationships. Water flows towards the mysterious and mystical side of relationship, and watery types are attracted and repelled by the 'energy' and 'vibrations' of others, unable to articulate the invisible thread that pulls them towards another or the impulse that drives them away. Water also idealizes the sphere of relationship and those who inhabit this terrain – siblings, partners, friends and associates. While fire may be conceptually idealistic about relationship, water is emotionally idealistic, often leading to unrealistic and dysfunctional relationships. Watery types are led by their feelings, aroused by empathy and compassion for another, which contributes to a power imbalance in relationship.

Separateness and independence forged in the houses of relationship is antithetical to water. With this element on these houses, the inclination is to bring sympathy, empathy and concern to the sphere of relationship. Often these feelings are not reciprocated and the individual feels unsupported emotionally. Water's power to obliterate emotional separateness can create enmeshment with others. This is experienced as the ability to feel the other's feelings (or at least what we *feel* is the other's feelings), to serve the other's needs and to care for our partner's insecurities. This is admirable; however, within the arena of equal relationship, some may experience this as smothering or invasive. For the watery person, this sense of abandonment and emotional inequality is enormously painful, yet ultimately necessary in learning the difficult task of separateness.

With water on the cusp of these houses we enter relationship with a sense of deep connection, moved by our need to nurture, fuse or merge with the other. With water on the third we may have experienced enmeshment within the sibling system. This could have manifested in many ways: being bound together in the sibling system because of a dysfunctional family atmosphere, through sharing inappropriate feelings with the siblings or through a powerful secret that binds siblings together. This could also manifest as being caretaker to the other siblings, or one of the siblings needing more attention and support than the others. Water here confuses boundaries, and when it is important to separate, the person may be unable to leave; when it is important to be there, the person may be unavailable. This is a difficult task that water learns here: to discriminate and draw boundaries in relationship, understanding that it cannot transform or save someone else.

Water is attracted by the sensitivity and creativity in others, drawn to their compassionate and caring qualities. Emotional manipulation, chaos, secrecy or moodiness are the shadows that may lurk underneath. But when water becomes conscious of its projections and is cognizant of maintaining boundaries, then warmth, emotional generosity and support are returned.

The third house: sibship

The third house symbolizes our primary encounters with others who shared our environment, mainly the sibling/s, but also other neighbourhood friends and primary schoolmates. While the third house suggests that siblings are equal, a hierarchy is created by the ordinal positions of the siblings. The beginning of the quest for equalitarianism is born out of the paradox of this situation. As siblings we each have our own unique orientation to the family which is defined by birth position and personal experience of the family atmosphere. In this system each sibling is an individual striving for equality. Age difference, physical size, intellectual capability, social adaptability and parental influence may create inequality amongst the siblings; however, 'in the majority of cases there is usually equivalence in siblings' feelings of acceptance for one another which allows them to relate as equals'.[2] For this reason the third house is critical, as it suggests how we may first experience peer relationship and the impact it will have upon subsequent relationships. We first test the response from the world through the reaction of our sibs, using them as a mirror to how we are received. As Salvador Minuchin says:

> Within this context [the sibling sub-system], children support, isolate, scapegoat and learn from each other. In the sibling world, children learn to negotiate, cooperate and compete. They learn how to make friends and allies, how to save face while submitting, and how to achieve recognition of their skills.[3]

The third house is the experimental ground for relating. Habitual behaviour in relating may find its origins in the third house. Expectations we have of relationships, patterns we repeat with partners or even our choice of mate may be more influenced by the sibling/s, and the third house, than we realize. The sign on the cusp of the house, its ruler and the planets in the third house illustrate the primary bond between ourselves and a sibling, and the potential pattern that is brought into adult relationships. The astrological statement may clearly describe the sibling or 'at least those qualities we project onto him or her'.[4]

Planets in the third house have reached the IC, the lowest and darkest point on the ecliptic and are now beginning to rise. Their descent has terminated and third house planets have turned, starting their ascent when they are fixed into our birth horoscope. The ascent towards the horizon symbolizes the third house planets' urge for consciousness and individuality. This rising momentum will be imprinted upon third house planets. Planets in the third will carry this experience of rising consciousness as they progress and transit into the fourth house sphere of family. Planets in the third suggest an encounter with the archetype of relationship through the siblings. Looking at the early themes of relationship with our sibs may inform us of patterns carried through into our adult relationships. The planets as well as the sign on the cusp are potent images of our sibling relationships.

PLANETS IN THE THIRD HOUSE

The Sun in the third house suggests an identification with the sibling/s, highlighting the role of the first or favoured one. This places the archetype of the personal father in the domain of the sibling, suggesting a composite father–brother figure. If the father was weakened, unavailable or missing, a brother or Solar daughter may have replaced him as the authority or fostering figure. Father may be seen as a close confidant or ally, combining his roles as a mentor/parent with a friend/equal.

Favouritism may have been an issue in the sibling system and father's favourite may have been seen to be acknowledged and encouraged more than the others. The Sun may have cast its shadow over the sibling system, splitting the system into those who were favoured by father and those not. A girl who was father's favourite may feel in a precarious position, caught between her brother and father. In adult life this may rearrange itself as feeling caught between her partner and son. This position suggests the individual may be the sibling who was most father-identified or the one most easily triangulated with father against the others, including mother. We may have a very different view of father from the rest of our sibs and are the one most sensitive to colluding with him. This suggests we may also be the one who 'looks just like father', but on a more subtle level, the one who has inherited more paternal ancestral complexes or treasures.

We could be aware that a sibling is more creative and dynamic, more confident and more popular if the Solar energy is being projected. Initially, the tendency may be to adore the sibling; this projection, however, will be gradually withdrawn when growing up. The sibling acts as a hook for our emerging identity. With the Sun here, it may be the sibling we identified as either a rival or a hero. Ultimately, we strongly identify with others, but may pass through stages of feeling unacknowledged or not appreciated, before we are able to claim an equal and authoritative position in our relationships.

The Moon in the third house locates the nurturing and mothering instinct in the sphere of the sibling, suggesting that a sibling may have provided a care-taking role or that we were placed in this role. The early sibling relationships would have a direct impact on our sense of safety and security, and be important in forging a sense of emotional security. Because of this emotional impact, there could be a strong attachment to the sibling if the sibling was the good mother, or conversely, a sense of alienation if constellating the dark mother. Given the Moon's propensity for symbiosis, separation from the sibling could have been difficult. Early separations (going to school, being taken care of by another, etc.) may have been traumatic if we were not adequately prepared. The Moon in the third carries an image of an older sister, one who may have shared in our upbringing, and one to whom we may still have a strong attachment. Whether there was a literal elder sister or not, we may have sought this sister–mother figure in our environment, or alternatively, made mother our sister. An early pattern of confusion between sister or equality and mother or dependence may continue into our adult relationships. A young boy with Moon in the third *and* a sister may feel the need or continue to expect 'women' to take care of him. While he is very comfortable with sisters and the world of women, he may be habitually drawn to women who will nurture and take care of him. This was one of the sibling statements in Carl Jung's horoscope. An important aspect which needs to be learned in the sibling system is not only how to communicate one's needs but how to fulfil them independently. Without this initiation in the sibling system, we will still try to make our adult relationships symbiotic and regressive.

The Moon in the third could point to the sibling who was closest to mother, mother-identified, and given the role of taking care of mother. Therefore this could be the sibling most at risk during the 'leaving home' stage, feeling great difficulty separating. The sibling story is woven around the image of mother and sister and includes the inheritance from mother and her siblings.

Mercury is the natural ruler of the third house and has an affinity with this territory and the sibling relationship. It is an image of the younger or middle sibling that feels both the need to catch up to older sibs as well as being the interpreter for the familial dynamics. Mercury is less attached to either parent than the Sun or Moon in the third. Its role is the messenger, the go-between, and in the third it takes the role as mediator and guide in the sibling system. Mercury was not the only messenger god; he often shared this capacity with the goddess Iris, but she delivered the message intact whereas Mercury often rearranged it to suit his purposes. The sibling may have played the role of messenger and *psychopomp*, being disconnected enough from the family dynamics to be able to reveal what was going on. In the myth of Hermes and Apollo, Hermes' envy of his elder brother prompted him to steal resources from him. These actions helped win recognition from their father, Zeus, the prevailing authority figure. In the third house, Mercury's task is to translate the envy or jealousy of sibling rivalry into a productive and satisfying solution.

With Mercury here, communication and interchange of ideas with the sibling was an important foundation for the ability to share our ideas and converse as equals. A difficult placement of Mercury could point to a feeling of intellectual inferiority with the sib which still affects our confidence today. Issues of learning, education, communication and conversation are derivative of the sibling experience. Mercury has an affinity with the sibling system which promotes the ability to be able to translate and decode both overt and covert messages between siblings, a skill taken into the adult world.

Venus in the third house suggests an encounter with the sister archetype. For a man, the image of sister becomes a potent feminine or anima image for him. If he has a literal sister, she will have played an important transitional role in carrying this internal soul image for him. The sister may have helped shape his image of a partner more than he might like to admit, and he may unconsciously find her image again in his adult relationships. Without a sister, the man would still seek this image of sister in his adult relationships.

A woman with Venus in the third may be unwittingly drawn into competition with her sisters. In Homeric tradition, Aphrodite (Venus) was half-sister and rival to Persephone, Athena and Artemis. Zeus decreed that Aphrodite had to share her lover, Adonis, with Persephone. Aphrodite charmed Paris so that he would choose her rather than Athena in the competition for the fairest goddess. And with Artemis, Aphrodite clashed over the young boy, Hippolytus. The mythic themes of sisterhood may be drawn up to consciousness through a clash of values or a similar love object. It is also through this relationship that social skills are developed. Sister could be an influence on our values, what we find attractive and how comfortable we feel in social circles.

With Venus in the third we look towards our sibs of either sex for experimentation with the process of relating and sexuality. The sibling system may be where we first recognized that the feelings of loving and valuing another could be different from the way we felt towards our parents or other adults. We could project our own sense of worth or value on to our sibs, seeing them as more attractive or social, a sibling providing a mirror for our developing sense of creativity and sexuality. It is through our earlier relationships with siblings or friends that we developed our tastes, what we find attractive and the social skills which influence us today. In later years, those with Venus in the third may yearn for a warm and supportive relationship with their siblings.

Mars has an affinity with the image of the elder brother, the warrior, the competitor, and in the third house these images may be brought into consciousness via the sibling.

Clients and students with Mars in the third have often told me stories of their experiences of aggression and even brutality from the sibling – being pushed down stairs, tied up and abandoned, and even of being rushed to hospital as older brother had stabbed younger sister with a kitchen knife. Because these situations occur when both sibs are young, and not adequately supervised, the family often makes a farce of the situation, deflecting the rivalry. Students, describing their experiences in class, often laugh along with their classmates when regaling them with a sibling story that is volatile and violent. With sibs we learn to defend and stand our ground, and with Mars in the third our aggressive and survival instincts are brought to consciousness, generally by a sib's taunting and goading. In many cases, sibling violence is not even reported to the parent and the secret brutality leads to alienation from the sibling. With Mars here we may first experience the aggressive instincts with a sibling. Some sibling fighting may be over territorial rights to the parent.

Mars also constellates the sexual instincts, and these too may be tested out with the sibling in various ways, ranging from sexual play to a consummation of the relationship. Siblings may want to test their sexual or physical virility with each other. The sibling system may be where we first experienced aggression, competitive feelings and anger. How these feelings were consciously managed will impact on our adult relationships, for unresolved sexual or hostile feelings towards the sib will certainly be constellated in our adult relationships. For a women, this placement of Mars suggests that a brother image is part of her internal masculine realm and a literal brother would be an appropriate hook for the externalization of this animus. Mars often seeks role models and strives to emulate them, and in the third house we may have chosen a sibling as one of our role models.

With Mars here, the sibling system is an important training ground for taming the aggressive and sexual instincts. Mars is the first planet outside the orbit of the Earth, a planet that is outside the Earth's system. When Mars is in the third house, we learn in the laboratory of childhood how to become independent and retain our individuality within a system.

*

Jupiter searches for a wider view of the horizon by questing beyond the familial; experiences with siblings prepare us for different beliefs, ways of life and cross-cultural awareness. Learning from our siblings and being open to their guidance and life experiences may be a valuable part of our education and socialization. In adult years, siblings and their families may continue to expose us to new ideas and adventures. Quite literally, I have often seen this placement representing many siblings; however, I suggest the statement of Jupiter in the third talks more of the wide panoramic exposure that the sibling may provide. The sibling system could be cross-cultural in that it may have included step- or half-siblings, or we may have met regularly with cousins or others who introduced us to different ideas and beliefs. We may have had the opportunity to travel and explore new places with our sibs, giving us an early appreciation of other ways of daily life, beliefs and ideologies.

Jupiter is a planet of socialization, and therefore siblings' social progress, their choice of studies, extra-curricular activities, etc. were important to us. They may have become a benchmark that we judged our own progress against. A sibling may also have been our guide to a wider social world, introducing us to new horizons of belief and culture. However, siblings could also be experienced as rigid and unwavering from their beliefs and with whom we are at odds. One of the sibs may play the role of Zeus in the sibling system, claiming dominion over the others and constellating a 'larger than life' figure. The early experience with our sibling–peers gives awareness of the need to feel spiritually compatible with our adult partners and friends. In later years we may find that although we may be physically, spiritually or morally distant from our siblings, the urge to reconnect is a catalyst for the examination of our own beliefs.

When Saturn is in the third house, the themes of authority, duty and responsibility may have been constellated for the first time with the sibling/s. I have witnessed Saturn in the third consistently with only and eldest children who feel they have been placed in positions of control and responsibility too early. There were many reasons for this; a common theme, however, was the sibling who filled a void left by an irresponsible parent. Often this placement also suggests wide age spacing between the sibs, so that they grow up virtually as only children, or for some other reason are not part of the sibling system. For an only child, this placement talks of the world of equals being overshadowed by the world of the adult. For eldest children, it suggests they were responsible for their younger siblings, setting the example of upholding parental law, often while their younger sibs broke the rules. There could be difficulty sharing or delegating as a result of sibling experiences. Issues around the division of labour may have caused resentment, as the individual may have felt he had a greater share of the chores than the others. Whatever the birth order, Saturn confers a sense of the lawmaker upon the individual who may feel obliged to discipline or direct his siblings. There could also be a tussle for the top position in the sibling system, feeling that the parent's approval was gained at the expense of feeling connected to the other siblings.

Another manifestation of this position could be the feeling of rejection by our sibs, or feeling completely alone and separate from them. We may feel the need to become self-reliant and not have to depend upon the siblings for support, encouragement or comradeship. It may become imperative to detach, withdraw or take care of ourselves on our own, contributing to an isolationist tendency. This pattern could be the foundation of feeling self-reliant in our adult relationships, not easily able to depend upon others.

In adult years, Saturn in the third house could also be demanding, as we again feel it is our responsibility to bring the siblings together. Issues around family gatherings, rituals or special occasions polarize the siblings again into their childhood roles. One of the greatest tests concerns responsibility and decision making for an elderly parent. With Saturn here, we learn to be responsible, but not at the expense of our own individuality. It is in the sibling system that we first learn how to delegate, discern and let go of control in appropriate ways. Learning to differentiate who is responsible and set the appropriate boundaries becomes an important lesson for Saturn in the third.

While Chiron is not classified as a planet, its archetypal imagery is too important to leave out of our planetary pantheon. Chiron, like the three older Olympian brothers, Hades, Poseidon and Zeus, was a son of Chronus and therefore was their half-brother and part of the Olympian family. Chiron was not awarded the same status as his half-siblings, an interesting image for Chiron in the third house. Here is the sibling who is exiled from the system or not granted the same status. As a sibling image Chiron represents the adopted sibling, the step-sibling, the sibling not wholly part of the sibling system.

When Chiron is in the third house, it points to a potential wounding that has occurred through our siblings, or the image that the sibling himself is wounded, handicapped or exiled. Chiron is the wound that is inflicted unintentionally; with Chiron in the third, this wound may have been inflicted by our sibling/s. This generally is not physical, although it may be; it is usually experienced through name calling or other forms of verbal abuse or wounding. The teleological level of the third house, I feel, has to do with the power of the *word*. With Chiron in the third, the poisonous arrows that are the wounding agent could be the sibling's verbal abuse. A child being branded stupid, ugly or illegitimate by his siblings can receive a lifelong wound. Chiron in the third is also highly sensitive to the feeling effect that flows beneath what is said; so the wound can also be inflicted by the dishonesty and trickery of the sibling.

The wound could symbolize that we feel exiled from our siblings, completely separate and not a part of the same system they belong to. I have often witnessed that this placement reflects the death of a sibling in the family, and the individual with Chiron in the third is the one who carries the unresolved grief of this loss, which is that sibling's wounding experience. Chiron in the third seems to be a dominant placement for those who have a handicapped sib. Ambivalence accompanies this aspect: there is a love of the sibling, but also a feeling that they missed out owing to the enormous attention focused on the handicapped sibling. The wound is opened through the relationship with the handicapped sibling.

Early patterns from the sibling system may be re-enacted later in adult relationships by drawing the wounded other into our orbit, constellating the primal polarity of wounding and healing again in relationships. Unexpectedly, our partners and friends may once again draw the sibling wound to the surface.

The outer planets describe experiences beyond the personal, and when placed in the third house suggest that the sibling may have magnetized images, feelings and experiences beyond our capacity to understand or integrate them. These outer planets in the personal house of the sibling may stir deeper, mythic and archetypal experiences which we can only begin to address in our adult years. With either of these planets in the third we are drawn into a larger and more collective story with our siblings. Since these energies seem to be larger than us, we may tend more to project them on to the sibling. Here we must acknowledge that the sibling–other has been the personal spokesperson for an impersonal archetype.

*

Uranus in the third house may suggest a sense of abandonment, separation or distance from the sibling. This archetype often suggests separation and splitting, therefore in the third, this may have applied to the sibling system. Uranus is disengaged and this may have characterized the nature of the sibling system. The sibs may have been highly differentiated, so much so that they may have nothing in common. They may have been separated for a variety of familial reasons including divorce, relocation, education or even the unexpected death of another sibling. Uranus' nature is sudden and unexpected, so this could characterize our relationship with a sibling, never knowing what to expect in the relationship. One day we may be welcomed into her circle of friends and the next, firmly rejected. This image suggests that the sibling is highly individualized, and, with the best-case scenario, we feel an individual within a system and that our sibling is also our friend. More often there may be a feeling of disconnection or alienation from the sibling. Uranus' sense of separation can be so severe that once the bond is severed it cannot be reclaimed. Therefore, with Uranus in the third, we could have experienced a sense of irreconcilable differences which led to an irrevocable separation from the sibling; or our feelings towards the relationship are frozen, remaining in contact, yet being virtually unreachable. It may be with a sibling that we first experience Uranus' ability to sever, detach, stand apart and split off from these feelings.

Within the sibling system we may have been the one to rebel or take a stance contrary to that of the others. We may have found our individuality by rebelling against the others. This early pattern of independence and individuality in relationship to our sibs will influence our attitudes towards relationships, continuing to seek out the different, the unusual and the unique in our partners and friends.

Neptune's urge to sacrifice may be a pattern lived out with our brothers or sisters, when placed in the third house. We may be the one to take the blame for actions perpetrated by our siblings or allow them to set us up, even use us. Neptune's urge to merge is so strong that we may discard our sense of self in order to experience this sublime union. We may feel that we are not giving up that much to the sibling when the self is fragile anyway. However, a pattern may be created that continues into our adult relationships. Ultimately, this sacrifice comes at a high price as it weakens our sense of independence. Quite literally, we may have had to sacrifice our education or our dreams for another sibling.

There may be a lack of boundary between ourselves and our sibs, so we may be highly sensitive to their psychic life. One of the most difficult Neptunian patterns in family life is to know intuitively what is going on but to have this continually denied by the other members. We then begin to mistrust our intuition and often feel that we are going mad. In this scenario, Neptune in the third becomes the classic 'identified patient' in the sibling system, manifesting the anxieties and the disease that is repressed by the other members of the system. In the third, the sibling could play the role of the liar, the deceptive one, even the mad one. Enmeshment with siblings is high and we are often unable to distinguish what the truth is. We may get caught up in the web of the sibling's deceit or addictions. Neptune in the third is a potent image of a primitive yearning to surrender oneself to the other, disappearing through fusing oneself with that person.

My experience of Neptune in the third is that it often describes a missing sibling, one who has disappeared or become estranged, leaving a void in our lives that we try to replace with friends. Equally, the missing sibling may be idealized so that the feelings of loss are numbed and defended by the idealization. Since the third house is the first of the houses of relationship, it is quite likely that the image of the missing sibling surfaces in our later relationships where we once again address the issues of sacrifice and invisibility in relation to our partners and friends. We are vulnerable to recreating a fused relationship and losing ourselves in it.

When Pluto is in the third house the underworld domain may be brought into consciousness through an experience in the sibling system. Often this may be through the experience of grief over the death of a sibling, a profound sense of loss that may continue to permeate life. The loss of the sibling may not be a conscious memory or literal event, yet this image may still be part of our psychic terrain. While there may be no awareness of a death in the family, we sense the shadow of loss in our sibling system. This may happen when a child is a replacement child, or when the family atmosphere is clouded by the unresolved grief of the parents.

The underworld could also be constellated through the experience of feeling dominated and controlled by the sibling. The sibling may have been manipulative, wielding power, confronting us with feelings of powerlessness and loss of control. Pluto's placement in the horoscope could locate one of the entrances to our underworld. Here in the third house, it is through our early relationship with our siblings that we are exposed to the underside of life, confronted with dark and dangerous feelings.

Within the sibling system we may have been coerced into keeping a secret or be privy to a secret we still feel obliged to keep. If the secret has gathered intense feelings of shame and guilt, it becomes a complex that keeps the participants in the secret bound together in an unholy alliance. Over time the sense of feeling powerful is distinguished as the secret is a constant reminder of being in the grip of something more powerful than oneself.

Pluto represents an innate aloneness, which we come to understand later in life as part of the human condition. As children this is difficult, since it feels threatening to our survival and our sense of well-being. With Pluto in the third, we may have felt alone in the sibling system which also felt painful and terrifying. Pluto constellates both extremes of the feeling spectrum and in the third we may have experienced either a deep sense of betrayal with a sibling or a deep sense of union and trust. It is in the sibling system where we may need to look first to understand our feelings of mistrust, suspicion and control, and we may need to return here to heal a primal sense of betrayal before we feel able to trust in an adult context.

The next house in the trinity of houses of relationship is the seventh. Unlike the third, it is above the horizon of the horoscope and therefore suggests more visibility or objectivity. Perhaps it symbolizes what we already know: that the arena of sibship below the horizon offered no conscious choice of the 'other', it is a non-consenting realm. But on the horizon of the seventh, our partners are consenting, at least consciously. Siblings are contained by the larger system of the family, whereas seventh house partners come from beyond the familial system. Into the seventh we carry the *a priori* pattern of the sibling along with our experiences of relating in the sibling system.

The seventh house: partnership

The seventh house is the sphere of equality on an adult level, where we encounter others who feel familiar and complement what we sense is missing in ourselves. The seventh house process embraces the experience of being with an equal other in a committed and intimate way. There is mutuality and reciprocity. Seventh house partners are not only marriage or life partners, but the business partner and others engaged in relating at an equal level of exchange. Partner contains *part*, the sense of being separate – apart, yet also able to join.

Traditionally, this is the house of 'open enemies'. Sibling rivalries may be re-enacted openly with our partners. In a contemporary context, the seventh house open enemy may be our own shadow material rather than a literal individual. However, the unconscious is marvellously astute at choosing individuals who embody these shadowy qualities. Whereas traditional astrology would ascribe seventh house qualities to a partner, contemporary astrology sees these qualities as mirror images of what is innate in the individual.

Psychological astrology stresses the propensity to project the seventh house planetary qualities on to the partner. While we remain unconscious of the seventh house energies, we continue to proclaim them as belonging to someone else, generally the partner. Seventh house planets are usually first recognized through a partner. The opus of the seventh house is the attempt to be more conscious of our inherent nature that is projected on to our partners. Projection, as Jung explained, is an unconscious defence mechanism; therefore the task is an eternal one. But becoming conscious of these projections provides a greater facility to be authentic in relationship. We enter a mystery in the seventh house where we are drawn to what appears as opposite and different, yet is only a partial reflection of what is still not conscious in us. What we sense is kin, congeniality, familiarity, yet not from the system we have known. The partner of the seventh house stimulates us to reunite with the missing parts of ourselves.

Projection is the mechanism that helps illuminate these unconscious aspects of ourselves through relating. The seventh house planets are the archetypal patterns that are catalysed as we enter into relationship. In essence they are part of the other side of ourselves, hence this is why they are so easily mobilized through the agency of the other. Again we are in territory that stirs the images of the missing other and shadow. This time, however, we are outside the familial alembic, and the family taboos no longer apply. Emotional involvement with the partner also begins to shift the loyalties away from the family of origin into another system.

The seventh house is an area of mutuality which suggests we become the carrier of our partner's projections, being drawn into a mutual collusion. The fifth house, the first in the developmental process of relating, is where unrequited love or one-way projections are more likely. Generally, there are three stages in the process of seventh house projection. First is the numinous stage: the bright side of the archetype is embodied in the individual to whom we are attracted. The qualities shine and we are in awe. Generally, the planetary energy is exaggerated or idealized, being drawn to the divine aspects of its nature. For instance, we may first meet the seventh house Mercury as the brilliant and witty genius; Saturn, the success story; or Pluto, the magnetic and intriguing therapist. Next comes the waning stage: the very qualities that mesmerized us are now annoying and uncomfortable. The shadow of the archetype begins to manifest. Mercury has become superficial and non-committal; Saturn is patronizing and cold; while Pluto is now obsessive and controlling. The seventh house planets reveal both sides of the archetype through the same partner. At this stage the integration of the presenting shadow material is possible. However, the possibility of regression is also available by choosing another partner with whom we can re-experience the magical first stage. The last stage holds the tension between the opposite sides of the archetype which we come to recognize as aspects of ourselves. The integrative process begins when we make conscious these qualities that the partner is living out for us. The seventh house, like the third, is a territory where consciousness occurs because of another. Planets in these sectors can be blatant; consciousness is not as subtle as the unconscious.

The sign on the cusp of the seventh house is also an important quality to us and is very often prominent in our partner's horoscope. The planets in the seventh house are representative of archetypal patterns constellated in the exchange between partners. As we have seen, they are generally first embodied in the partner before they are consciously able to be successfully integrated into our lives. There is an analogy between the arrival of the partner and the birth of a sibling. Powerfully conflicted feelings of love and rivalry, fascination and anger are constellated with the seventh house other.

The seventh house is the western horizon – the Hesperides of the horoscope. It is twilight, when the light elongates the shadows and we prepare to meet the dark. The partner awakens an earlier stratum of psyche where unresolved or incomplete issues with the sibling may enter into our current relationship. The open enemy may be our unresolved rivalries, left-over anger or unfinished challenges with our siblings that rearrange themselves with our partners. The seventh house experience is directly influenced by the earlier effect and residue of our sibling relationships. Into the seventh house we drag our unresolved sibling relationships. Unconsciously, we may have entered a new relationship in reaction to this unresolved material with a sibling.

Partners can also become the target for unresolved hostilities that siblings cannot confront each other with. The partner is then triangulated in the sibling relationship. This is confirmed by a family therapist when writing of the importance of sibling issues in new marriages:

> Siblings may also displace their problems in dealing with each other on the intrusion of a new spouse. Predictable triangles are especially likely between a husband and his wife's brothers or between the wife and the husband's sisters.[5]

Equally, it may be a partner's sibling who enters into the triangle. We may be able to express intimacy with a sibling-in-law that we find difficult with our sibling.

Toman's premise was that adult partnerships replicating the sibling infrastructure were more complementary and therefore more successful. His theories showed that the sibling experience directly impacted upon adult relationships (see Chapter 4, 'Exploring Birth Order'). In dealing with issues between couples, I find it enormously valuable and revealing to ask about their sibling constellations: their position in the system, sibship size and gender, age spacing, etc. These details can often open up the imagery of both the third and seventh houses and reveal issues from the sibling system that are infiltrating the current relationship. Third house planetary energies that are still projected on to the sibling or unexpressed in us, will find a new venue in the present relationship

The sister–brother marriage is a mythic pattern, perhaps best seen in the relationship of Hera and her brother, Zeus. While the later myths focused on their power struggles and dysfunctional marriage, the earlier stories told us of their secret marriage and sacred union. This sacred union was their sibling marriage, the level which contains the equality and companionship in all relationships. The seventh house experience rests on the third house, and the relationships of the seventh house include the archetypal layer of the sibling marriage. Opposite-sex siblings may have been a temporary carrier of the anima or animus, and transferring this powerful connection to another partner will undoubtedly awaken intense feelings between the sibling and the partner.

The third house's consciousness of separateness prepares us for the fourth house merger with the family, just as the seventh prepares us for union with the beloved in the eighth. The seventh house prepares us for the eighth house intimate encounter, where what is exchanged within the relationship is of equal value.

The eleventh house: friendship

The eleventh house represents our encounter with equals in the community outside the familial setting, which includes the 'social others' – colleagues, associates, acquaintances, friends and professional equals. This is the house of groups, of organizations, reminiscent of our first experience of an organization – the family. While the eleventh house depicts the group, not bound by blood or kinship ties, nevertheless our experiences of family will be stirred. As a member of the group our relationship to the other group members will magnetize the unconscious memory of our links to our earliest peers, the sibling/s.

Hopes and wishes are traditional key words for the eleventh house and here is where we hope and wish for a better future. However, in the eleventh we are still prone to recreating the unresolved familial issues in groups and associations, impeding this progress.

Like the seventh house, the eleventh is above the horizon, but in the eastern hemisphere where the focus is on the individual. As individuals we are contained by the larger system of society, subject to its laws, influenced by its ethos and bound by its taboos. Our eleventh house symbolizes the larger community, the groups, social structures, and the circle of friends and associates that populate society. This is the sphere where we take our place in the community and once again become part of a system. Our sibling system was the microcosm of this larger social sphere. The experiences in the sibling system directly impact on our ability to feel comfortable in other social systems.

The last house of relationship is where we meet our extra-familial peers. Minuchin says:

> When children contact the world of extra familial peers, they try to operate along the lines of the sibling world. When they learn alternative ways of relating, they bring back the new experiential knowledge into the sibling world.[6]

Roles and positions have already been forged in the sibling system, and we instinctively take these into our relationships in the broader community. Our impact on society and society's impact upon us is related to our primary experiences in the sibling world.[7]

Our eleventh house relationships feel familiar as they too are kin: allies who are kindred spirits. Hopefully, the spirit that inspires and infuses us is the common link in our friends and colleagues. In a way, the eleventh house is a return home to the missing other through a sense of congeniality and enjoyment of the shared spirit of life. Congeniality literally means 'with the generations', an apt description of the eleventh house process of shared community. In the eleventh we can find the sense of belonging to a larger family, being individuals in a larger collective. This is an important aspect of the eleventh house as we learn here to be separate from the collective, which inherently prepares us for rescuing the collective soul of the twelfth house.

However, the group of friends, the group of colleagues, the organizations we join reawaken the incomplete sibling experiences and rivalry once again is experienced. Our group experiences are often regressive, reminding us of the infantile behaviour with our siblings, fighting for the attention of the parent who is now embodied as the leader of the group. If we have not yet learned to feel an equal, then we will react to perceived acts of favouritism bestowed on the rival colleague or group member. In this respect, therapy groups are hotbeds for sibling transference. Adults are vulnerable to playing out incomplete sibling hostilities and rivalries in their professional associations and organizations, as well as their therapy groups. Festering sibling rivalries may pollute the equilibrium of the organization. Sibling behaviour of acting up within the group, bullying, gossiping, conspiring with the other group members stems from the feeling of inequality. Quite often members of groups can polarize into their sibling positions of first, middle, last or only. Birth position may be replicated quite literally in our professional world. This certainly was apparent in the psychoanalytic circle, and astrologically consistent with both Freud and Jung's eleventh house Mars.

It is in the eleventh house in the quadrant of the horoscope that represents social development where we play out the quest for equality on the world stage. Alfred Adler suggested equality started in the earliest social system with the siblings:

> unless children feel equal, mankind will never be well grounded in social feeling. Unless girls and boys feel equal to one another, relationships between the two sexes will continue to pose the greatest problems.[8]

No longer is equality 'having what the others have', but being valued as an equal individual within the group. In the eleventh house, equality is not having the same as everyone else, but being an individual. In an adult context, an equal share is held by each group member even if one or more members receive more attention and time. Hopefully, as adults, we have introjected enough autonomy to be able to feel concern and equality in our adult relationships.

The eleventh house can also be the territory where we redeem our conflicted sibling relationships. A loving friend, an encouraging colleague or a supportive group are healing agents for earlier wounds inflicted in the sibling system. We may also be able to accomplish in the larger world what we could never do in the sibling world. Planets in the eleventh house are symbols of the psychic territory we may revisit in our peer relationships in the world. But these planets are also dynamic energies seeking expression in the world, an expression they may not have been able to find in the earliest social system with the sibs. While we are influenced by our sibling system we are not bound to it, and the eleventh house is the arena where we can amend this. Now we are able to choose our brothers and sisters in the eleventh house. They come from the same spiritual tribe and generally look forward in the same direction as we do, carrying the same hopes and wishes for the future. They are partners, equals and kin in our worldly family. This is brotherhood and sisterhood.

It is in the sibling sub-system where we must first learn about equality. The first experience of this form of equality and sense of mutuality of concern occurs primarily in the sibling group. Our estranged or disengaged siblings may present themselves through others we encounter in the world beyond family. The link between the three houses is natural; however, if these houses are astrologically linked in an individual horoscope, then this pattern becomes more evident and visible in the individual's life, as shown below:

- The ruler of the third house cusp in the seventh or eleventh house.
- Gemini on the cusp of the seventh or eleventh house or planets in Gemini in these houses.
- Mercury in the seventh or eleventh house.
- Planets in the third house in aspect to planets in the seventh or eleventh house.
- Planets ruling the cusp of either the seventh or eleventh house in the third house.
- The ruler of the third house in aspect to the ruler of the seventh or eleventh house.

Outer planet transits through these houses have a prolonged influence on how we experience relationship and how patterns of relating are shaped. The Moon's progression through these territories not only records the emotional effect and reactions to relationship, but remembers these earlier reactions in its adult circuit through the horoscope (see Chapter 13). When natal planets in these houses are aspected by transit then issues arising from the sibling relationship may be stirred and brought to consciousness.

Each of these three houses precede the water houses, the territory of soul-making and the ground of the ancestors.[9] In essence, each of the water houses is a larger container for the relationships that are encountered in the houses of relationship. The family system contains the sibling relationship; the tribal system, the partners; the collective, our friends and colleagues. Our relationships are inextricably linked to a larger picture.

Notes

1. Salvador Minuchin, *Families and Family Therapy*, 59.
2. Victor G. Cicirelli, *Sibling Relationships Across the Lifespan*, 2.
3. Minuchin, *Families and Family Therapy*, 59.
4. Howard Sasportas, *The Twelve Houses*, 50.
5. Monica McGoldrick, 'The Joining of Families through Marriage: the New Couple', in *The Changing Family Life Cycle*, Betty Carter and Monica McGoldrick (eds), 228.
6. Minuchin, *Families and Family Therapy*, 59.
7. For fascinating research and discourse on the sibling influence on our political lives, see Louis H. Stewart, *Changemakers*; Frank J. Sulloway, *Born to Rebel*; and Albert Somit, Alan Arwine and Steven A. Peterson, *Birth Order and Political Behavior*.
8. Alfred Adler, *What Life Could Mean to You*, 124.
9. For a thorough examination of these houses in connection to family and ancestry, see Erin Sullivan, *Dynasty: the Astrology of Family Dynamics*, 170–94.

11

The Astrological Houses

Exploring the Process of Relating

Since contemporaries outside the family are treated like the siblings, these first relationships to the brothers and sisters become important factors in determining the individual's social attitudes.

Anna Freud[1]

The houses of relationship should be differentiated from contemporary astrology's 'interpersonal houses'. Included in this category are the fifth to eighth houses, the second quaternary of houses where self-development through interaction and relationship beyond the family of origin occurs.[2] These houses track our psychological maturation through our interrelationships with others outside the family. But it is the familial experiences that directly impact on the formation of these relationships.

The interpersonal houses

THE FIFTH HOUSE: NARCISSUS' REFLECTION

The cusp of the fifth house symbolizes the threshold between the family of origin, our childhood and primary emotional attachments, and the world beyond family, our adulthood and new emotional relationships. The cusps of all the fire houses, one, five and nine, represent a form of birth. The fifth house cusp marks an important initiatory phase in the life of the individual and the family – the moment of leaving home, or 'birth' into the adult world. In a developmental way this cusp talks of the separation of the individual from the security of the family matrix. In myth, this is the hero's emergence into the world. One of the common motifs of the hero is that he is an exile, separated from his homeland. The fifth house speaks of the separation from the primal place of belonging, home and family, so that we may consciously continue with the larger task of individuating. The latter phase of the heroic motif is to return home, like Odysseus. First, the hero must leave in order to build the ego strength and consciousness to claim the inheritance of his ancestral home.

The fifth house of 'love affairs' is the first experience of relating to someone outside familial territory. It is the realm of Narcissus where the first stages of relating are self-orientated, and the 'other' is the mirror for the self. Love, often idealized lust at this stage, enters our lives and challenges us to leave the familiar, redirecting our emotional attachments away from the family. Relationship in the fifth is about supporting or denying the process of creativity and self-expression, not always about equality. Relating is passionate and exciting, but often is only a means of self-reflection, not equality or commitment. The partner, at this stage, is not equal but either a regressive romantic fantasy or a catalyst to encourage the creative quest.

It is into these interpersonal houses that we bring our experiences from the family of origin. Our fate here is to recreate some of the familial patterns in the relationships we encounter including the patterns forged with our siblings. Sibling experiences have helped mould our sense of worth, individuality, separateness and, ultimately, the strength to be able to feel equal in a peer relationship. These experiences have helped us to formulate when we may need to go it alone or when we need to belong.

Narcissus is an interesting example of the first encounter with self and an other outside the realm of the family. Our most popular account of Narcissus is from Ovid's *Metamorphoses*.[3] The nymph, Liriope, was swept away in a river. The river-god ravaged her while she was imprisoned in the waters, and from this union she gave birth to a beautiful child, Narcissus. As an adolescent, his pride in his beauty was so inflated he was unable to share himself with another; no youth or maiden could inspire Narcissus' heart to love. While he was young his mother consulted the seer, Tiresias, to ask if her son would live a long life. Tiresias suggested that Narcissus would live a long life only 'if he never was to know himself'. But the fate of not knowing himself was not to be.

While hunting, Narcissus becomes lost in the woods and encounters the nymph, Echo. She has been condemned by Juno for her incessant chatter and now is cursed to repeat only a portion of what has been said. She falls deeply in love with Narcissus, but he is cold and unresponsive and rejects her. In the mythic scene between the two, the devastating power of unrequited and unequal love is demonstrated. After Echo embraces Narcissus, throwing her arms around the man she adores, he cruelly rejects her: 'Away with these embraces! I would die before I would have you touch me!' Narcissus is disgusted. But Echo can only mirror back the last part of the sentence: 'I would have you touch me!' In her painful rejection, grief destroys her body leaving only her voice, yet her fascination with Narcissus continues. She too has been trapped by his addictive power of self-love. In the fifth house we begin self-exploration through the reflection others mirror back to us.

Nemesis, the goddess who personifies divine retribution, fulfils the prayer of Narcissus' spurned lover – 'May he too be unable to gain his loved one!' The rest is mythological history; Narcissus finds the clear pool, falls in love with his own reflection and dies from the painful fires of self-love that consume him. The fifth house concerns love we are able to express to others through our creative self. But if we cannot begin to withdraw the projections we unconsciously cast on to the other, we risk remaining transfixed by our own reflection.

It is Pausanias[4] who refers to an older version of the myth that has been overlooked by the popularity of Ovid's story. Pausanias tells of Narcissus' twin sister who was similar in physical appearance and character to the beautiful young boy. They loved one another intensely. She died in her youth and Narcissus was able to keep her alive by imagining it was his sister's reflection, not his, that was in the mirror of the clear pool. Like Pollux's grief for Castor, Narcissus is unable to feel complete without his twin sister. He still searches for this missing other externally, imprisoned in a world where no other relationship is possible. Questing for the missing half keeps the individual fixated on the outer image of the other, defending the pain of the primal separation. Again, myth reiterates the theme of the missing twin, reinforcing the sibling image as a double of the self.

An inability to separate from the sibling inhibits the facility to love another. If we have not yet managed to separate from the sibling, we could carry this into our relationships outside the family. Like Narcissus, we may only be able to see the sibling's image reflected back to us in each new encounter.

We commence the journey into our adult relationships with embedded images and feelings of our experience with siblings. Somewhere in the psyche the sibling, or lack of one, represents the first available relationship. This primary relationship may be before any gender differentiation, therefore the sibling complex recreated in adult relationships could stem from a sibling of either sex. Castor and Pollux are a same-sex pair, unable to differentiate. Narcissus and his sister are separated, unable to be reconnected. The fifth house is the beginning of knowing ourselves through our reflected image in the mirror of others, and beginning to internalize these projections.

THE SIXTH HOUSE: HESTIA'S HEARTH

The sixth house, while often referred to as a sphere of 'unequal' relationship, is where a more conscious process of self-reflection can occur. This sphere symbolizes the psychological processes that take place before we are ready consciously to enter the sphere of equal relationship, represented by the seventh. The daily rituals of the sixth create a coherent experience of ourselves that paves a way for the sharing of daily life. The work and service of the sixth is directed to the maintenance of our well-being, which is strengthened through the process of self-reflection. This contributes to the ability to be conscious of our sense of self within relationship. Here, we are engaged in the sphere of the goddess, Hestia.

The sixth house is Hestia's territory of sacred space where the focus is on our internal self. Of the three Olympian sisters, Hera, Hestia and Demeter, it was Hestia who remained unviolated by her brothers. Her threshold is sealed and within her precinct the focal fires of the self are kept alight. Hestia in Greek is the image of the hearth. No god can move across her threshold unless invited. She represents the aspect of self that cannot be violated. In her sibling constellation she is the only one who does not get caught up in the familial dramas and remains uncontaminated by the family bickering. One sister, Hera, is identified with her brother–husband Zeus, while the other sister, Demeter, is identified with her daughter, Persephone. Hestia is not identified through another family member but with the internal core of her own self.

As a custodian of the sixth house, Hestia represents the focused tasks of day-to-day living. It is here, for the first time, we may separate what is exclusively personal from what is familial and collective. The process of discrimination is awakened and the boundaries between our private self and the self we share in relationship are made conscious. Hestia is an image of sacred space and her sense of spatiality creates an internal hearth where aspects of our self can congregate. Around this hearth of our interior self may gather the guests and ghosts we welcome across our psychological threshold.[5]

The sixth house has many levels including our urge for well-being and health. The sixth house cusp and planets help delineate what daily rituals are imperative to maintain well-being. This is also the territory within the process of relationship development where we can find our inner core exclusive of an other. Like Hestia we may find our own hearth not violated by familial toxicity. She also honours the continuity of the family. Hestia's tradition brings the coals from the hearth of the mother to the new bride's home, honouring the legacy she is to bring into the marriage. The sixth house prepares us for the union of the seventh.

In the 'Homeric Hymn to Hestia', Hermes is equally honoured. Hermes is the natural ruler of the sixth house and is the guide of souls to the door of Hestia. He is the outer voyager; Hestia is the inner journeyer. In growing up, we have daily contact with the sibling and learn to be private within this context. It is in the sixth house we learn to honour the sense of privacy, while also participating in relationship. Frequent contacts with our siblings and sharing the daily rituals of preparing food, eating, cleansing and housekeeping with them, may have influenced our ability to hold both our privacy and publicity successfully. The sibling is an integral part of maintaining our well-being, and in a similar way to the sixth house connection between Hermes and Hestia, the sibling may be the link to our interior world.

Mercury rules both Gemini and Virgo, and therefore the third and sixth houses. Siblings share a large portion of daily life in growing up and sibling themes are recreated with those we share our adult day-to-day activities with, mainly our co-workers. But Mercury also reminds us of the language and culture we share with our siblings. While the Geminian side suggests the sibling influences on our learning, ideas and speech, the Virgonian side suggests their influence on our internal world. Siblings may develop an inner language between them and be linked together on a level below consciousness. Therefore siblings are often symbols of the inner and spiritual life, and myth portrays this inner link.

Penelope, the wife of Odysseus, was depressed and worried over the safety both of her husband and son. Athena shaped Iphthime, Penelope's sister, into a dream image and wove her into Penelope's dreams, where she supported her sister by being hopeful and optimistic about the future. Penelope was comforted by her sister's closeness to her even though she knew her sister's home was far away. 'Take courage, let not your heart be too altogether frightened,' Iphthime whispered, and the inner link that bound the sisters together healed Penelope's suffering.[6]

Another Greek myth demonstrates the subtle language of the sibling bond. Philomela had been raped by the husband of her sister, Procne. He cut out her tongue and imprisoned her so that she would never be able to tell. He then told his wife that she had died. In her captivity, Philomela wove a tapestry showing the forced rape, the dismemberment of her tongue, her imprisonment, and through the language of images told her story. A servant of the house where she was imprisoned delivered the tapestry to Procne who instantly read the story. Procne then released Philomela and together the sisters confronted their betrayer. Sixth house signs and planets may be influenced by the powerful language of the sibling realm. Our daily rituals and interior world is moulded and shaped by the sibling relationship.

The seventh house is also part of the interpersonal quaternary. Belonging also to the trinity of relationship houses, the seventh house is the quintessential house of relationship (see Chapter 10).

THE EIGHTH HOUSE: PSYCHE'S DESCENT

In the eighth house we enter territory where we risk exposing the deepest and unknown aspects of the self. We return to a mysterious sphere where love penetrates our strongest defences and we are rendered vulnerable and out of control. Once again we risk being annihilated by the lover's betrayal, abandonment or death. The first time we were vulnerable and exposed to the powerful bond of love and betrayal was with our caretakers, the custodians of our fourth house. This realm of relating confronts us with the possibility of the loss of the beloved.

The eighth is a burial ground where the ghosts of previously incomplete relationships may haunt us. Here rests the power of the unresolved issues with the family and the ancestral legacies. The ancestral ghosts, the undertow of the parental marriage and the invisible realms of each partner's familial past flow beneath the eighth house union. The eighth reconnects us back to the fourth house family of origin, and family complexes that we have inherited are ready to surface.[7] Sibling themes come forward in the eighth when they have been part of the larger theme of ancestry. Hence, a sibling death or estrangement which has not been grieved in the family may surface now, needing to be dealt with. The legacies, literal or moral, will be addressed with our sibs. The eighth house is where the resources of the family are shared with our equals, our partners and our sibling/s.

The eighth house evokes the image of the *catabasis*, the journey into the Underworld. Siblings can often be catalysts for this journey through their envy, jealousy or betrayal. Psyche's labours, which included the descent into the Underworld, were the direct result of her sisters' jealousy and betrayal.

Psyche had been forewarned about her envious sisters by her partner Eros. However, Psyche wanted her sisters to see her fortune and share in her happiness. Ignoring Eros' warning, Psyche arranged for her sisters to visit her fabulous palace. Her sisters were immediately envious when they saw their younger sister's palatial home and heard of her delirious happiness. Together they planted doubt in Psyche, until she believed what the sisters told her: that she was married to a monster. Finally she took her sisters' advice and defied her husband. Against his commands, prompted by her sisters, she raised the light to discover the truth about who he *really* was. To her dismay, in the flickering candlelight, she did not see a monster but the god of love himself. Breaking her agreement to her god–husband, Eros, she is exiled from her home. Eventually she petitions her mother-in-law, Venus, for her help in being reunited with her beloved. Venus, however, is furious with her and demands Psyche fulfil the impossible tasks she sets for her. The fourth and final task is her descent into the Underworld, a place synonymous with the eighth house confrontation with death.

Psyche is in an unconscious relationship with Eros as she is not allowed to know who he is. His mother, Venus, still haunts their relationship as he has not separated enough from her to be with Psyche. In not being permitted to fully know her lover, Psyche cannot completely participate in an authentic eighth house relationship and so regresses. Her envious sisters are her agents of consciousness who constellate the eighth house betrayal. Ironically, it is the betrayal that allows Psyche to be conscious and know the truth of her marriage. The triangle formed with Psyche, sisters and husband is reminiscent of the eighth house triangles that defend intimacy. When betrayal breaks the triangulation, then the ego is confronted by the truth. The descent begins and like Psyche we journey towards a more honest and authentic relationship.

The interpersonal houses describe the process of the development of relationship from the narcissistic experience of self-love through to the dynamic and moving experience of intimate love. These houses mark our departure from our family of origin to the place where we risk recreating the familial patterns once again in our own adult lives, within our relationships and our families of choice. And the sibling relationship is reworked and recreated throughout this process of relating. Since it is an *a priori* relationship, the sibling like the parents will arrive in the midst of our adult relationships.

Hierarchy and equality

The third, seventh and eleventh houses symbolize relationships that are peer based and therefore conditional and interdependent, rather than unconditional and primarily dependent. This can be contrasted with relationships that are symbolized by the successive trinity of houses four, eight and twelve which are known as the 'houses of endings'.[8] In these houses we encounter relationships that are hierarchical and compatible with the vertical axis of the ancestors, the MC–IC axis. Relationships in these houses of endings confront us on the deepest levels, constellate unconscious or hidden agendas and are formulated more on symbiosis, unconditionality and the need for merger, union and loss of self, unlike the houses of relationship where connection is based on a more conscious awareness of separateness, duality and difference. In these houses the urge to regress is strong and relationships can be more inflexible. These houses of endings draw us back to the collective, ancestral, tribal and familial patterns that often require the breaking of a taboo in order to free ourselves. Personal identity, separate from the larger container of family, tribe or collective, is formed in the air houses. Relationships in the watery sphere bind those involved on a psychic level, where the emotional life below the horizon of consciousness is forever felt and registered by the other.[9] Relationship is as much about what is not visible as what is, as much below the horizon of consciousness as above. Here the unconscious process binds the participants together in a mysterious way. The psychic terrain in the houses of relationship is not, by nature, as binding.

Astrological themes in the houses of relationship that could symbolize potential disturbances or inhibitions to the natural development of separateness, equality and individuality, hence relationship, can be seen when antithetical energies influence these areas. For instance, if a planet inclined towards unconditionality, dependence or fusion, such as the Moon or Neptune, were placed in one of the houses of relationship, then we are alerted to an inherent conflict. When people with this placement enter into the world of equal relationship, their natural inclination would be to convert this sphere into a dependent realm, a place neither the individual nor the other would find satisfying. Neptune's urge either to idealize or sacrifice would create chaos in this territory while the Moon's instinct to protect and defend would inhibit the necessity of individual experience which is the opus of these houses. If one of the ruling planets of the fourth, eighth or twelfth houses were placed in one of the houses of relationship, there may be an innate tendency to confuse these different realms. The pattern may be formed early in life, then played out with partners or colleagues. We may try to recreate the pattern of enmeshment with a partner, unaware that we instinctively avoid equality. With the Moon in the third, we may have learned early to be a caretaker of others. If an authoritative archetype like Saturn were in these sectors, then the confusion between hierarchy and equality would be possible. If Saturn were in the third, the urge to be in control of the sibling system or feel the sense of duty/responsibility to our siblings may take precedence over the need to be equal, distorting the adult view of equality in later relationships. Pluto, inherently inclined towards the cyclical process of birth, death and rebirth, in one of these houses, would dominate the urge for equality, bringing to the relationship the issues of power and love. If Pluto were in the third house, the early issues of power and control may have dominated the effort to be separate.

The natural urge to forming equal relationship may be complicated by the Moon, Saturn, Neptune or Pluto in the houses of relationship. When they are in the third, this experience may have occurred early in the sibling system affecting our ability to feel equal in our adult relationships. Ultimately the third, seventh and eleventh houses prepare us for the conscious experience of closeness and union symbolized by the subsequent trinity of houses.

Notes

1. Anna Freud, *Indications for Child Analysis* (Hogarth Press, London: 1969).
2. Houses 1–4 are the personal houses; houses 5–8, the interpersonal houses; and houses 9–12, the transpersonal houses. Each contains four houses which correspond to the elements:

    houses 1, 5 and 9 are the Houses of Life (fire);
    houses 2, 6 and 10 are the Houses of Substance (earth);
    houses 3, 7 and 11 are the Houses of Relationship (air);
    houses 4, 8 and 12 are the Houses of Endings (water).

3. Ovid, *Metamorphoses*, Book 3.83–7.
4. Pausanias, *Guide to Greece*, vol. 1, trans. Peter Levi (Penguin, Harmondsworth: 1971), 376.
5. For amplification on the etymological connection to Hestia as the goddess of hospitality, hence host and ghost, see Barbara Kirksey, 'Hestia: a Background of

Psychological Focusing', in James Hillman (ed.), *Facing the Gods* (Spring, Dallas, TX: 1980), 110.

6. Homer, *The Odyssey*, Book 4.787 ff.

7. See Brian Clark, *Eros: the Sacred Site of the Eighth House* (Astro*Synthesis Series, Melbourne: 1991).

8. Howard Sasportas, *The Twelve Houses*, refers to these houses as 'The Trinity of Soul', 130–32.

9. For further amplification on the water houses, see Erin Sullivan, *Dynasty: the Astrology of Family Dynamics*, 170–94.

12

Sibling Themes and the Horoscope

Consultant astrologers will find it useful to question clients about early sibling relationships.

Howard Sasportas[1]

Astrological indicators of sibling patterns contribute not only to a greater understanding of our relationship to brothers and sisters, but to many of our adult relationships as well. Some of the sibling issues I see frequently in my practice are described below.[2]

The handicapped sibling

A handicapped child presents the family with a new set of demands and dilemmas. The handicapped child needs more attention, placing strain on the parents, their time and resources; more tension, stress and frustration leak into the family atmosphere. This pressure placed upon the parental marriage may severely damage the primary relationship. Other siblings may feel neglected and in competition with a rival they cannot overtly compete with. They are faced with a host of complex questions about why and how it happened. This disruption to 'normal' family life quickens their maturation, and often the others define themselves in reference to the handicapped sibling. The functionality of this situation is directly proportional to the attitudes and actions of the parents. Not all families with handicapped children are disadvantaged; in fact, I have experienced families where a handicapped child has been the catalyst that brings the family together, inspiring love and devotion. The handicapped child becomes a focus for the family as well as a healing agent.

The birth of a handicapped sibling can constellate a myriad of feelings amongst all family members: each feels differently and each plays her or his own role. Feelings of compassion, pity, shame, guilt, blame, love, regret and wonder flood the family atmosphere. It is important that the siblings of the handicapped child are able to express these feelings without judgement, and have an open forum to express both their bewilderment and frustration. Without this openness, the family atmosphere is darkened and the children are left to absorb the negative and repressed feelings. Without an avenue of expression, siblings are unable to exorcize feelings of guilt and self-blame.

James was approaching his Saturn return when he came for a consultation. He belonged to the generation born in 1966 with the Uranus–Pluto conjunction opposite the Chiron–Saturn conjunction. His Saturn return was not only complicated by these planetary aspects but also by the simultaneous Chiron opposition. James, the youngest of three brothers, had a younger sister who was severely mentally retarded. When he was four she was placed in an institution, and he remembers seeing her only a few times during her life. She died when he was twenty-one. James had Venus conjunct the Saturn–Chiron conjunction, and it was during his first waxing Chiron square that his sister died.[3] He had Neptune in Scorpio in the third house, Scorpio being on the cusp of the third. When I first asked him about his siblings he did not mention her. He only mentioned his sister after I had tried to articulate some of the relational themes in his horoscope. She was missing, lost, invisible – a mystery. For James, his only sister represented an incomplete and unknowable relationship, a recurrent pattern in James's adult relationships which he presented at the beginning of our consultation. Through our discussion James realized that the metaphorical journey back to acknowledging and accepting his sister was necessary to complement the journey forward into relationship. He had carried both the rage and sadness over the loss of a sister for his brothers, but now James felt sure enough of his own loss to grieve.

When a handicapped sibling is exiled from the family, the remaining siblings are at risk of identifying with the parental values, fearing they may be banished as well. Gerald told me during our consultation that when his brother with Down's syndrome was institutionalized, he decided to be the success that he knew his father wanted him to be. Gerald became a successful lawyer at the expense of his innate urge to travel and adventure. But at the age of thirty-nine he decided to give up the corporate world and see what else was out there. This magnetized the fear of being banished and exiled by father's disapproval, yet also constellated a deep sense of grief over the loss of his brother.

Other sibling/s can act out and become rebellious in order to divert the attention away from the handicapped child. Vicki expressed concern over the behaviour of her eldest son, Christopher. Her younger son, Jacob, had been severely crippled in a car accident. Jacob, however, was feisty and competitive and had a will that Vicki almost believed could make him walk again. The spirit and life force that flowed through her damaged son was not evident in Christopher. However, this had not always been the case. It was after Jacob's accident that she noticed the change in Christopher. Christopher had a Neptune–Mars conjunction in the third house squaring the sixth house Moon. I wondered if he felt that, were he disabled like his brother, his mother would favour and attend to him more, as she seemed to do for Jacob. Identification with the damaged sibling may align us with a victim role.

There will be many differing issues and scenarios with a handicapped child in the family. Allowing space for clients to tell their story is often empowering enough, but to match this with the astrological symbols can provide a setting for reconciliation to take place. Joan felt she was able to honour her relationship with her handicapped brother through her greater appreciation of the astrological symbols in her horoscope.

Joan is a second child and in the middle, between two brothers. Her younger brother was born when she was five years old. While her mother was in hospital for the birth, Joan stayed with her mother's elder sister. She vividly recalls the day that her mother and younger brother came home from the hospital. She returned home, rushed to the front door of her house where her mother greeted her. Joan's new baby brother was in her mother's arms. The excitement turned to curiosity then bewilderment when Joan saw a plaster cast around her brother's leg that dangled below the blanket that he was wrapped in. She remembers feeling perplexed by what this could mean.

The birth was a shock for the whole family. It was not until the day Martin was born that Joan's mother knew he had Down's syndrome. He was born blind and also with a club foot. It was the club foot that was wrapped in plaster, the first image Joan associates with her baby brother.

Joan has the Sun in Sagittarius opposite Mars in Gemini and both are squaring Chiron in Virgo. Both personal masculine planets are squaring Chiron. When Martin was born, the Sun had progressed to the exact degree of Mars and Chiron. Martin also had the same three planets in aspect, but the Sun and Mars were conjunct in Pisces squaring Chiron in Sagittarius. Chiron in Sagittarius was transiting Joan's Sun within one minute of arc when he was born, the transits being Martin's horoscope. Martin became the living symbol for Joan of both the Chiron–Sun transit and her natal

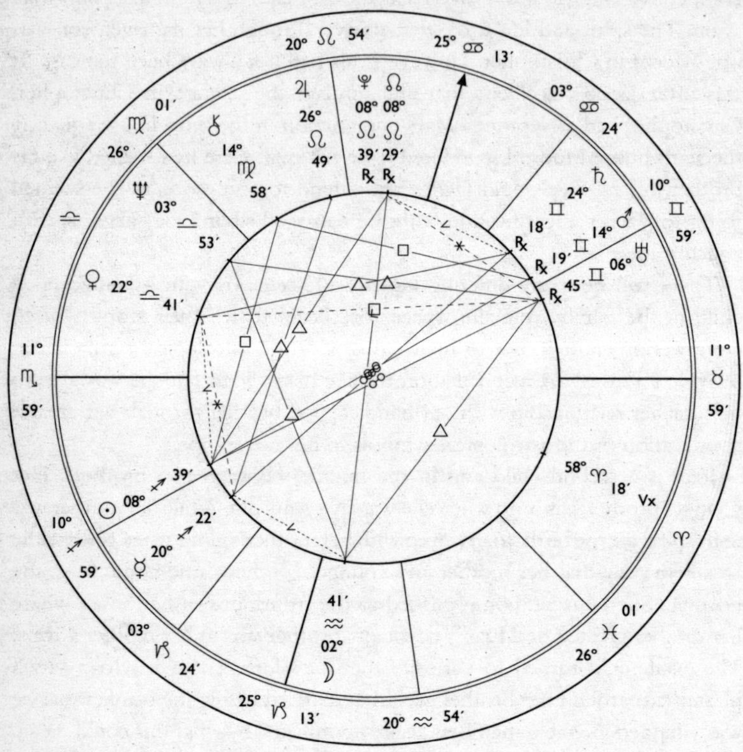

Figure 12: Joan's horoscope.

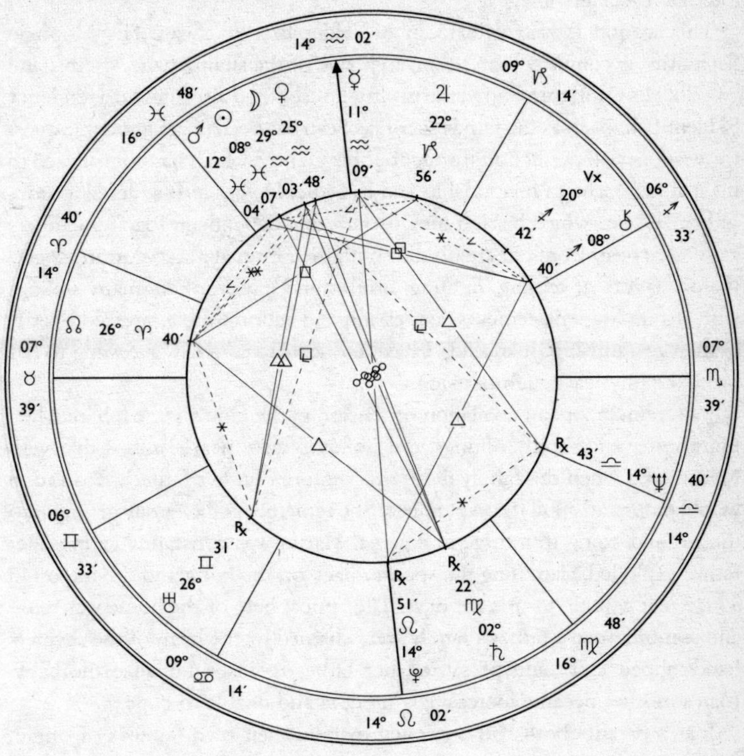

Figure 13: Martin's horoscope.

T-Square: the image of the wounded brother. While he was alive, she loved and cared for him, attending to the wounds that were also part of her own internal masculine images.

This wound is also evident in her elder brother, Sean. His Moon in Sagittarius is conjunct Joan's Sun, an image of the sibling pair, Artemis and Apollo. His Capricorn Sun in the twelfth house could also suggest a tendency to identify himself as the family sacrifice. Sean has been on an insatiable quest for wisdom and perfection throughout his lifetime which has contributed to his inability to be in relationship and to settle. He has also suffered a series of breakdowns which has left him insecure and dependent. Joan remembers a different Sean from her childhood. With their mutual Mars–Moon aspects there was lots of teasing, fighting, bruises and injuries. Like many siblings with strong Mars placements, aggression and action were expressed overtly in their relationship. Joan said, 'I have the scars to prove it', referring to her brother's physical rough-housing.

Joan remembers an escalation of tension in the family atmosphere when Martin arrived. Family outings and holidays were nearly impossible with Martin, and when the family did try to venture out, her father's frustration would erupt and spoil the experience. She remembers the family getting into the car and going to a drive-in cinema. Martin was constantly crying. Her father exploded, slamming the speaker back on the hook and driving off in a rage that wouldn't settle for days. The atmosphere of the home was tense and sombre. Joan's father's family were shamed by the birth of the severely handicapped child and pressured her father to institutionalize the baby. Joan's mother became increasingly tired, ill and unable to cope.

Joan's parents both had a missing male in their own families of origin, so the shame and helplessness associated with their own earlier losses may have been triggered by Martin's handicap. Her father was a twin. His brother had disappeared under shameful circumstances, becoming estranged from the family. Joan's father had not heard from his twin brother since their separation. Her mother's father had died when Joan's mother was two. The youngest of four girls, Joan's mother was left in a household completely dominated by women. Joan's Pluto–Moon opposition in the parental fourth to tenth houses suggests that she was susceptible to mother's psychic atmosphere of loss and grief. The Chiron–Sun aspect can often resonate with an image of a damaged, lost or wounded masculine figure which is literally carried by the males in the family. Often, the damaged masculine figure is eclipsed by the feminine which becomes part of a familial theme,

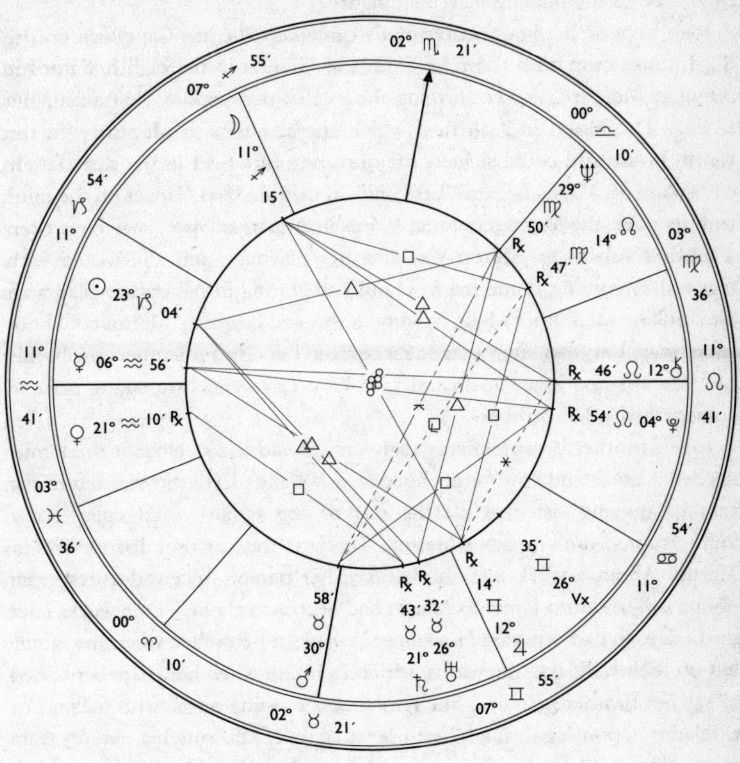

Figure 14: Sean's horoscope.

influencing the surviving family members. Both aspects in Joan's horoscope suggest a high susceptibility to absorbing the familial grief and loss constellated around the missing masculine figure.

Joan became her younger brother's caretaker. She has Capricorn on the third house cusp with the ruler Saturn in Gemini in the eighth. Saturn is opposite Mercury, also confirming the role of the responsible one for the sibling. The Moon in Aquarius (which she shares with Martin) is in the fourth house and could suggest the nurturing of a peer in the early family environment. Martin became 'her child'. Martin also has Cancer on the third with its ruler, the Moon, conjunct Venus in Aquarius. Sister may have been a mother substitute. Martin was also her playmate and she would look forward to coming home from school and getting in his crib to play with him, pulling each other's hair, making noises and laughing. Martin could not see or walk but Joan knew that he recognized her. She remembers the bonds of closeness and love she shared with him. Love and care-taking became entwined with her brother.

Joan's mother became increasingly unwell and it was evident the family needed a break and so a family holiday was planned. Martin was left in the care of nursing sisters while the rest of the family could enjoy some uninterrupted time 'without Martin'. This was the last time Joan ever saw Martin. About a week into the holiday, her parents received a desperate phone call to return home as Martin had become very ill. Three weeks later he died. Joan had not seen him since she had said goodbye when the family left on their holidays. She was at a friend's house when her parents phoned to say her brother had died. She remembers running home with feelings of exhilaration pouring through her: a sense of relief knowing her parents were released from a huge burden, yet crazily mixed with tremendous grief at her loss, and guilt for the torrent of emotion she was now experiencing. No one paid attention to Joan's feelings and she felt alone in her grief. In retrospect, Joan is confused as to why she didn't see her brother in the month before he died; something feels incomplete, a chapter not finished, a wound that still aches when she imagines how she might have said goodbye differently.

For six weeks after the funeral she can still recall mourning her brother, draping herself over his crib and sobbing uncontrollably. The astrological portal to the Underworld of Joan's eighth house is Gemini, now opened through the loss of her brother. The loss of a handicapped sibling constellates a variety of mixed feelings which complicates the grief. Joan felt the spectrum of feelings, but she also felt no one else understood her grief, as no one else was openly mourning or talking about what happened. The loss of a child is such a tragedy that a veil of silence is drawn with the intent to protect the surviving children. However, the silence isolates children in their grief and they are left bewildered that no one feels as they do, confused and angry for being left, and suspicious that the rest of the family is withholding something. The feelings of anger and guilt become shameful for the child who is not supported through this passage. Shame breeds silence and then secrecy. In this atmosphere of unspoken grief the child's instinct to survive colludes with the silence of the other family members and to protect the parent. Survival for Joan, with the Moon–Pluto opposition across the fourth to tenth axis, could now mean taking care of her mother.

The silence of the grief and the inability to express feeling divided the family. Sean was also wounded by the inability to resolve his grief, perpetuating an eternal quest for the divine. This eternal quest for the lost other could be suggested by his Jupiter in Gemini opposite his Sagittarian Moon. These are the planets first encountered as he leaves the parental domain of the fourth and tenth houses. Searching for the lost loved one is part of the normal grieving process. With unresolved grief this could turn into an eternal quest. This is a mythic sibling theme: Pollux searches for Castor, Cadmus for Europa and Narcissus for his sister.

Joan's Moon is in the third degree of Aquarius. At her brother's death, Uranus was in the third degree of Leo, the transiting opposition signalling a separation from a secure object. When Uranus transited the Moon in Aquarius, these images were once again stirred. The progressed Moon in this time circled the horoscope one and a half times, and now was progressing through the third house allowing Joan to feel, remember and relive the earlier images of her brother. Forty-one years after he had died the feelings towards her brother were still alive in her.

After Martin died, the family atmosphere changed. Joan was now the youngest child and she recalls her mother paying much more attention to her and fussing over her. When a sibling dies there is a reshuffle of sibling position. Now the baby of the family, Joan felt more attended to by both her parents. The price for this attention – her lost brother – evoked guilt. When a child dies in the family the parents turn their anxiety of loss on to their surviving children. But with the loss of a handicapped child, the everyday pressures the parents have carried are lessened. Joan's mother was less depressed and tired and had more time to spend caring for Joan. Her father was less frustrated, and also had more time to spend sharing a mutual love of theatre with his only daughter.

Martin died a month before Joan's twelfth birthday. She had just had her first Jupiter return which was complicated by the conjunction with Pluto, an interesting symbol for the relief and the grief both associated with Martin's death. Two days before Martin died the Jupiter–Pluto conjunction was exact. Her initiation into adolescence was in the shadow of a literal loss which became entangled with the natural mourning rituals of her girlhood that was passing. Shortly after Martin died, Chiron in Aquarius transited her fourth house Moon. When Chiron retrograded and returned across her Moon, Joan contracted polio. For six months she was paralysed, immobile and unable to walk – as Martin had been. This is a grieving response. Through identifying with the lost sibling, the sibling is kept alive. It is not uncommon for a surviving sibling to find a way to express the grief that has not been allowed its place in the family: illness, mood swings, destructive behaviour, depression are all methods of expressing loss.

Sean has Pluto opposing Mercury in Aquarius. For the eighteen months after his brother's death, transiting Uranus opposed Mercury (similar to Adler's transit when his brother died) and transiting Chiron conjoined Mercury. The Pluto/Mercury contact is an image of the loss of a sibling and the transit has synchronized with the literality of the psychic theme. When a child dies, the surviving siblings are at risk of identification with the dead sib. Parents and friends often collude with this in order to commune with the loss. In identifying with this loss, Sean may have unconsciously become the damaged one. This would also ensure that the familial image of the damaged man is lived out in the family, healing the masculine wound that is buried deep in the family. Sean now carries the wound overtly. His numerous breakdowns have contributed to his isolation and depression; his sacrifice may be the heroic act of burying the family complex. Each sibling grieved in his or her own way.

The sibling constellation that includes Sean, Joan and Martin is the final one for this line of the family as neither Joan nor Sean have children. Martin had Pluto conjunct the IC, the end of the line. Joan described Martin as her child and his death may have been one of the factors that contributed to her not having children. For Joan, she lost not only her beloved brother but a son. Their relationship has many astrological significations of a powerful relationship that transcends the bounds of time – the ascendant–descendant axis is reversed, Joan's Mercury is conjunct Martin's Vertex, while Martin's

Mercury is conjunct Joan's South Node. As Joan's parents come closer to death, she is concerned about Sean's welfare. Without her parents, only Joan and Sean are left to carry the family legacy.

The loss of a sibling

The death of a child in the family is a trauma that engulfs the whole family in a powerful grief. It is such a tragedy I often wonder how any family member survives. Yet surviving and returning to life are quite different. It seems that to return to life the process of grief must be as fully spent as possible. This entails a descent into the unfamiliar nether regions. Like any descent into Pluto's domain, we require proper instructions and a wise guide. For the siblings of a dead child, their guides are their parents. Instructions are gleaned from the parents and other adults' reactions and behaviour. Grief is a powerfully singular and personal experience. Children need guidance through this overwhelming time, which is doubly difficult for parents lost in the depth of their own grief.

Freud and Adler both lost a brother and that had a potent impact upon their psychology. Jung survived at least three siblings who came before him, and while not affected overtly by sibling loss, none the less he was born into a family atmosphere where his survival was in the shadow of the dead siblings. In the late nineteenth century, with childhood mortality rates high, the concern over the loss of a child, and certainly sibling grief, was not a priority. Until recently, the attitude of the medical profession was to advise the grieving parent to have a replacement child, unaware of the powerful legacy of the dead sibling.[4] A century later, in the Western world, sibling death through childhood diseases is minimal. Now this loss takes place more noticeably through suicide, car accidents, drowning or other events that seem unfair and untimely. Recognizing the need to facilitate the surviving siblings' grief is a priority. Grief that remains disenfranchised isolates children. They feel insecure and fearful of their own mortality, often cut off from their parents' care and attention when they need it the most.

The death of a child often creates anxiety in the parents about their surviving children, leading to over-protective or anxious parenting. The surviving siblings may also feel as if they are living in the shadow of their dead sibling. The family atmosphere has dramatically altered, and the members are more cautious and reticent about what to say or do. A reshuffle of roles and positioning takes place in the sibling system to accommodate the void left in the family. These are often parental manoeuvres that attempt to defend the loss. The remaining siblings may also identify with the lost sibling and fill the void created in the family dynamics. Sean was left to carry the wounded masculine for the family after his brother's death. What is needed is the ability to be able to express the complexity of feelings and the depth of grief that arise during these times.

Until recently, it was commonly accepted that parents needed to shelter their children from the grieving process to allow them to have as 'normal' a life as possible. Grief cannot be closeted that easily. The secrecy of the grief, while of good intent, turns toxic for the surviving siblings. Unresolved and hidden grief lingers in the family atmosphere and stifles the psychological well-being of the surviving children. Bank and Kahn make an important point about parental grief:

> if a part of the parent has died with the child, that parent, who was narcissistically invested in the child, will be likely to mourn unhealthily and involve the other children in that pathological grief.[5]

Part of the surviving sibling may have also died. Astrologically, the traumatic impact of sibling grief is most noticeably constellated around the archetype of Pluto in relationship to the third house or similar astrological combinations (Scorpio on the third house, Pluto in aspect to Mercury, etc.). The archetype of Chiron is also often involved in the loss of a sibling. Surviving siblings encounter Pluto, the archetype of death, mortality, loss and finality, at an early age. Chiron's archetypal process also confronts the child with the transitory nature of incarnation, opening a wound that becomes part of their psychic life.

Dorothy had just turned forty-eight when she first came for a consultation. A few weeks later, she phoned to ask if she would be able to make a series of appointments to continue to explore the theme that had surfaced during the first session. The theme was the death of her sister. Transiting Pluto was retrograding in opposition to her Sun in the third house, and over the next few years would continue on to conjunct her South Node and oppose her Mercury, which was conjunct her North Node in Gemini, also in the third house. Progressed Mars in Gemini would also be conjoining her Mercury over the next few years. The timing seemed appropriate.

Dorothy was the eldest child. Her only sibling was a sister born when she was two years old. When her sister was born, Dorothy's progressed Sun had moved into Gemini (Mercury, the Moon and Uranus are in Gemini natally) conjoining her North Node.[6] Her sister had the Sun in Scorpio exactly opposite Dorothy's Mars–Venus conjunction while her sister's Moon–Venus conjunction was exactly opposite Dorothy's Moon–Uranus conjunction in Gemini. These astrological images helped us to imagine what Jean may have been like. Dorothy had no memories of her sister except one, which she had spent her life trying to avoid. With her Moon in Gemini, which was also conjunct Uranus on the IC, she had lost an important part of herself with her sister, a part of herself she had sought to redeem in other relationships. Dorothy also had Chiron in Scorpio, conjoining her Sister's Sun, which filled out a T-Square with Saturn and the Venus–Mars conjunction.

Dorothy was nearly six when the accident occurred. The family was visiting friends in the country when the two girls wandered off, unnoticed by the parents and other adults. Near the house was a billabong where ducks would congregate. Curious about these creatures the girls ventured towards the pond. Jean slipped and fell into the pond and drowned. Dorothy cannot remember what happened next. Her main recollection is constantly feeling the wall of silence that greeted her whenever she walked into the room where her parents were. She said she remembered listening at doors while her parents argued and fought and blamed each other, but as soon as she entered the room a veil of silence descended and her parents would not speak, either to her or to each other. Her sister was never mentioned again in her presence. It was as if she had never existed.

Dorothy remembers the rest of her childhood as frozen, numb and disconnected. Interestingly, this had been the initial reason for the consultation as these were her feelings in her present relationship. Uranus is on the third house side of the IC conjunct the Moon. Uranus on the IC or a Uranus–Moon aspect is often synchronous with a disengaged or dismembered familial atmosphere, where the feeling life is severed and cut off. No one helped her through her grief or her enormous guilt over what had happened. I asked where her sister was buried; she did not know and had never thought to ask. She remembered she was not allowed to go to the funeral. That day she was sent to a neighbour with whom she was extremely uncomfortable. She felt alienated and abandoned, but also responsible, guilty and alone. Shame accompanied the guilt. Having no adequate emotional support systems to help her through the grieving process, Dorothy's secret guilt impeded her emotional development.[7]

The transit of Pluto was helping Dorothy remember. Through our consul-

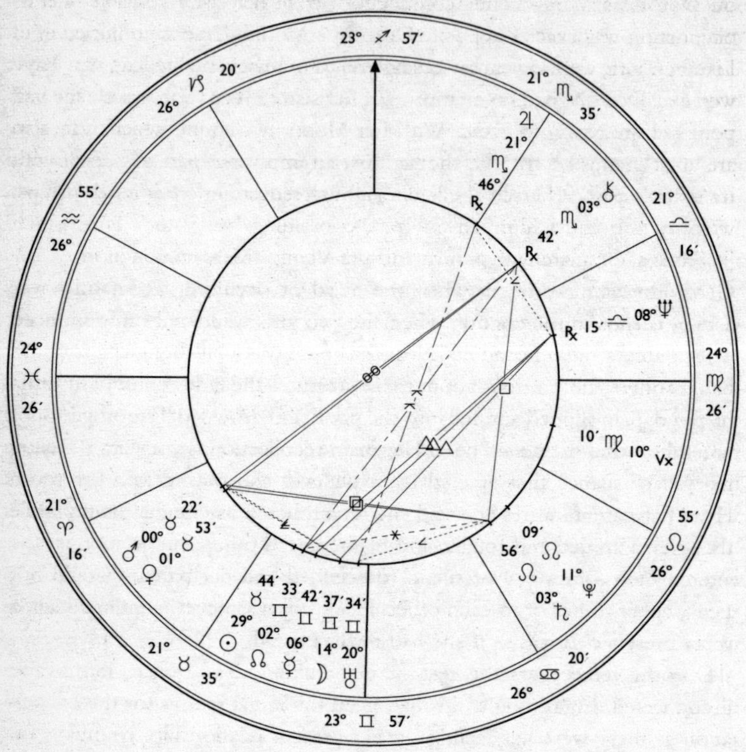

Figure 15: Dorothy's horoscope.

tations, she had an opportunity to go back and try to reconstruct what happened with her sister, allowing herself to grieve, letting the grief thaw out the feelings that had been frozen half a lifetime ago. Grief is a cumulative phenomenon, therefore we are wary of opening the channel to buried grief. Like Pandora, we feel we may unleash all of our darkened feelings on to the world. This is a common feeling with Plutonic energy: we experience it as potentially annihilating and obliterating when it is unexpressed; yet once we are able to express the energy, the experience is one of release, relief and transformation. Pluto demands enormous respect and to honour its own wisdom and timing is important.

The loss of a sibling is a potent psychological demarcation in one's life. Gena has a Pluto–Mercury conjunction in the third house. When she was a few months old, her mother became pregnant. The child was stillborn. The familial story was that her brother was stillborn because Gena's mother had to nurse and take care of her continually. Kubler-Ross points out that blame is part of the grieving process,[8] yet Gena became the target upon whom the blame was fixed. The grief was turned to guilt and no one recognized that Gena had lost a brother, only that mother had lost a son. Howard Sasportas also suggests that Pluto–Mercury in the third complicates the grieving process of the surviving siblings:

> I drew up the chart of a woman with Mercury conjunct Pluto in the 3rd house whose younger brother died when she was only six years old. At the age of twenty-eight, she was still walking around believing that something she had said or done was the cause of his death.[9]

Sexuality

Ovid tells us the story of the opposite-sex twins, Byblis and Caunus, and the passionate desire the sister Byblis had for her brother.[10] At first, Byblis thought that her desire was normal; however, over time her actions revealed she was obsessed by her love for her brother. She would dress for him, be anxious about her appearance in front of him, and began to fantasize that she lay in his bed with him. Byblis was tormented with desire for her brother and struggled to reconcile the fact that she could not do what the gods were able to do. Oceanus married his sister Tethys, Saturn was wed to Rhea and even Jupiter married his sister Juno! As a mortal, Byblis was not free to love her brother sexually.

Byblis eventually decided to send her brother a letter confessing her passionate love for him and her delirious possession by Cupid. On reading the letter, her brother became enraged, disgusted, at his sister's suggestion of incest. But his sister was possessed by this love and continued her approach towards him. Finally he felt he had no choice but to flee to a foreign shore where he established a new city. The abandonment by her brother drove Byblis mad with grief. In her hysteria, she decided to pursue him. But her grief was so debilitating she was unable to travel very far, falling upon the wooded trail and crying herself to death. Nymphs of the forest pitied her and changed her tears into an everlasting fountain. These continuous tears are an apt reminder of the violated taboo of brother–sister incest, a taboo that is broken more often than we would imagine by siblings.

Antiquity was aware of the range of feelings in the brother–sister relationship, from those of extreme closeness through to indifference, from sacrifice to sexual desire. In contemporary society, the taboo on brother–sister sexual attraction is rarely spoken of. There is a silence about the feelings of love, desire, ambivalence and even loathing that are an integral part of the dynamic of brother–sister relationships. Little is mentioned about the brother–sister incest taboo, even though it has been reported that the probability of violation of this taboo is five times more likely than adult–child incest.[11] The high incidence of the broken taboo must be connected to the collective denial of the power of the brother–sister bond. While the sibling bond remains unconscious, the archetype remains imprisoned in the dark. Guggenbuhl-Craig is perceptive on this point. In re-visioning the state of marriage, he discusses exiled archetypes that are banished, becoming pathological or obsessive. He acknowledges the sibling archetype as one of these condemned archetypes, and suggests that with the changing zeitgeist of relationship we may be able to become more conscious of its reality:

> the archetype of the siblings will again be able to be lived out – the Artemis–Apollo relationship – and the intimate, persistent, all-encompassing love between brother and sister will no longer be condemned as incest or unhealthy bond. (Interestingly enough, the sibling relationship was less pathologised and less understood as 'incest' in Queen Victoria's time than it is today.)[12]

Jung spoke of the brother–sister incest in archetypal, not personal, terms, acknowledging its psychic presence but nothing about its embodiment in actual sibling relationships. Freud's follower, Ernest Jones, acknowledged that 'erotic experiences between brother and sister in early childhood are exceedingly common'[13] but that they were, in essence, an extension of the Oedipal drama. Myth acknowledges what early psychoanalysis did not: that sexuality between siblings is a powerful force in its own right and may have repercussions for the rest of one's life.

Sexuality and sexual curiosity are also part of same-sex sibling relationships. We compare ourselves to our same-sex siblings, and often 'sexual roles' are assigned by other family members: 'he's a heart breaker', 'she has all the right moves', 'he's got a great body', 'she's the sexy one'. They are all part of family life. Same-sex siblings can be models for our sexual progress as we watch their forays into the world of sexuality. Rivalry erupts again in adolescence and siblings can be wounding by deriding the way we look, mocking our attractiveness and criticizing the way we dress or our choice of friends. While this is part of adolescence, for some these are wounds that have affected their sense of body image and sexuality.

Sexual play between siblings, especially those who spend a lot of time together, seems a natural extension of their relationship. Once the curiosity is satisfied, the experience is often forgotten or safely contained. When the family atmosphere is bound in a moral strait-jacket, then this can lead to guilt, shame and a 'dreadful' secret. In a polluted family atmosphere, siblings may turn to one another for solace and comfort. In this refuge, siblings sometimes engage in sex as a means of feeling loved. Sibling incest is more frequent than we care to admit; it can happen once, or continue over a period of years. Sibling incest is complex as it occurs between two relative equals and is not always power based. In most cases it remains a dark secret between the two siblings that is skilfully repressed. For many, the first time they share the secret is with their therapist many years later. As astrological counsellors we are witness to the healing power of disclosure.

Margaret had transiting Uranus just rising over the descendant and beginning its opposition to the Moon in Leo, snuggled on her Cancer ascendant. She had just completed the astrological transit of Pluto across her Sun–Mercury conjunction. To explore the wider picture, and the new possibilities surfacing with Uranus across the western horizon opposing the Moon, I asked Margaret what images she remembered from around the age of twelve, half a Uranus cycle ago. This is what we discussed.

Margaret and her brother Edward, who was two years older, were both children of a wartime romance. Their father was fighting in Europe at the time of both their births. Their mother had always made a point of telling

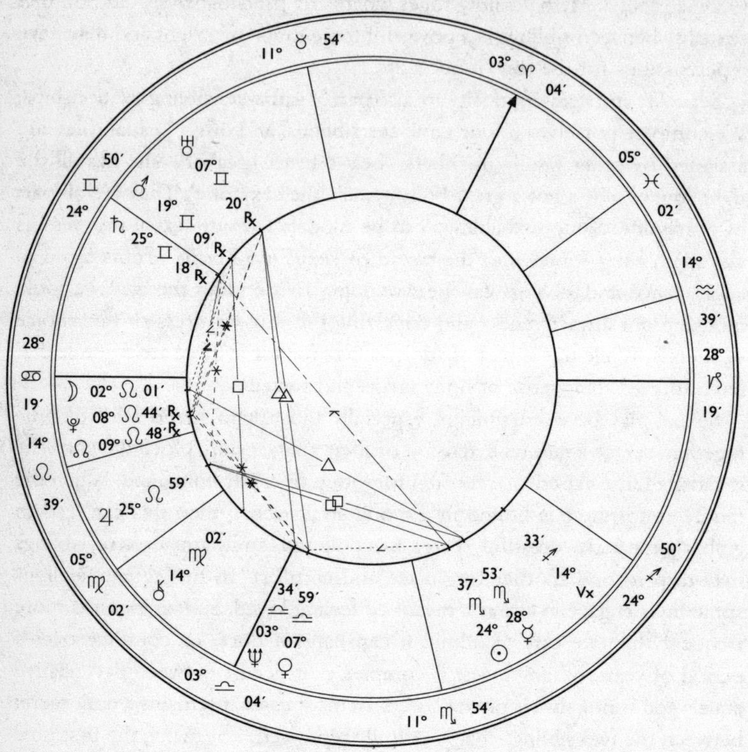

Figure 16: Margaret's horoscope.

the children that he had wanted her to have an abortion when she became pregnant with Edward. Edward became his mother's 'little man' and, as Margaret saw it, the favourite. She has no memories of living with her father and her first memory of him is the day he left the family. She was four years old.

Margaret with her mother and brother had emigrated to Australia to be with their father. But instead of living with him, they moved in with her mother's brother. The tension in the household was so high, they left to live with her father's sister. I wondered how much unresolved sibling fate lay underneath the surface of her parents' families. Margaret has lost a lot of childhood memories, but with Neptune exactly on the IC, conjunct the IC ruler, Venus and a Pluto–Moon conjunction, there *was* a lot to forget!

Father left the family to be with his pregnant girlfriend. When Margaret was seven, her mother remarried a man that her brother introduced her to. Margaret believed this was arranged so that her mother would be taken care of, absolving her uncle of responsibility. Mother's brother chose an interesting caretaker and replacement: the new husband was severely crippled and hunchbacked and, as Margaret describes, 'horrible to her and Edward'. The children were constantly left alone and Edward was expected to supervise his sister. Edward, who had been replaced by the step-father, began withdrawing from Margaret and his mother. Margaret felt rejected by both her brother and mother, who became pregnant immediately after her marriage. Margaret felt displaced by her new half-sister, and passed into what she described as the darkest years of her life. Saturn transited the IC, over her Neptune–Venus conjunction and through the fourth house. Saturn's stark reality challenged any ideals or fantasies she may have harboured about home.

Margaret's physical development happened early. In the suffocating atmosphere of the home, her only bright light was her brother. She would do anything to win his favour. He was her hero, her father–brother, the only constant male and constant love in her short and turbulent life. Margaret has Mercury, ruler of the third house, conjunct the Sun in Scorpio in the fifth, perhaps an image of this fusion of the heroic figure of father–brother. This conjunction is also square to her Jupiter, inflating the heroic masculine image. Edward's Saturn–Moon conjunction sits exactly opposite her Sun–Mercury, providing the Sun–Moon contacts so potent in sibling synastry. But Margaret also has Chiron in the third house squaring her retrograde Mars, portraying an inherited, wounded masculine figure, experienced first through her father, then embodied in her step-father, but then ready to be transferred to her brother.

Margaret described her brother as sensual and attractive, and when she was twelve years old she submitted to his sexual curiosity. She loved her brother and felt, as lovers do, that she would do anything for the loved one. Margaret remembered thinking, 'if this is going to make him care for me, so be it'. She had sex in her bedroom with him. 'Straight after there was an immediate sense of grief and I felt I had lost him forever,' she said. It never happened again, was never mentioned again, and has remained a secret between them. But, to this day, Margaret still says she has never loved another man the way she loved her brother, and wonders what fate drew them together so passionately yet also kept them apart. Edward joined the army the year after, and Margaret was left alone. Another half-sister was born, estranging Margaret even more. She was in her own world, alone.

Margaret said she could not separate the shame that she experienced with her brother from the overall shame that she has always felt about sexuality. She was fascinated yet repulsed by her mother's sexuality and her relationships. Her brother was an attractive young man who always had girlfriends, and her father's affairs were legendary. Margaret swung between the romantic idealism of her Neptune–Venus and the intense needs of her Pluto–Moon, both intimately connected to her parents' legacy and the sexual atmosphere of her family home.

Many of the threads of Margaret's life were reconnected over the years when Pluto transited her Sun–Mercury conjunction. Her divorce was finalized, her natural father and the daughter she had relinquished made contact with her in the same year, and her step-father died. Endings, beginnings, as well as the bringing up of many childhood memories, were all part of the process. She has now returned to the memory of her brother and the love that she once shared and knew with him. Margaret knows more consciously that her father's abandonment, her step-father's coldness and her brother's desertion are not fated to repeat themselves. Uranus' transit into the seventh house and opposing the Moon was a separation from these patterns and an opportunity to move beyond them. Margaret describes a family atmosphere congruent with the climate where sibling incest is likely to manifest: an unstable home, an absent and deserting father, an intruder (step-father) who divides loyalties, a lack of affection or attention. Within this atmosphere, the sibs turn to each other for comfort.

Returning to the mythic themes reminds us of the necessity to acknowledge the powerful erotic bond that may appear in the sibling system. As adolescence awakens our sexuality, the archetypes of Venus and Mars are brought to life and embodied, archetypes also constellated in our relationship with siblings. Margaret had Venus in Libra while Edward had Mars in Aries, both planets in their ruling signs suggesting the potency of these energies. Margaret's Mars is squaring her brother's Venus, an aspect whose friction is fascinating and erotic.

Sibling secrets

Family secrets divide and weaken the family. Because they are generally charged with feelings of shame, guilt and regret they are banished from view to protect the family and its members from humiliation, embarrassment, social stigma and exile. Secrets are often consciously kept to protect children. It is ironic that in spite of these good intentions the secret will return to haunt these children. Family secrets are never protective as children naturally live closer to the world of the unconscious, the location where the secret is banished. The archetype of Pluto is intimately connected with both the toxic and dark effects of the secret, as well as the healing power of disclosure. With Pluto in Sagittarius, we are becoming more aware of our collective and familial secrets and shame. As Pluto continues its transit in opposition to our personal and social planets in Gemini, we will also become more aware of the secrets carried by and through our sibling system. Sagittarius offers us a word of caution about being over-zealous or conceptual about these recovered secrets, most of all not to construct moral ideologies around them. The healing power of Pluto is contained in the process of descent, to recover that which has not had its due burial rights.

The sibling system can also carry potentially damaging secrets which either separate or fuse the siblings together. Secrets inhibit honesty and intimacy, so no matter how close we feel we are to the sib, the power of the secret denies real closeness. The secret also introduces a power differential into the relationship, as one knows while the other does not. Trust is broken and may never be restored. One sibling may be asked to hold a secret about another sibling which puts both in a difficult position. Sometimes, all the siblings will know a secret but not know who knows. The sibling and family atmosphere is flooded with suspicion, lack of trust, insularity and anxiety.

John is the youngest of five children. When he was seven his oldest brother died in a boating accident, or at least this is what he was told. Jeremy, the eldest, was John's favourite sibling, the brother he admired and the one who cared and looked out for him. What John did not know, but the rest of the family did, was that Jeremy had shot himself. His parents had decided that the truth would be too much for the baby of the family, and the protective secret of seemingly good intent became what estranged John from the rest of his sibs. When John was nineteen, the age Jeremy had been when he died, he became engaged in a violent argument with his eldest sister. John was now the last one at home. He was acting up and, as he puts it, 'going through a rough patch'. This was upsetting his parents and the sister stepped in to support them. John and his sister hurled angry remarks at each other, and in the passion of the moment his sister screamed that he was 'just like his damn brother and why didn't he go and blow his head off too'. The Plutonic secret had come out and grabbed the innocent. Suddenly, betrayal, grief and rage were unleashed. He now knew why he hadn't felt part of the family all these years. This scenario is similar to what a family therapist describes here:

> Estrangement can be created through various subsystems of the family according to who knows, who doesn't know, and who doesn't know who knows. If a parent tells two siblings a secret about a third sibling, a secret alliance is formed between the two siblings and the parent, estranging the third child.[14]

Sometimes the spell of a secret is broken by genuine care and love and the urge to forge an authentic and intimate relationship. We know we must purge a secret before we can feel free of it. Amy is the third of four sisters. She describes the four of them as friends and now, in their adult years, their families have become close, sharing birthdays and holidays and the usual family rituals. But the three youngest share a secret about their oldest sister that is gnawing at Amy. Jane, the eldest, was sixteen when she was violently raped, became pregnant and had an abortion. Their parents had been divorced the year before and their father had just remarried. The trauma shook the family and Jane believed only her parents and the authorities knew what happened. She went to live with her father who 'took care of all the details'. Her younger sisters were told that Jane had gone to live with their father to take advantage of the school near by. Jane returned home a few months later and the separation from her sisters was not questioned because of all the family upheavals: their mother's adjustment, adolescence and acquainting themselves with their new step-mother. It was the step-mother who told Amy and her two sisters what had really happened to Jane. She also warned them not to tell anyone else for fear of reopening the whole ugly episode.

Twenty-five years later, Amy is haunted by feeling dishonest and says she often feels like an impostor with her sister, especially when her sister has been so supportive and approving of her. I asked Amy what she felt she must do. We explored the consequences. Pluto was natally conjunct the Moon in the twelfth house and she was just approaching her Pluto square. Pluto ruled the third house where the transit was taking place. One of the most powerful transiting combinations is when an outer planet is aspecting itself and also in aspect to an inner planet, recapitulating its natal theme. The psyche is ready to experience something powerful. She knew what she had to do. She wanted to take the risk and speak out, for, as she said, it was important to have an honest and intimate relationship with her sister. She felt empowered by the astrological image of her chart that spoke about her difficult task.

Secrets are powerful forces that inhibit the feelings of closeness and security in our relationships. However, it is prudent to differentiate between what is a secret and what privacy is. Attempting to be open, ridding ourselves of the dread of the secret, does not imply random disclosure as witnessed on American daytime television. Communal catharsis, public divulging and group purging are popularized New Age remedies, passing for the healing of familial wounds. Secrecy is Pluto's realm and his epithet of Hades was 'the invisible one'. Healing is done within the privacy and the intimacy of the human bond that has been damaged by the secret. Privacy is also an important aspect of the sibling bond, as we learn to be private within this system, to care for and nurture what is sacred to us. The difference between privacy and secrecy is that privacy helps define who we are, not deny who we are. We learn to be private to honour our sense of self, yet we hold a *secret* to deny a part of ourselves. When the secrets become collusive with others, as in a family secret, then the system is fractured by its own powerlessness and inability to be authentic.

Twins

Twins have held a perpetual fascination, as witnessed by the inclusion of the archetypal pair in the zodiac, the circle of life. We have already met the mythic twins of Castor and Pollux, Helen and Clytemnestra, Apollo and

Artemis, Etocles and Polynices, Byblis and Caunus, Zethus and Amphion and Narcissus and his sister. In this space I cannot do justice to the complexity of twinship, except to acknowledge twins and other multiple births as a special and significant category of sibship. While astrological research has spasmodically appeared on twins, a comprehensive and thorough examination of this unique area is still needed.[15] Psychological researchers are nearly as fascinated by this area as they are with birth order, and as Pluto in Sagittarius continues to reflect the opposite sign of Gemini, then perhaps more insight will be forthcoming.

Genes aside, twins face the same dilemmas as their other siblings except that the process of separation may be more intense and difficult. Having shared the same womb, their definition of themselves and orientation to life is fixed much more firmly on the other. Finding individuality in the constant presence of a mirror is perhaps the fate of the twin, who may differentiate through polarizing into the shadow side, or conversely through positive identification and merger. From an astrological point of view, twins share the same main chunks of their horoscopes and individuation is attained through their separate ways of approaching these patterns. They may divide up the horoscope or utilize the same planetary patterns in very different ways. The detailed techniques of astrology yield many ways to investigate difference between twins, but the main patterns of the horoscope are the same. What is more fascinating is how the twins weave their own story with the same material!

Raymond Brandt, the publisher of the magazine *Twins World*, said: 'I'm sixty-seven, and my identical twin died when we were twenty. I love my wife and sons in a very special way, but my twin was one half of me, he was my first love.'[16] Twins remind us of the intensity and primacy of the sibling bond.

Twin births are becoming more common for many reasons, including the use of fertility drugs and the later age of women having children which increases the chances of twins. Research is also suggesting that many solo births originally started as twins. Ultrasound has shown twin pregnancies which have become single pregnancies, the phenomenon known as 'the vanishing twin' syndrome. Archetypes are powerful images, and it seems that the archetypal imagery of Gemini and the missing twin may even be part of a genetic intelligence. A young client, with Gemini on the cusp of the twelfth house and the Moon in Gemini opposite Neptune in the sixth house, expressed that she felt as if she had lost a twin and was perpetually searching for her. She might have been!

Wendy also has Gemini on the twelfth house cusp with Saturn in this house. Saturn is involved with the Moon and Mercury in a Yod pattern and is the apex of a T-Square with Venus and Neptune/Chiron. The Neptune–Chiron conjunction falls exactly on the IC with Chiron taking the third house side, Neptune the fourth. Mercury rules both the twelfth and third houses and is opposite Pluto. The powerful aspects focusing on the twelfth house Saturn draw our attention to the collective and familial realms of the twelfth. But the twelfth house also supplies us with pre-birth images or perhaps illustrates how the feeling life of a mother can be absorbed by a baby while *in utero*.[17]

Wendy's mother suffered a horrible trauma when three months pregnant with Wendy. She was standing on the porch of her mid-western home waiting for her daughter, Patti, to cross the street. It was Patti's seventh birthday, and both mother and daughter were excited about the celebrations planned. A car swerving down the road, totally out of control, hit and knocked Patti down before smashing into the tree which brought it to a halt. Patti was killed instantly, and the family discovered later that the woman driving the car had suffered an epileptic seizure. The loss of the sibling is reflected in the images of Wendy's horoscope: Pluto opposite Mercury, ruler of the third; Chiron on the third house side of the IC; Moon opposite Uranus. The family atmosphere of the missing sister can be seen through Chiron–Neptune conjunct the IC opposite Venus, the ruler of the IC, both squaring Saturn in the twelfth. But Patti's was not the only life lost that day.

When Wendy was ten she was rushed to hospital as the attending doctor thought her appendix had ruptured. However, the problem was later traced to a growth, the size of a grapefruit, connected to the spine. Part of the bowel had to be removed in the operation and, because of the complications, the doctors thought Wendy had little chance of surviving. It was Easter, 1955. Progressed Mars was conjunct natal Mercury and progressed Mercury was just separating from the Sun. By transit Uranus was exactly on her ascendant with Jupiter close behind. These two planets would conjunct the next month just over one degree from her ascendant. Wendy did survive. The emergency of the Uranian experience often allows us to be separate enough from the trauma – through shock, disbelief or numbness – to survive such tumultuous events. But eleven years later, complications arose and Wendy was back in hospital; infection from the first operation was beginning to have an adverse effect. The doctors operated again.

The progressed Sun was now squaring Uranus. The progressed Sun, as

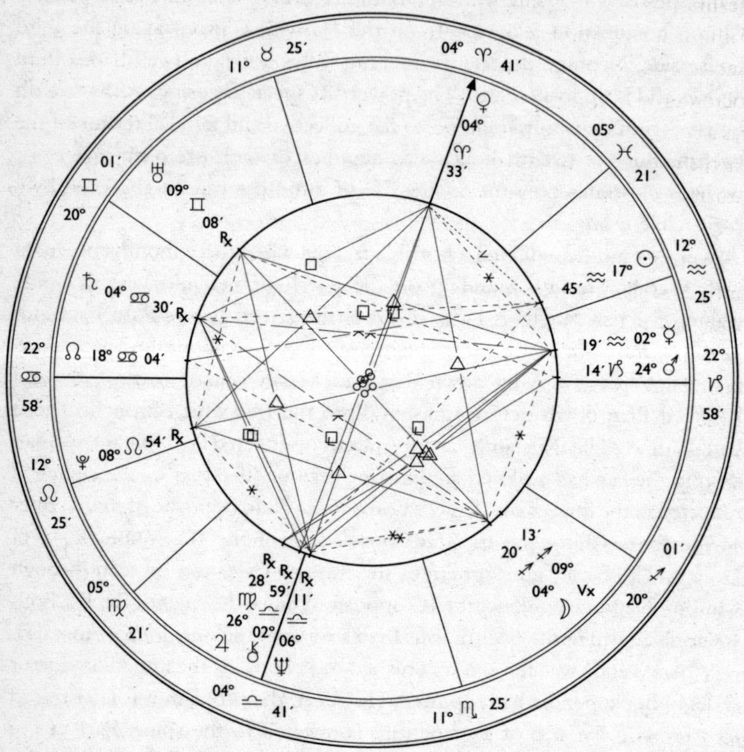

Figure 17: Wendy's horoscope.

her evolving ego strength, was ready to identify the part of herself she had been severed from. The Moon was progressing through the third house for the first time contributing to the consciousness of Wendy's sibling story. Within days of the operation Uranus and Pluto were making their second exact conjunction in her third house. It was after this operation that the doctors told Wendy what had been removed eleven years before. Wendy was a surviving twin and during the traumatic episode in her mother's womb, her twin was absorbed. Part of her twin had become adjoined to her spine. Saturn rules the spine, and in myth he interred his progeny. Saturn, in Wendy's twelfth house, described the pre-birth atmosphere.

Wendy's legacy of losing both siblings on the same day, before she was born, is clearer to her now. The fears of death that haunted her are manageable. The Pluto transit across her Moon and opposite Uranus with Uranus simultaneously transiting the Mercury–Pluto opposition, activated the powerful familial legacy. Twins serve as a literal reminder of the potency of the sibling bond. The twin image of fusion and merger is what we long to regress to. Yet twins also remind us of the inevitable sense of separateness and the quest to claim our singularity.

The opposite of twinning seems to be the fate of an only child. Only children have their own unique quest in learning how to cooperate, share, compete, separate, and experience the duality of feelings towards those they love. They have no literal siblings, except for their peers, upon whom to practise in their early years. Whereas the twin reminds us of the difficulty in separating and forging our individuality, the only child may find the difficulty in sharing and compromising. The only child's familial system is parentalized, and differentiating the structured hierarchical world from an independent equal system may be difficult.

Sibling issues are not just confined to childhood. As adults we search for ways to reconnect and rediscover our sibling bond, and these relationships are explored further in the final chapter.

Notes

1. Howard Sasportas, *The Twelve Houses*, 51.

2. The cases where charts are shown all belong to the generation with Uranus in Gemini, 1942–9. Saturn was also in Gemini from May 1942 to June 1944 (see also Appendix). Clients from all generations are influenced by the sibling relationship but this generation perhaps was more able to demonstrate its collective impact.

3. For more on the cycle of Chiron, see Brian Clark, *Keys to Understanding Chiron.* Two excellent sources on Chiron and its cycle are Melanie Reinhart, *Chiron and the Healing Journey* and *To the Edge and Beyond.*

4. One of the most chilling reminders of the replacement child was Adolf Hitler, three siblings died before he was born.

5. Stephen Bank and Michael Kahn, *The Sibling Bond*, 273.

6. Having the Sun, Moon and Node close together suggests Dorothy was born near the time of a Solar eclipse. This occurred the day before she was born. The cycles of eclipses are powerful images.

7 . For amplification on guilt and sibling death, see Robert Krell and Leslie Rabkin, 'The Effects of Sibling Death on the Surviving Child: a Family Perspective', in *Family Process* 18 (December 1979), 471–7.

8. Elisabeth Kubler-Ross, *On Death and Dying* (Macmillan, New York: 1969), 50–56.

9. Sasportas, *The Twelve Houses*, 189.

10. Ovid, *Metamorphoses*, Book 9.215–21.

11. Laura M. Markowitz, 'Shared Passages', in *Family Therapy Networker* 18, no. 1 (January/February 1994), 27. Reporting of sibling incest to authorities is frequently not done. The secret is maintained by the siblings. If the incest is revealed, then the family often closes in to contain the event, attempting to hide the shame rather than deal with it. Hence accurate statistics of sibling incest are difficult to maintain. But family therapists, social workers, psychologists and family sociologists all report the high frequency of occurrence.

12. Adolf Guggenbuhl-Craig, *Marriage Dead or Alive*, trans. Murray Stein (Spring, Zurich: 1977), 58.

13. Ernest Jones, *Hamlet and Oedipus: the Oedipus Complex as an Exploration of Hamlet's Mystery* (Doubleday, New York: 1958), 157–8.

14. Peggy Papp, 'The Worm in the Bud: Secrets Between Parents and Children', in Evan Imber-Black (ed.), *Secrets in Families and Family Therapy* (W. W. Norton, New York: 1993), 68.

15. Suzel Fuzeau-Braesch, 'An Empirical Study of an Astrological Hypothesis in a Twin Population', in *Personal and Individual Differences* 13, no. 10 (February 1992), 67, concluded positively that 'a psychological profile, based upon astrological differences connected with the respective moments of birth of twins is discernible to a certain degree which is statistically impossible to attribute to chance'.

16. Jill Neimark, 'Nature's Clones', in *Psychology Today* 30, no. 4 (July/August 1997).

17. Howard Sasportas refers to the twelfth house as a pre-birth image: see 'The Stages of Childhood', in Liz Greene and Howard Sasportas, *The Development of the Personality*, 101–2. Interestingly, Sasportas says: 'if Saturn is in the twelfth, then Saturnian feelings pass from mother to developing embryo via the umbilical cord', 26. Tad Mann's technique also includes the twelfth house as part of the process of gestation that starts with the ninth: see *Life-Time Astrology* (Allen & Unwin, London, 1984), 175–9.

13

Adult Relationships Between Siblings

Transits, Progressions and the Evolving Sibling Relationship

Unlike all other organisations, families incorporate new members only by birth, adoption or marriage, and members can leave only by death, if then.

Betty Carter and Monica McGoldrick[1]

Our sisters and brothers are part of our sibling and family systems for life. For many siblings, leaving home marks the beginning of a gradual movement away from the familiarity of the sibling relationship and out into the world. Even though contact may continue, there is less daily involvement between siblings. Regular meetings between adult sibs generally occur for anniversaries, birthdays and ritual holiday gatherings. This contact, often in the family home, exerts a tremendous pull back to the past, and rather than meeting siblings as they are now, we engage with them as they were then. The tension of growing apart is abated by this regression to the past. Quite instinctively we slip back into the old patterns of relating, find our old niche and claim back our comfortable roles, share the memories rather than our current lives and sentimentalize rather than feel. Sharing the way it used to be inhibits the forging of an adult relationship with our siblings. Instead, we continue to sacrifice a new relationship for the comfort of what we had. Adult relationships may also become complicated by our siblings' partners, their new families or lifestyles. Primary loyalties have shifted from the family unit, forcing us to readdress sibling relationships. To establish adult relationships demands that we also accept sibs' significant others.

The author of the book *Original Kin*, Marion Sandmaier, explores 'the search for connection amongst adult sisters and brothers'. In fact this is the sub-title of her book, reminiscent of the Geminian theme of questing for the sibling–other. She writes of her own journey of reconnection and reconciliation with her estranged brother. In one poignant moment she describes the unique bond between siblings. They have just shared a funny story and she observes her brother's reaction. She says: 'I leaned back and watched my brother, who was shaking with glee like a ten year old. And I understood in that moment that my brother and I belonged to each other in a way that nobody else in the universe ever would or could and that it was going to be worth the continuing struggle to stay in each other's lives. And it seemed important at that point to communicate my feelings to him on this subject.'[2]

Removed from the family atmosphere, adults are challenged to find a mature relationship with their siblings. Restoration of the sibling bond 'that nobody else in the universe' could replicate is often an integral part of mid-life and beyond. While this can take the form of a literal reconciliation with our sibling/s, it is most important as an internal journey of reconnection with the sibling archetype. Adult siblings may continue to place their brothers and sisters in the same roles they had in childhood, by still competing and persisting with rivalry, avoiding the formation of a new relationship. What we may in fact be avoiding is the consciousness that our early familial experiences have bound us into a common destiny. The sibling relationship survives throughout our lifetime, unlike our parents who leave us, or our children who join us. In this way, the sibling relationship is unique as it may be the only familial relationship that spans the course of our lifetime: the only possible lifelong companion is the sibling. They provide a continuity from childhood through to adult life.

What makes this bond so unique is the shared past of the familial bond. Siblings are co-participants in the family drama, witnesses to our early years and the custodians of memories long forgotten. Sometimes we may wish to forget the memories that are reflected back. When the pain of living with our siblings has been too great, then adult estrangement protects us from the wounds reopening and becoming reinfected. The memories of who we were in the past that are carried by our sibs are powerful. As Laura Markowitz puts it:

> Siblings are the living remnant of our past, a buffer against the loss of our own history, the deepest, oldest memories of us as we were almost from the beginning. But in these memories lies a terrible power: every time we see our siblings, they hold up a mirror before us, forcing us to look at an image of ourselves that may be either comforting or devastating, perhaps evoking self-acceptance and pride, perhaps shame and humiliation.[3]

The death of the parents will be a turning point in the sibling system. This is the crucial stage that will either bring the siblings closer together or keep them in isolation. Without the parents, hierarchy is altered. Childhood has truly gone and the siblings no longer have the parental buffer. The parental inheritance is announced and this can reawaken rivalry. Favouritism in the parental legacy can be a blow that the sibling relationship may never be able to recover from. In other instances, I have witnessed the fight for the parental legacy bring siblings together. Two sisters, estranged since their early twenties, joined forces when their father died to contest his will. Their father's will decreed that his *de facto* partner would receive everything, including their mother's estate, inherited by their father when she died. Their father had told each of them they would inherit everything when he died. Therefore they were suspicious that his partner had forced him into signing a new will. During the trial, the sisters re-found their relationship. They were the only ones left from their family of origin and externalizing the fight for their father's inheritance provided a setting for coming to terms with their shared familial legacy.

The astrological movements in the horoscope cannot determine how the adult sibling relationship will develop – that is in the hands of the individual – but they do suggest when the archetypal image of the sibling may be highlighted. Throughout the passage of our lives, the effect of the sibling relationship will be constellated through other adult relationships, not only the primary sibling relationship. The sibling world is an archetypal world that not only seeks its expression in our future but has its roots in our and our ancestors' past. Transits and progressions are powerful images that are reflective of the evolving relationship with both living and deceased family members. Transits are systemic since a major transit to one family member's horoscope affects the other members, including the siblings.[4]

I will now explore some of the progressions and transits that could synchronize with the evolution and understanding of the sibling relationship.[5]

The progressed Moon: our emotional archives

The secondary progressed Moon is the most appropriate astrological tool for tracking the emotional development and evolution of an individual. The progressed Moon's movement registers our emotional reactions, the impact of the familial atmosphere and the climatic changes that occur in the family system. The Moon has no personal container in the early years, being contained by mother and the family, and therefore participates freely in the feeling life. Through the 'participation mystique' the child feels, senses and records the moods and feelings of the family members within the system. The Moon registers and remembers these feelings and the emotional reaction to them, becoming the record of our feeling life. Hence the progressed Moon represents the archives of all that we have tasted, touched, wanted, smelt and felt. Memories are mostly unconscious, stored in the psyche as images, symbols, feelings and instinct, or imprinted in the body. Lunar memory in the body may be stored in the adrenal or olfactory glands, the tension in the muscles, or our allergies and illnesses. These primal Lunar responses may find their way into consciousness through our eating habits, our moods, our body shape and also the emotional patterns repeated throughout our adult relationships. The Moon is habitual and it is through its steady progression throughout the horoscope that we can become conscious of the feeling life that underlies our emotional responses.

The progressed Moon circumvents the horoscope three times in an average life span, symbolizing the three distinct developmental stages of the youth, the adult and the elder. The average time to progress through a house is two and a third years, a period when the emotional life is focused on a particular sphere. The light of the Moon reflects the feeling life, instincts, habits, emotional patterns and motives, as well as the level of emotional safety and security in the territory it is passing through. Progressing through a house, the Moon points to areas of life we are becoming sensitive and responsive to, as well as the sphere of our lives where we need to assimilate a greater sense of emotional security.

Matrilineal tradition separates the Lunar cycle into three phases, symbolized as the maiden, the mother and the crone. Lunar goddesses were threefold in nature: the youthful and unattached maiden represented by the New Moon, the woman of power as mother and equal as the Full Moon, and the crone, wise woman and elder of the Dark Moon. For example, Hera is associated with three phases of life, reflected by her names Pais, the maiden, Teleia, the fulfilled and Chera, the solitary. Applying this threefold nature to the progressed Moon suggests that during its first revolution (from 0 to 27.3 years old), the Moon is absorbing, recording, gathering experience, feeling, and participating in the feeling life of the tribe. Emotional maturity is marked by the completion of its first revolution at the age of twenty-seven. By then, we have recorded every emotional experience available to us. Its second journey through the horoscope (from 27.3 to 54.6 years old) is now the phase of adult life, when new emotional and personal attachments are formed. We begin to remember and relive our earlier emotional experiences in an adult context. A greater choice about our emotional responses and an ability to differentiate our feelings from those of others is part of our maturation.

The third circuit of the progressed Moon (from 54.6 to 82 years old) initiates us into the elder phase of life, the wise woman, grandmother, tribal elder and crone, when emotional experiences are more anchored and directed, less reactive and instinctual. Our emotional attitudes are more integrated and understood and add to a sense of well-being for the whole community. These phases correspond with the contemporary family life cycle of child, parent and grandparent, that the ancients saw as the maiden or child, the mother or bride and the crone or widow. The three generations of the family are continually part of the progressed Lunar cycle.

In terms of the sibling relationship, the progressed Moon is of most interest when it is progressing through the houses of relationship, especially the third house. When the Moon progresses through the third, the archetype of the sibling will be activated. In the first cycle, an important emotional statement in relation to the sibling may have been recorded – recognizing feelings of love or care towards a peer, sharing with others, familiarity with the duality of feelings or the comfort of companionship. Equally, darker feelings may have been registered such as intense rivalry, brutality, betrayal or feeling unsafe in relationship, mistrusting of companionship. Wendy (see Chapter 12) was told that the growth originally removed from her spine was connected to her lost twin when the Moon progressed through the third house for the first time. The progressed Moon in the third reflected light on the mystery of her lost siblings. The third is the first terrain of consciousness and as the Moon progresses through here, deep emotional or feeling life may be brought into consciousness. An emotional event such as the birth, separation, initiation or rite of passage of a sibling may have been registered by the Moon in its first passage through the third house. As the Moon progresses through the third house, for the first time we become aware of the feelings towards sibling/s and their impact on future relationships. Planets in the third house and the patterns they suggest will be triggered as the Moon progresses through this sector. The natal pattern of the sibling relationship is consciously felt and recorded.

As the progressed Moon moves through the third house in its second and adult cycle, the focus is turned back to the primary relationship with the sibling. I vividly remember attempting to amplify to a client the image of the progressed Moon's passage into the third house. It had just entered this sphere of her horoscope. When I mentioned the sibling relationship, she exclaimed: 'I just heard from my brother last month and he is coming down to visit me next week.' Not particularly eventful for most, but for this woman, who had been estranged from her brother for over twenty years, it was momentous. This meeting was an attempt at reconciliation. The image that always remained with me was that the progressed Moon 'hit' the third house cusp, and bells (literally, in this case the phone) went off. The second passage of the Moon through the third house may revive incomplete sibling themes. As adults we are in a position to examine the early relationship more clearly and sometimes more objectively. The Moon also acts as a loosening agent as it progresses through the chart, breaking up the psychic complexes and resistances that defend this territory. As it progresses through the third, it may catalyse some of our earlier memories of our sibling relationship. We saw in Chapter 5 how Susan's dream of her brother facilitated her understanding of the impact that her protective and enmeshed sibling relationship had on her present relationships. As the Moon progressed through the third, Susan was better able to manage her negative feelings that had been hidden behind her protection of her brother. This pattern began with brother and continued to repeat itself in her adult relationships with men. The third house progressed Moon ignited the memory of how this pattern began. The psyche's propensity for dream images as a messenger to the ego's realm is important, as the sibling may appear in the dream to alert us to the shadow material that is being unearthed. This is Lunar memory. This passage of adult life brings to light a more conscious understanding of our sibling dynamics. Instinctively we may find ourselves drawn to reconnect with our siblings, attempting to nurture the early relationships.

During this phase of adult life, when the Moon progresses through the third, we may be drawn into the examination of our sibling relationships and their impact on our current relationships. We may now be ready to enter into adult relationship with our siblings. If this is not possible, we may recognize the need to relinquish it and mourn the loss. During the second passage we will recall whether we felt comfortable or were able to feel that we belonged in the sibling system; we have more emotional latitude as to whether we are going to connect with our sib/s in a personal and individual way. With the Moon progressing through the third, we are more able to discern the individuality of our sibs and not just see them as members of a group, or keep them fixed in the role they played in our childhood.

The Moon is our emotional barometer and indicator of how best to vent our feelings. As the Moon progresses through the third house, in its third and final phase, we come to find peace and reconciliation in the sibling relationship. During this phase we are most likely drawn together because of an important transition in the family life cycle: the death of a parent or another family member, the birth of a grandchild, the rite of passage of one of our children, grandchildren or member of the extended family. This progression will also draw to the surface the feelings regarding our relationships with our partners and friends, the sibling substitutes of our lives. Lunar memory will recall much of the relationship with the sibling over the life span. With its third movement through this house, it consciously addresses our sense of communal belonging and whether this applies to our siblings. As it moves through the third towards the IC in this phase, consciousness is turned towards the 'end of life', providing a nest and a sense of security for the latter years. This may or may not include the sibling.

While the progressed Moon's passage through the seventh or eleventh house may not speak directly of the sibling relationship, this is often highlighted as these spheres connect us back to our earlier sibling relationships. It is during the first cycle that these links are probably more visible, when our forays into relating are often witnessed and shared by the sibling. The progression of the Moon through the seventh house focuses on the adult relationship, while the progression through the eleventh focuses on our social circles of friends and colleagues. The shadow of the sibling is ready to be constellated in these situations whether they are personified as the other in the triangle with our partner or appear as the rival other in our professional life. The connection between our adult relationship and the sibling is apparent when the progressed Moon crosses the descendant in its second cycle. Here the psyche is sensitive to relational issues and is beginning to recognize the patterns in our adult relationships. Quite often I have seen that the sibling other becomes important again at this time, as a representative of the primal sense of comfort in relationship. The Moon through the seventh will reflect light on the relational pattern in one's life and often brings the incomplete aspects of the sibling relationship into the present one.

The progression of the inner planets

The secondary progression of the other inner planets may also inform us of the evolving sibling relationship. The progressed Sun may be active at the birth of a sibling which complements Freud's premise that the birth of a sibling is a jolt to consciousness and the first sense of being separate for an elder child. This coming to consciousness through the facility of the sibling or the sibling image could also be reflected in the adult progressions of the Sun. The progressed Sun is a symbol of the development of conscious life, the growing sense of self and identity in the world. As the Sun progresses, we expand our tolerance and awareness of differences to accommodate and include other ways of being. With the birth of a sibling we need to be more tolerant and are initiated into our own sense of individuality. This developing sense of individuality and difference is constantly tested in the sibling system, as it is in all our relationships. I see the progressed Sun as an important indicator of our growing awareness of self in our relationships with others: siblings, partners, friends. The Solar progression is also synchronous with the growing ability to feel more centred in ourselves and the development of a strong ego container. This allows us to move through narcissistic stages and be more conscious of tolerating differences in others. The progressed Sun is the creation of the capacity to begin to tolerate shadow and foreign aspects in others and is often synchronous with important turning points in relationship.

Progressions of the Sun to other inner planets may signal sibling themes. The progressed Sun's aspects to Mercury, Venus and Mars are those I have found to be the most significant for identifying sibling issues or themes. The progressed Sun in aspect to natal Mars could trigger the awareness of rivalry, competition, an intruder in the environs, aggressive feelings, as well as a sense of independence and separateness. With this progression we may become more aware of our individuality and how we express this sense of independence and energy. This may be intimately tied to the experience of a sibling who may have been the original catalyst for this sense of individuality.

The Sun's progressed aspects to Venus signal a growing consciousness of our self-esteem, sense of value and personal tastes, as well as our comfort: relating and feeling equal and attractive to others. An emphasis on our sense of body image, sensuality, creativity and sexuality may come to light. These are components of the earlier sibling relationship which now could be released into consciousness. If Venus is later in zodiacal longitude than the Sun, we will experience the progressed Sun conjunct Venus at some point in the first half of life (maximum age approximately forty-eight), an important progression to note for the herald of an important relationship, recalling the earliest layers of the sibling relationship. In contemporary astrology, this is more an image of the inner marriage, a consciousness of valuing the self or the love of the self. However, this 'marriage' may also stir the archetype of the brother–sister marriage and awaken the earlier images of love and sexuality experienced through our siblings. It is an image of union but often I have seen the progressed Sun in aspect to Venus as a reconciliation with the sister for either sex. Ultimately, it is the consciousness of our own internal sister and feminine figure.

The progressed Sun's aspects to Mercury will speak most directly of the sibling pattern and the astrological combination may speak of the necessity of clarity, understanding and reconciliation in our sibling relationships. It may also signal the conscious need to separate and claim equality in the system. Again, if Mercury is ahead of the Sun in zodiacal longitude, the Sun will progress to a conjunction within the first twenty-eight years of life. In reference to the sibling, this progression suggests becoming conscious of the dynamic of the relationship and its impact on how we express ourselves and communicate effectively with our current partner.

The progressed Mercury is a symbol of the evolving relationship with our siblings. Its change of signs offers us greater tolerance and scope in our sibling relationships and its aspects to the other planets may bring about a greater understanding of the relationship dynamics.

When Mercury is retrograde natally, it is more intently focused on a specific area. If an individual has Mercury retrograde, then during the years spent at home with the sibs the progressed Mercury is focused on a specific zodiacal ground. This symbolizes the intensity of the relationship. Mercury retrograde may be symbolic of a much more deep and complex relationship to the sibling. The progressed change of Mercury's direction can also be significant in marking a distinct change in the sibling relationship. As it turns direct, the progression may signify a turning away from the intensity and focus on the sibling. As Mercury moves from a retrograde to a direct position, we may feel a greater sense of freedom within our sibling system, being more capable of accepting the complexity of the relationship. The planet aspected by the progression of Mercury would symbolize the sibling dynamic or theme that is ready to be seen in a different light.

Progressed Venus or Mars may be linked to the evolving relationship with either a sister or a brother. Both are important in their progressed aspects to the other planets in the horoscope, as well as the years they may change direction. Margaret (see Chapter 12) had her retrograde progressed Mars enter the square to her natal Chiron when she had the incestuous experience with her brother. The natal Chiron/Mars square was triggered by progression. As well, progressed Venus was trine her natal Mars stimulating the Mars/Venus themes of sexual exploration. When Margaret came for a consultation, her progressed Mars was stationary going direct. Her progressed Venus was opposite her natal Uranus, trine her natal Pluto and sextile her natal Venus, all suggesting a powerful new alignment with her sense of self-worth and sexuality/femininity. The powerful progressions of Mars and Venus were synchronous with her beginning to feel free of the sexual shame of her earlier relationship with her brother. The adult progressions were now able to forge a new image of her brother.

The progressions of Venus and Mars are often synchronous with the formation and sustaining of adult relationship, therefore there is a possible sibling undertow. Because these archetypes are often embodied by a literal sister or brother, the progressions may also parallel important turning points in the siblings' lives.

The impact of the outer planets' transits

Transits in our adult years may be helpful indicators to times when the sibling themes and dynamics are in focus and when reconciliation or separation may be more appropriate in our sibling relationships. The prime indicators would be when the outer planets are transiting the inner planets, especially Mercury, Venus or Mars, or the angles of the horoscope, more notably the ascendant–descendant axis. Transits to the Sun and Moon, as well as the MC–IC, may present sibling dynamics, but they are probably connected to the parents and family. As the Sun, Moon or Meridian is transited, the family system, which contains the sibling system, is affected. The issues may be systemic, familial or generational, and may not necessarily speak exclusively of the sibling relationship, although the sibling could be the identified one during the transit.

Uranus' cycle in our adult life presents what has been relinquished. The transit of Uranus can bring the severed parts of our lives into consciousness – the separations, the unlived aspects, the untravelled roads. What was abandoned, split off or dismembered is met again as Uranus' cycle impacts upon our lives. What Uranus shatters is the fixity that the ego has employed to keep these aspects of self away from consciousness. With reference to the sibling, the Uranus transit may offer an opportunity for reconnection and reconciliation or, conversely, may break the symbiotic tie.

Neptune loosens the bonds that keep us blind to our larger potential. The planet's cycle is synchronous with the times of life when there is less certainty, clarity and direction. What is missing presents itself through yearnings, fantasies and dreams. In an adult context, the transits of Neptune help to formulate a spiritual perspective, as the ego is forced to confront the difference between what can be incarnate and what cannot. All the outer planets conspire to break down the ego defences and constructs, encouraging the authenticity of self; however, Neptune's nature is more evasive and illusive. All boundaries of time, priority, identity and certainty are subtly shifted and rearranged until the ego feels lost. A sacrifice is demanded so the initiate may be able to move on. For siblings who are enmeshed and have been unable to separate from their symbiotic bond, this transit could help dissolve the web of their relationship. For siblings who are disengaged, there could be a longing to bond with the lost one.

Pluto brings about a much more definite encounter with the underworld of the self. In an adult context, Pluto transits reveal unresolved loss, activating an encounter with grief. Pluto is synonymous with disclosure, revelation and remembering. The past returns so that we may let it go, and the shades ask to be properly buried so that life may be renewed. In the context of the sibling, there is now the necessity to mourn these losses, confront the secrets and strive for a more authentic and intimate bond. We may be ready to deal with what keeps us compulsively bound to the sibling image, letting go of the residue of unexpressed feelings towards our earliest companions.

The outer planets' transit to Mercury are a potential indicator of a shift in the sibling dynamic. Mercury symbolizes how we negotiated our place in the system, found our niche and were able to find our unique expression in the larger group. Mercury's role as a guide, the patron of travel and as *psychopomp*, is important as well. During a transit to Mercury, the sibling may guide us to another level of understanding. The transit may not always manifest as a literal sibling who embodies the role of guide or fellow traveller, but it will be a similar substitute. Transiting Pluto to Mercury brings the Underworld god into the sibling system, exposing the truth of the relationship. Perhaps the sibling needs to disclose a secret in order to heal the relationship. The death, or threat of death, of one of the siblings may become an issue. Mercury was the guide into Pluto's domain; during this transit the sibling may be the guide into an unknown aspect of the past, an agent of revelation or the trickster who uncovers the darker aspects of the self. In our adult years this would bring an intensification of the relationship, and a need for honesty and integrity with the sibling. However, some of the resentment and powerful feeling towards the sib may first have to be expurgated. If we cannot do this, then we must face the fear of letting the relationship go.

Transiting Neptune to Mercury confronts our ideals of the sibling relationship, the illusions that we may have carried to defend a sense of feeling disappointed in the relationship. The dynamic as we knew it may be dissolving; there is a loosening of the bond and a potential new one emerging. Certainly this transit may synchronize with the image of the internal sibling appearing in dreams, memories, visions, reconnecting us to the image of the lost sibling. The individual may feel lost, directionless and unable to navigate using old maps and theories; however, the inner guide through this shifting landscape may be a figure inspired by the sibling.

Uranus to Mercury symbolizes separation from the sibling. This could be a conscious awareness of either a sibling or partner entering or leaving our space. If there is a crisis of accession, this may be accompanied by feelings of suffocation, a lack of space, and feeling invaded. If this is a crisis of disengagement, the separation may constellate abandonment, accompanied by feelings of panic, anxiety or relief. Consciousness towards the sibling is heightened. In our adult years, Uranus reconnects what has been severed, so this may be an image of the reconnection to a sibling from whom we are separated.

Transits to Venus may awaken our relationship to the inner feminine, partially shaped by our relationship to sister. If we have a sister, then this may synchronize with the literal relationship to her. However, if we do not have a sister, this transit may awaken the sister archetype in our relationships. With Pluto transiting Venus, a woman may be aware of the need to deal with her dark feelings towards her 'sisters', now incarnate in a rival, an associate or acquaintance. This transit offers the confrontation with the darker feeling side, carried by a sisterly double or the sister herself. For a man, a powerful Eros is awoken, which may confront the brother–sister taboo; he may be aware of a dangerous force making him face up to his feelings. Ultimately, the man's desires lead to a confrontation with intimacy and a sense of equality and fairness in his relationships. In adult years, this transit facilitates more comfort with the darker sides of his own internal feminine, represented as the dark sister.

Neptune to Venus engages us with the creative power of the feminine and the sister archetype. We may feel the need to relinquish a personal relationship to find the creativity or spiritual union that we seek. As an adult, this transit may suggest that we are able to negotiate more equality in our relationships and break the enmeshment or the victim role played out with the sister. We may be drawn to engaging with the sister archetype as creatrix and muse. This is a 'soulful' transit that stirs the longing for the other half, an image often carried by the sibling archetype.

Uranus' effect by transit is to shock, to jolt us into consciousness. Transiting to Venus, we may be shocked to locate feelings we are disconnected from. Both sexes may be more capable of separating from the ancestral feminine images, confirmed through familial experiences. Uranus offers a radically different perspective: our severed sister relationship may present for reconciliation, or our symbiotic relationship with our sister may be shattered. A new perspective on the feminine is becoming conscious.

Similarly, transits to Mars may speak of the brother image being stirred, literally or psychologically. Fraternal themes range from rivalry to loyalty, fratricide to sacrifice. For sisters, mythic brothers were protective and heroic, but sometimes, like Apollo, too controlling. The mythic brother could also be their partner and spouse. Transits to Mars will awaken these themes. For a woman, her internal brother, her equal and partner, is constellated. For a man, the outer planets' transits to Mars awaken the brotherly themes of rivalry and competition, or challenge and support. As an adult, he may have to confront both the inner rival and ally in order to forge a truce between the warring aspects of himself. This transit often presents a literal threat or challenge to the man, personified by a brother-figure, which constellates his desire and urge to be independent.

Pluto transiting a woman's Mars may stir powerful feelings to be equal in relationship or to venture independently to claim her own desires and destiny, contacting the powerful figure of her own internal brother. For a man, this transit may awaken the incomplete feelings with his brother, healing archaic feelings of resentment and powerlessness. With Neptune transiting Mars, a woman may have to sacrifice her old way of being in relationship to the brother-figure to find her new partner. This dissolution of the bond to the external brother may be necessary to facilitate the emergence of her own heroic and independent animus image. A man may face disappointment with his brother having idealized the relationship. Through this transit the complexity of the enmeshment with the brother or brother-figures becomes apparent for both sexes. Uranus to Mars stimulates the desire to challenge the brother, to separate from his dominance and be independent. The Uranus–Mars transit is a call to equality with the masculine and the opportunity to forge a unique and liberating relationship with the brother.

With the outer transits to Venus or Mars, the literal brother or sister may become a living symbol for dynamic internal changes that are taking place in our lives. These transits could also signify the urge to resolve the relationships with our siblings who are intricately part of our lives and whose influence contributed to shaping our relational patterns.

Into the third

Jupiter and Saturn will transit through the third house more than once in an average life span. Jupiter's nature by transit is to magnify what is inherently ready to be brought to consciousness. If nothing is ready to be dealt with then nothing happens: more of nothing *is* nothing. But if a dilemma is festering, Jupiter's tendency is to blow it up. In the third, I take note of any unresolved issues around the siblings. Jupiter's gift is the ability to put the situation into a life context, endowing it with meaning and strengthening the facility to grapple with bigger issues.

Because Jupiter's cycle will return every twelve years to the third house, there are opportunities over one's life to expand one's understanding in relation to the sibling. An only child may feel more able to relate to a wider system, as Jupiter transits the third, while an elder may feel less inclined to be stuck in the role of responsible one. The transit could also be lived through one of our siblings who may go back to university, travel overseas, become affiliated with a new church: the sibling being the catalyst for our own inner change. As Jupiter moves through the third, it is interesting to take note of the developments with our siblings, as they are indicators of what may be shifting inside ourselves.

Saturn will transit the third house three times in an average life. Like the progressed Moon, the transits of Saturn divide the life into three phases. Saturn represents the building of ego structures through concentrated effort and dedication. As it passes through the third, the opus may begin its focus on the sibling issues. Its transit of the third in our adult years may synchronize with establishing a more mature relationship with our siblings, engaging together as adults. Saturn's cycle leads us further into the world, and therefore is constantly suggesting separation from dependent structures, as its purpose is in establishing autonomy and self-regulation. Saturn is the formation of boundary, and as it passes through the third the boundaries between the siblings may be examined. It may be necessary to find an autonomous voice, learn to speak for ourselves and define more clearly the nature of the relationship. Saturn is about responsibility, and we may now be more inclined to say what we need to say to our siblings in order to commit ourselves to a more honest relationship. The reality of the Saturn transit may redefine our sibling responsibilities, re-examining our roles and coming to new arrangements and agreements about the management of familial tasks. The consequences of our relationship to siblings could become visible. We may feel alone and separate from our sibs, and take the responsibility for trying to bridge the distance. A new foundation for these relationships and relationship in general may be laid.

The outer planets' transit of the third may not happen in a lifetime but if it does, the transit will be for a long period of time.[6] Sibling issues may be brought to the surface when these planets aspect other planets while they transit the third house sphere. Uranus, Neptune or Pluto transiting the third house may exacerbate our relational patterns. If these transits occur when we are younger, they may symbolize the lifelong imprint the sibling relationship marks upon our adult relationships.

Outer planets rising across the descendant may also bring sibling themes sharply into focus. This is especially significant when the planet may be in the third house natally. With the planet moving from the third into the seventh, the larger area of relationship is examined and the primary influence of the sibling becomes of utmost importance. The planet crossing the descendant may signal a sibling re-entering our lives, or the shadow of the sibling archetype rising up to conscious awareness.

Uranus was rising over Margaret's descendant (see Chapter 12) when she discussed her sexual encounter with her brother for the first time. Transiting Uranus in our youth may symbolize what we split off from, or cut out; but in our adult years the transit may bring back what was disenfranchised. What may have been necessary to separate from when we were younger may not be necessary now: the ego is stronger and the psyche demands a chance to integrate what has been disconnected. In this way the Uranus cycle is a powerful link back to what has been severed.

Marian has Neptune in the third house and has always described her relationship with her sister as difficult. She recognizes now how often she rescued her sister by taking the blame for her and suffering the parental punishment for something her sister was ultimately responsible for. When

Neptune transited her descendant, Marian's sister, Jennifer, came back into her life. Jennifer had escaped from an abusive relationship and moved in with Marian. As adult sisters they were redefining their relationship. Their estrangement was being confronted and Marian felt she coped better with her sister and was more aware of her instinctive tendency to rescue her sibling. Their arguments were more honest and their feelings were now overt.

Chiron's cycle is less obvious owing to its irregular orbit transiting the sign of Aries in nearly eight years while spending less than two years in Libra. Each generation will experience differing crisis points in its fifty-year cycle.[7] Chiron's transits through the third house, as well as the seventh and eleventh, and to Mercury, Venus and Mars, should be noted for sibling themes. The transits of Chiron in adult life synchronize with reopening earlier wounds so that the innate consciousness and intelligence, which is part of the wound itself, can be released for healing. Chiron's cycle may parallel the healing of wounds incurred in our sibling relationship.

Towards Aquarius

As mentioned from time to time in this book, the outer planets' transits at the dawn of the new millennium signal an individual awareness of a global family. With Uranus and Neptune both transiting Aquarius, the collective definition of equality, shared space, individuality, and fair shares becomes paramount. Pluto mirrors the Geminian theme from its residence in the sign of Sagittarius, and draws our primal experiences of being a sibling to the surface. The archetype of the sibling is being constellated and therefore it will be seen more often on our television and film screens, in our consulting rooms and, more personally, in our own lives.

As we focus more on this primal relationship we become more aware of its uniqueness. The sibling is the witness to our lives, a companion throughout the life cycle, a confidante of our early secrets, an ally against the tyranny of the parental system, a friend when we felt insecure, our first partner, a rival for the top spot and a link back to the earliest memories. It is a multi-faceted and unusual relationship. We share the same genes and family history with our siblings, yet we are allotted our own individual fate.

The new millennium heralds a new age which speaks of global equality. But this vision of sisterhood and brotherhood – *siblinghood* – will first constellate our own unique experiences within the sibling system, promoting a coming to consciousness of the sibling archetype lost under the exclusivity of the hierarchy and patriarchy.

Notes

1. Betty Carter and Monica McGoldrick, 'Overview: the Changing Family Life Cycle – a Framework for Family Therapy', in *The Changing Family Life Cycle*, Carter and McGoldrick (eds), 5.
2. Marian Sandmaier, *Original Kin: the Search for Connection Among Adult Sisters and Brothers.*
3. Laura M. Markowitz, 'Shared Passages', in *Family Therapy Networker* 18, no. 1 (January/February 1994), 69.
4. Erin Sullivan, *Dynasty: the Astrology of Family Dynamics*, 206, describes the impact of transits on familial patterns.
5. When referring to progressions, I will be referring exclusively to secondary progressions which use the equation: 1 day = 1 year. This is my preferred system of progressions/directions, as it keeps the ratio of the planet's speed and its direction intact: see Brian Clark, *Secondary Progressions* (Astro*Synthesis Series, Melbourne: 1992).
6. For a description of the outer planets transiting the third house, see Howard Sasportas, *The Gods of Change.*
7. See Brian Clark, *Keys to Understanding Chiron.*

Appendix
Birth Data Used in the Text

Birth details, along with the source of the birth data for Freud, Adler and Jung, are noted with their horoscopes. Birth data used in Chapter 12 is listed below. The data is from the clients.

Joan	2 December 1943	4.30 a.m. GDT	37S49 1444E58
Martin	27 February 1949	11.00 a.m. GST	37S49 144E58
Sean	14 January 1942	7.50 a.m. GDT	37S49 144E58
Dorothy	22 May 1947	1.35 a.m. GST	33S52 151E13
Margaret	17 November 1943	9.30 p.m. BST (GMD)	51N06 000W43
Wendy	6 February 1945	4.20 p.m. CWT	41N39 092W21

Glossary

A PRIORI derived from the Latin to suggest being there from the first place or inherent.

ALEMBIC a glass or copper vessel used by alchemists for distillation. Psychologically, the image is significant and used to describe a symbolic vessel or container.

ANIMA from the Latin meaning 'soul' and used in both Jungian and popular psychological jargon to represent the unconscious feminine side of a man.

ANIMUS from the Latin meaning 'spirit' and used in both Jungian and popular psychological jargon to represent the unconscious masculine side of a woman. Jung developed this in reference to his conceptualization of the anima and suggested each were archetypal.

CATABASIS refers to a descent into the Underworld.

CHAOS from the Greek suggesting 'yawning void', a chasm from which creation comes into being.

CONJUNCTIO an alchemical term used to describe the marriage of opposites, the union of the male and female, the King and Queen, Sol and Luna and the combination of Mercury and Sulphur.

COSMOGONY from the Greek *cosmos* meaning 'world' or 'universe' and *gony* meaning 'genesis' or 'beginning', hence the beginning of the universe. For the Greeks, cosmos was also beauty and order, hence the birth of beauty or an ordered universe. The term refers to the myths of creation.

COSMOS the world or universe and also beauty and order, all important to the ancient Greeks.

HESPERIDES the nymphs of the setting Sun who lived in the extreme Western sphere. The descendant is on the Western horizon where planets, including the Sun, set, hence my term 'the Hesperides of the horoscope'.

HIERO GAMOS a Greek phrase meaning 'sacred or holy marriage' referring to the union of the deities, for instance the sky-god and the earth-goddess.

IDENTIFIED PATIENT the member of the family or group who is manifesting symptoms which originate from their identification with the familial shadow and material repressed in the family. This individual is 'identified' as the one with the problem, but actually is carrying the burden for the family.

NODAL EVENT a term used in family therapy to suggest a defining point in the family life cycle. Astrologically, a 'node' refers to the intersection of the ecliptic with a planet's orbit, hence a central point in a system. The Lunar Nodal cycle of 18.6 years is a defining point in both the individual and family life cycle. These points (returns) occur at the ages of 19, 37, 56 and 74.

OPUS while generally used to describe a major musical composition, it is also used to suggest psychological work or a life task.

PARTICIPATION MYSTIQUE in Jungian terms this is an archaic connection between the unconscious of an individual and objects or people, allowing access to their unconscious lives which results in a potent unconscious bond. Originally an anthropological term describing the participation in a tribal unconscious.

PSYCHE from the Greek meaning 'soul'. The concept of psyche and soul changed throughout antiquity.

PSYCHOPOMP from the Greek *psyche*, meaning 'soul', and *pempo*, 'to send off'. The term refers to a guide of souls into the Underworld, whether they are dead or alive. This was a role given to Hermes by Zeus.

PUER from the Latin meaning 'child', generally referring to a man who is still bound to youth. The *puer* is also known as the *puer aeternus* which is from the Latin meaning 'eternal child', and generally refers to the masculine, whereas *puella* generally connotes a girl. In Jungian terms *puer aeternus* is used to describe a man fixed in adolescence, unable to commit or grow into adulthood, owing to his unconscious tie to mother. His archetypal counterpart is the Great Mother.

SHADOW the Jungian term for personality traits, attitudes and characteristics which are not conscious in the individual. These include both light and dark aspects banished into the unconscious by the ego, its conscious representative.

SYNCHRONOUS from the Greek, *syn* meaning 'together' and *chronos* meaning 'time', hence 'happening at the same time'.

SYSTEMIC refers to a system as a whole, not just one part. In family therapy it refers to the total organism of the family.

TRIANGULATION refers to the enmeshment of three individuals. Triangulation in sibling relationships usually involves two siblings and the partner, friend or colleague of one of the sibs. However, potent triangles also exist between two siblings and a parent and sometimes between three siblings.

Bibliography

ALFRED ADLER

Adler, Alfred, *What Life Could Mean to You*, trans. Colin Brett (Oneworld Publications, Oxford: 1994).

Ansbacher, Heinz L. and Rowena R., *The Individual Psychology of Alfred Adler* (Basic Books, New York: 1956).

Stepansky, Paul E., *In Freud's Shadow: Adler in Context* (Analytic Press, Hillside, NJ: 1983).

SIGMUND FREUD

Clark, Ronald W., *Freud: the Man and his Cause* (Jonathan Cape/Weidenfeld & Nicolson, London: 1980).

Costigan, Giovanni, *Sigmund Freud: a Short Biography* (Macmillan, New York: 1965).

Freeman, Lucy and Stream, Herbert, *Freud and Women* (Frederick Ungar, New York: 1981).

Freud, Sigmund, *The Standard Edition of the Complete Psychological Works of Sigmund Freud*, trans. from the German under the general editorship of James Strachey, in collaboration with Anna Freud, assisted by Alix Strachey and Alan Tyson (24 vols; Hogarth Press, London: 1953–75).

Fromm, Erich, *Sigmund Freud's Mission: an Analysis of his Personality and Influence* (Allen & Unwin, London: 1959).

Gay, Peter, *Freud: a Life for Our Time* (W. W. Norton, New York: 1988).

– (ed.), *The Freud Reader* (W. W. Norton, New York: 1989).

Grosskurth, Phyllis, *The Secret Ring: Freud's Inner Circle and the Politics of Psychoanalysis* (Addison-Wesley, Reading, MA: 1991).

Jones, Ernest, *Sigmund Freud: Life and Work*, vol. 1: *The Young Freud, 1856–1900* (Hogarth Press, London: 1956).

Krull, Marianne, *Freud and his Father*, trans. Arnold Pomeras (Hutchinson, London: 1986).

McGuire, William (ed.), *The Freud/Jung Letters: The Correspondence between Sigmund Freud and C. G. Jung*, trans. Ralph Manheim and P. F. C. Hull (Princeton University Press, Princeton, NJ: 1974).

Masson, Jeffrey M. (trans. and ed.), *The Complete Letters of Sigmund Freud to Wilhelm Fleiss, 1887–1904* (Belknap Press of Harvard University, Cambridge, MA and London: 1985).

Paskauskas, R. Andrew (ed.), *The Complete Correspondence of Sigmund Freud and Ernest Jones, 1908–1939* (Belknap Press of Harvard University, Cambridge, MA and London: 1993).

Roazen, Paul, *Freud and his Followers* (Alfred A. Knoff, New York: 1975).

Slipp, Samuel, *The Freudian Mystique: Freud, Women and Feminism* (New York University Press, New York: 1995).

CARL JUNG

Adler, Gerhard and Jaffe, Aniela, *C. G. Jung Letters*, trans. R. F. C. Hull (vols 1–2; Princeton University Press, Princeton, NJ: 1973–5).

Carotenuto, Aldo, *A Secret Symmetry*, trans. Arno Pomerans, John Shepley and Krishna Winston (Pantheon Books, New York: 1984).

Hannah, Barbara, *Jung: his Life and his Work* (Michael Joseph, London: 1976).

Jung, C. G., *The Collected Works of C. G. Jung*, trans. R. F. C. Hull et al. (20 vols; Routledge & Kegan Paul, London and Princeton University Press, Princeton, NJ: 1953–79).

– *Memories, Dreams, Reflections*, trans. R. and C. Winston (Pantheon Books, New York: 1973).

McGuire, William (ed.), *The Freud/Jung Letters: The Correspondence between Sigmund Freud and C. G. Jung*, trans. Ralph Manheim and P. F. C. Hull (Princeton University Press, Princeton, NJ: 1974).

McLynn, Frank, *Carl Gustav Jung* (Transworld, London: 1996).

Schultz, Duane, *Intimate Friends, Dangerous Rivals: the Turbulent Relationship between Freud and Jung* (J. P. Tarcher, Los Angeles, CA: 1990).

MYTHOLOGY AND CLASSICS

Gantz, Timothy, *Early Greek Myth* (vols 1–2; Johns Hopkins University Press, Baltimore, MD: 1993).

Homer, *The Iliad*, trans. Richmond Lattimore (University of Chicago Press, Chicago: 1961).

– *The Odyssey*, trans. Richmond Lattimore (Harper Perennial, New York: 1991).

The Homeric Hymns, trans. Charles Boer (Spring, Dallas, TX: 1970).

Kerenyi, C., *The Gods of the Greeks,* trans. Norman Cameron (Thames & Hudson, London: 1951).

– *The Heroes of the Greeks*, trans. H. J. Rose (Thames & Hudson, London: 1959).

– *Zeus and Hera: Archetypal Images of Father, Husband, Wife*, trans. Christopher Holme (Princeton University Press, Princeton, NJ: 1975).

Ovid, *Metamorphoses,* trans. Mary M. Innes (Penguin, Harmondsworth: 1955).

PART ONE: PSYCHOLOGY AND THE MISSING SIBLING

Bank, Stephen and Kahn, Michael, *The Sibling Bond* (Basic Books, New York: 1982).

Bradshaw, John, *The Family* (Health Communications, Deerfield Beach, FL: 1988).

– *Family Secrets* (Bantam, New York: 1995).

Carter, Betty and McGoldrick, Monica (eds), *The Changing Family Life Cycle* (Allyn and Bacon, Boston, MA: 1989).

Cicirelli, Victor G., *Sibling Relationships Across the Lifespan* (Plenum Press, New York: 1995).

Douglas, Claire, *The Woman in the Mirror* (Sigo, Boston, MA: 1990).

Downing, Christine, *Psyche's Sisters: Reimagining the Meaning of Sisterhood* (Continuum, New York: 1990).

Dunn, Judy, *Young Children's Close Relationships: Beyond Attachment* (Sage Publications, Newbury Park, CA: 1993).

Dunn, Judy and Kendrick, Carol, *Siblings: Love, Envy and Understanding* (Harvard University Press, Cambridge, MA: 1982).

Ellenberger, Henri, *The Discovery of the Unconscious* (Allen Lane, London: 1970).

Ernst, Cecile and Angst, Jules, *Birth Order: Its Influence on Personality* (Springer-Verlag, Berlin: 1983).

Fanos, Joanna, *Sibling Loss* (Lawrence Erlbaum, Mahwah, NJ: 1996).

Foster, Patricia (ed.), *Sister to Sister: Women Write about the Unbreakable Bond* (Doubleday, New York: 1995).

Grosskurth, Phyllis, *Melanie Klein: her World and her Work* (Jason Aronson, Northvale, NJ and London: 1986).

Hall, Nor, *The Moon and the Virgin* (Harper & Row, New York: 1980).

Harding, Esther, *The Way of All Women* (Harper & Row, New York: 1975).

Hillman, James, *The Myth of Analysis* (Harper & Row, New York: 1978).

– *Healing Fiction* (Station Hill Press, New York: 1983).

Kiell, Norman (ed.), *Blood Brothers: Siblings as Writers* (International University Press, New York: 1983).

Lamb, Michael and Sutton-Smith, Brian (eds), *Sibling Relationships: their Nature and Significance across the Lifespan* (Lawrence Erlbaum, Hillsdale, NJ: 1982).

Lasky, Judith and Mulliken, Susan, 'Sibling Relationships and Mature Love', in Judith F. Lasky and Helen W. Silverman (eds), *Love: Psychoanalytic Perspectives* (New York University Press, New York: 1988).

Leon, Irving G., *When a Baby Dies: Psychotherapy for Pregnancy and Newborn Loss* (Yale University Press, New Haven, CT: 1990).

Leonard, Linda, *On the Way to the Wedding* (Shambhala, Boston, MA: 1987).

Lewis, Michael and Rosenblum, Leonard (eds), *Friendship and Peer Relations* (John Wiley, New York: 1975).

McDermott, Patti, *Sisters and Brothers* (RGA Publishing, Los Angeles, CA: 1994).

McNaron, Toni A. H. (ed.), *The Sister* (Pergamon Press, New York: 1985).

McNeely, Deldon Anne, *Animus Aeternus: Exploring the Inner Masculine* (Inner City Books, Toronto: 1991).

Minuchin, Salvador, *Families and Family Therapy* (Tavistock/Routledge, London: 1991).

Sandmaier, Marian, *Original Kin: the Search for Connection Among Adult Sisters and Brothers* (Dutton, New York: 1994).

Satir, Virginia, *Conjoint Family Therapy* (Science and Behavior Books, Palo Alto, CA: 1983).

Somit, Albert, Arwine, Alan and Peterson, Steven A., *Birth Order and Political Behavior* (University Press of America, Lanham, MD: 1996).

Stein, Robert, *Incest and Human Love* (Spring, Dallas, TX: 1984).

Stewart, Louis H., *Changemakers: a Jungian Perspective on Sibling Position and the Family Atmosphere* (Routledge, London: 1992).

Sulloway, Frank J., *Born to Rebel* (Pantheon Books, New York: 1996).

Sutton-Smith, Brian and Rosenburg, B. G., *The Sibling* (Holt Rinehart & Winston, New York: 1970).

Toman, Walter, *Family Constellation* (4th edn; Springer, New York: 1991).

Waskow, H. and Waskow, A., *Becoming Brothers* (Free Press, New York: 1993).

Wiehe, Vernon and Harding, Teresa, *Perilous Rivalry: When Siblings Become Abusive* (Lexington Books, Lexington, MA: 1991).

Winnicott, D. W., *Home is Where We Start From* (Penguin, Harmondsworth: 1990).

– *The Child, the Family and the Outside World* (Penguin, Harmondsworth: 1991).
– *The Piggle: an Account of the Psychoanalytic Treatment of a Little Girl* (Penguin, Harmondsworth: 1991).

PART TWO: THE ASTROLOGY OF SIBLINGS

Clark, Brian, *Keys to Understanding Chiron* (Astro*Synthesis Series, Melbourne: 1991).
Cowger, Barry, *Reconstructing the Real You: Applying Astrology to Family Psychology* (Mercurius, Scottsdale, AZ: 1992).
Edis, Freda, *The God Between* (Arkana, London: 1995).
Greene, Liz, *Relating: an Astrological Guide to Living with Others on a Small Planet* (Samuel Weiser, New York: 1980).
– *The Astrology of Fate* (Allen & Unwin, London: 1984).
Greene, Liz and Sasportas, Howard, *The Development of the Personality* (Samuel Weiser, York Beach, ME: 1987).
– *The Inner Planets* (Samuel Weiser, York Beach, ME: 1993).
Reinhart, Melanie, *Chiron and the Healing Journey* (Arkana, London: 1989).
– *To the Edge and Beyond* (Centre for Psychological Astrology Press, London: 1996).
Rudhyar, Dane, *The Pulse of Life: New Dynamics in Astrology* (Shambhala, Berkeley, CA: 1970).
– *The Astrological Houses* (CRCS Publications, Sebastopol, CA: 1986).
Sasportas, Howard, *The Twelve Houses* (Aquarian, Wellingborough: 1985).
– *The Gods of Change* (Arkana, London: 1989).
Sullivan, Erin, *Saturn in Transit* (Arkana, London: 1991).
– *Dynasty: the Astrology of Family Dynamics* (Arkana, London: 1996).

Index

References to figures are in italics and n. refers to a footnote.

NEW AGE BOOKS FOR MIND, BODY & SPIRIT

NEW AGE BOOKS FOR MIND, BODY & SPIRIT

ARKANA CONTEMPORARY ASTROLOGY

Series Editor: Erin Sullivan

Dynasty: The Astrology of Family Dynamics Erin Sullivan

'If it is familiar, it is familial'.

Erin Sullivan's latest book is a breakthrough both in astrology and psychology. *Dynasty* makes gripping reading and shows us that astrology is the only system that demonstrates the complexities of the family as an organic whole; its place in the collective; and the role an individual plays in carrying on the ancestral line.

Individuals in the family-system are interwoven in a fabric which simultaneously both enhances and diminishes their individuality. To date there is no book dedicated to family patterns, the psychology of family dynamics and family-systems in natal astrology. Not only does this book fill a gap in astrological literature, but also adds an essential new dimension to the psychology of families and groups.

The five personal case-histories in *Dynasty* are fascinating life-stories of her clients – Erin Sullivan writes their stories with both compassion and accuracy weaving together various methods of analyzing and working with individuals and their families. There is 'Mohsin', the adopted man; a story of autism; a poignant story of a woman whose child rejected her in utero (Freud had it half right!); and the compelling story of a woman who carries the whole of her ancestral line, a deeply moving tale which verifies our personal links to our own ancestors – links that defy linear time.

NEW AGE BOOKS FOR MIND, BODY & SPIRIT

ARKANA CONTEMPORARY ASTROLOGY

Series Editor: Erin Sullivan

The God Between Freda Edis
A Study of Astrological Mercury

Hermes – the Roman Mercury – started as a crafty boy-god and violator of women but then developed into a miracle-worker and spiritual guide. Every aspect of his complex personality offers rich insights.

Mercury is often treated as a light-weight planet which over-emphasizes the intellect and ignores the emotional side of life. By drawing on mythology and a series of compelling case histories, Freda Edis shows that it can be far more. People who feel stuck – endlessly repeating the same unsatisfactory patterns of behaviour – and need to confront the darker aspects of themselves can find inspiration in stories of Hermes's descent into the Underworld. His love affair with Venus, and the birth of their hermaphrodite child, has much to teach us about reconciling the male and female within ourselves.

The God Between explores Mercury's role as Eternal Child, Rapist, Trickster, Traveller, Healer and Alchemist; his aspects to the other planets; and how he operates in the different houses and signs. Psychological astrology, it concludes, offers illumination, to anyone who truly wants 'to walk the path of deeper self-knowledge'.

NEW AGE BOOKS FOR MIND, BODY & SPIRIT

ARKANA CONTEMPORARY ASTROLOGY

Series Editor: Erin Sullivan

The Gods of Change Howard Sasportas
Pain, Crisis and the Transits of Uranus, Neptune and Pluto

Major changes or crises in our lives are usually signified by the transits of Uranus, Neptune and Pluto in our birthcharts.

Although Uranian disruption feels quite different from Neptunian confusion or the pulverising impact of Pluto, it is the transits of the outer planets that most often mark our personal turning points. Each offers its own distinctive dilemmas, its particular type of trauma, test or trial. In this impressive book Howard Sasportas blends his deep knowledge of psychology with moving case histories from his work as an astrologer in order to illuminate what happens as the outer planets transit the chart. In this way, he suggests, we can learn to collaborate with the inevitable, to find the meaning and pattern behind periods of upheaval and to discover new depths in our-selves. Above all, we can learn to use our life crises as opportunities for growth and development.

NEW AGE BOOKS FOR MIND, BODY & SPIRIT

ARKANA CONTEMPORARY ASTROLOGY

Series Editor: Erin Sullivan

The Psychology of Astro*Carto*Graphy
Jim Lewis with Kenneth Irving

'A horoscope's reach should exceed the birthplace's grasp, or what are the heavens for?'

We can only grow by learning to assimilate and accept repressed aspects of ourselves. Such spiritual breakthroughs, according to traditional astrologers, tend to occur at specific times, or during a major relationship. Astro*Carto*Graphy builds on the crucial insight that they are also linked to particular places. Maps developed by Jim Lewis can help us predict where we are likely to find fame or love, face up to our emotional needs or perform important acts of assertion. This superb book, completed by Ken Irving after Lewis's untimely death, explains the essence of the system with vivid, in-depth case studies, descriptions of the fundamental properties of each planet and analysis of how geography impinges on their influences. A radical combination of astrological ideas with depth psychology, Astro*Carto*Graphy offers us a uniquely rich and subtle way of understanding ourselves.

NEW AGE BOOKS FOR MIND, BODY & SPIRIT

ARKANA CONTEMPORARY ASTROLOGY

Series Editor: Erin Sullivan

Crossing the Threshold Linda Reid
The Astrology of Dreaming

People live their lives on two distinct planes: the conscious, ego-oriented level and the unconscious level of the soul.

The unconscious mind reflects on and interprets the experiences of our day to day lives and attempts to make sense of them through the symbolic language of dreams. It is important for psychological wholeness to be aware of and listen to what our dreams are telling us. In this seminal book Linda Reid blends an expertise in astrology with a pro-found understanding of dream imagery and intent, to demonstrate how we can benefit from the healing dynamics of dreaming.

Breaking new ground in astrological counselling, *Crossing the Threshold* describes how to use a dream chart to connect the unconscious experience with the conscious, allowing the psyche to heal itself through understanding and acceptance of dream imagery. The work is enriched with numerous case studies which examine the dynamics of astrological dreamwork and demonstrates its significance as a tool to self-realization.

NEW AGE BOOKS FOR MIND, BODY & SPIRIT

ARKANA CONTEMPORARY ASTROLOGY

Series Editor: Erin Sullivan

The Karmic Journey Judy Hall

Why are we here and what can we learn from our experience?

Karmic astrology postulates that we are eternal spiritual beings whose past-life patterns can be identified in the birthchart along with the purpose of the new incarnation. Judy Hall's exploration follows the theme that 'the soul chooses a time to be born because the astrological pattern fits the experiences needed for the present stage of growth'. Karmic astrology thereby adds another dimension to the understanding of the inner processes of life through an awareness of the pattern of cause and effect laid down in the past, and deepens spiritual perception by linking into a greater reality.

The author utilizes a wealth of case histories to show how an individual's horoscopes might reflect karma carried forward from previous incarnations and at times suggests therapeutic options for their present one. Also touched on are famous people, including the Kennedy family, Marilyn Monroe, Debussy, Jacqueline du Pré, Lenin, Joe Orton, Elizabeth Kubler-Ross, Martin Luther King and Bob Geldof. A celebration, in all, of that 'place of infinite possibilities' – one's own being.

NEW AGE BOOKS FOR MIND, BODY & SPIRIT

ARKANA CONTEMPORARY ASTROLOGY

Series Editor: Erin Sullivan

Chiron and the Healing Journey Melanie Reinhart
Updated edition

With the discovery of Chiron in 1977, and also further 'Centauric' bodies since 1992, a new dimension has been added to the study of astrology.

This study of Chiron has become established as a classic text, demonstrating a rare combination of careful research, innovative thinking and inspired interpretation. Melanie Reinhart explores the mythic figure of the Wounded Healer or Shaman in psychological and astrological terms, for this archetypal pattern is active within all forms of the healing process. Her work is rich in anecdotes from diverse mythologies, and includes a thoughtful historical and religious perspective. Detailed material on Chiron through astrological house, sign and aspect is included, as well as Ephemerides from 1900 to 2030. This book is an indispensable reference for all those seeking to understand Chiron's meaning in the horoscope.

'The author's grasp of mythology, history and man's evolutionary thrust combines well with her experiences as astrologer/therapist . . . an excellent book, an exciting introduction to the Chiron myth and its meaning in the birth chart, and a work which every astrologer must have' *Astrological Journal*

'This could possibly be the best book that will ever be written on the most recently discovered planet, Chiron. I doubt that anyone will ever surpass it; it is superb' *Prediction*

'Thoroughly researched, profound and well-written' *Astrology and Medicine*